The Practitioner's Blueprint For Logical and Physical Database Design

The Practitioner's Blueprint For Logical and Physical Database Design

Eric Garrigue Vesely

Principal, *The Analyst Workbench*
Visiting Lecturer, *Institute of Systems Science*
National University of Singapore

PRENTICE-HALL, Englewood Cliffs, NJ 07632

Library of Congress Cataloging-in-Publication Data

Vesely, Eric Garrigue, (date)
    The practitioner's blueprint for logical and
physical database design.

    Bibliography: p.
    Includes index.
    1. Data base management. 2. System design.
I. Title.
QA76.9.D3V46   1986   005.74   85-25680
ISBN 0-13-694267-9

Cover design: Ben Santora
Manufacturing buyer: Gordon Osbourne

Printed in the United States of America

10 9 8 7 6 5 4 3 2 1

ISBN 0-13-694267-9   025

Prentice-Hall International (UK) Limited, *London*
Prentice-Hall of Australia Pty. Limited, *Sydney*
Prentice-Hall Canada Inc., *Toronto*
Prentice-Hall Hispanoamericana, S.A., *Mexico*
Prentice-Hall of India Private Limited, *New Delhi*
Prentice-Hall of Japan, Inc., *Tokyo*
Prentice-Hall of Southeast Asia Pte. Ltd., *Singapore*
Editora Prentice-Hall do Brasil, Ltda., *Rio de Janeiro*
Whitehall Books Limited, *Wellington, New Zealand*

Contents

Foreword

This book is dedicated to the small band of courageous men and women who are fighting both the user community and the data processing community to bring order to data. They must convince both communities to relinquish their cherished homonyms, synonyms, and aliases and also convince programmers to use honest, complete, user-meaningful data names. This book provides a blueprint for achieving nirvana.

"The real world has little interest in elegant solutions to finite problems."

P. K. Nayak in *High Technology* Magazine.

Acknowlegments

Many people in different organizations have contributed ideas and material for this book. I thank all of them, especially George Blatt, McAuto; Peter Harris, ADPAC; Ken Orr, Ken Orr & Associates; David Reiner, CCA; Carol Schulman, DDI; Lisa Thompson, ADPAC; and Al Travis, Peat Marwick.

The preparation of the text and most of the figures required dedication and many hours of labor. I would like to thank Julie Harris, Glen Koue, Michael Szuromi, Kevin Thompson, and Steve Wortheimer.

I have written many articles. I thought that this book would be a collection of articles. In this case, it wasn't—it was a difficult undertaking! I thank Don Deussen, Andy Grove, Bill Miller, and Sigrid Rupp for providing the environment; I especially thank Lisa Thompson for her continued support and encouragement.

A special thanks to my production editor—Sophie Papanikolaou—who had to put up with an author half way around the world.

Finally, I would like to thank my editor—Karl Karlstrom—for gambling on an unknown author to publish this book!

Caveat

This book lists, and/or describes, and/or evalutates many structured methodologies, "workbench" and productivity software packages, database management systems, and so on. I apologize for any omissions or inaccurate descriptions and evaluations. The fault is mine but all mistakes were honest. I welcome all comments for inclusion in the second edition if there is one. Please send comments to:

Eric Garrigue Vesely
Attn: College Editorial Dept.
Prentice-Hall
Englewood Cliffs, NJ 07632

The Practitioner's Blueprint For Logical and Physical Database Design

1

Overview of Design Philosophy

The objective of logical and physical database design is to provide all user information correctly within an acceptable user time frame. The definition is simple; the execution difficult. Figure 1.1 is a generic dataflow of the design cycle advocated by this book and author. The major divisions are logical[1] and physical database design.

The *logical database* (model) graphically portrays the attributes of the user data independent of software, hardware, or computer. The model uses final normal form (defined in Chapter 8) and displays the association between the relationships.

The *physical database* is the actual schema and subschemas developed by a database designer to implement the logical database on a specific database management system (DBMS) on a specific computer configuration.

The major activities in the design cycle include: (1) the logical database and (2) the physical database.

LOGICAL DATABASE

Defining the Application Boundary

The design cycle is normally initiated by a user request to data processing to automate some of their manual procedures. Assuming that the project is funded or approved,[2] the

---

[1]ANSI/SPARC uses the term *conceptual model*. I prefer *logical* because it represents the actual data, not the concept of the data.

[2]This book assumes that a design methodology (such as DSSD, PRIDE, SDM-70, STRADIS, etc.) is in place and that a formal review procedure is used. Normally, the review procedure is some form of structured walkthru.

1

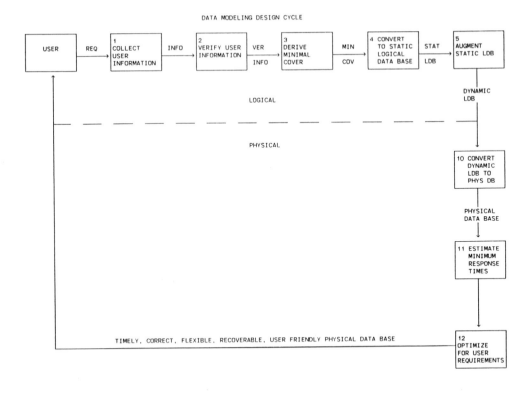

Figure 1.1 Data Modeling Design Cycle

first major activity is to ascertain the boundary of the application (i.e., what user functions are to be automated). The recommended vehicle is an entity (context) diagram (see Figure 1.2) that defines the external interfaces and the application. The approved diagram is the foundation on which the design cycle is built.

Data Collection

The dataflows in the entity diagram represent the universe of data for this user application. The dataflows must be defined by the data elements (an atomic unit of data that cannot be subdivided) that flow in each dataflow. The recommended vehicle is one of the structured analysis tools:

1. *Dataflow diagrams* (Gane/Sarson, SADT, Yourdon)[3]
2. *Data decomposition* (HIPO, Jackson, Warnier/Orr)[3]

---

[3]This is not the complete set of structured analysis tools but represents the best known and most popular.

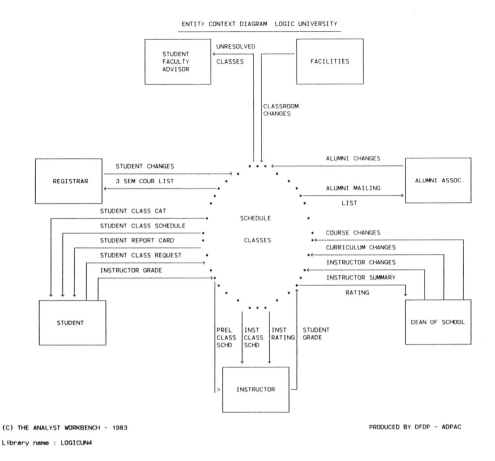

ENTITY CONTEXT DIAGRAM LOGIC UNIVERSITY

Figure 1.2   Entity Context Diagram: Logic University Class Scheduling

A basic objective of the structured analysis tools is to collect the data.

Data Verification

The data collected by the structured analysis tools should represent the universe of data for this user application by data elements. The next major activity is to verify that the data elements collected actually do represent the universe of data.[4] The actual verification method is dependent on the structured analysis tool used. The logical procedure is to verify that:

---

[4]Many authorities have cited significant statistical evidence that the cost to correct errors increases exponentially as the design cycle progresses. Consequently, this design cycle stresses maximum consistency checking between activities.

1. All input data elements are updated and used for output.

2. All output data elements are derivable from input data elements.

Entity Type Analysis

The collected data elements represent the attribute types of various entity types. An entity type is a person, place, thing, or concept that the user wishes to store data about. Examples are:

```
          Customer      Product      Employee
          Warehouse     Ledger       Government
```

An attribute type is a data element containing a single piece of information about an entity type:

```
          Name          Weight        Sex
          Social Security Number   Address
```

An attribute value is an acceptable definition of the attribute type: i.e.,

```
          Sex = Male (M) or Female (F)
```

The objective of this activity is to determine the entity types for this user application from the structured analysis diagrams.

Data Clustering

The previous activities have defined the attribute types (data elements) and the entity types. The objective of this activity is to cluster (assign) each attribute type to its entity type. Again, the structured analysis diagram is used as the source document.

Normalization

About 1970, E. F. Codd of IBM introduced the concept of using set theory in reducing data to its absolute minimum (minimal cover). This set of rules is called *normalization* and progresses from first normal form (1NF) through "final" form (FNF). Proper utilization of normalization eliminates redundant data and provides logical serial correctness. An additional benefit is that normalized output is in the form of tables (flat files) which are user friendly and therefore user verifiable.

Optimization

The process of normalization often creates tables that have identical primary keys.[5] Optimization is the process of identifying these tables and combining them into a single relation.

Generalization

The objective of normalization is to eliminate redundant data. Perfect application of the rules can still allow redundant data if entity instances (an occurrence of an entity type) are classified as entity types. For instance, if a database design contains the "entity types" student, instructor, and alumni, then a graduate student who is an instructor would have redundant information stored in three places.

The object of this activity is to examine the association between "root tables"[6] to determine if they are entity instances of a more general entity type. If they are, the tables should be combined. For instance, students, instructors, and alumni should be combined into an entity type of

```
Student-Instructor-Alumni
```

This combination achieves the basic objective of eliminating redundant data by storing basic information, such as name, address, phone-number, etc., once—not three times.

Graphic Model

The result of generalization is the logical database in Codd relational format. This format is complete and could be used as the basis for future work. However, most human beings prefer graphic representation (a picture is worth 1000 words). This design cycle recommends conversion to a graphic model.

Foreign Keys

The graphic model derived from the generalized Codd relational notation is the static picture of the logical database. It shows the association of tables derived from each other; it does not show other possible logical pathways.

---

[5]A table is a normalized flat file (two-dimensional array of data elements); each table must be uniquely identifiable by a data element or elements and that element(s) is the primary key.

[6]The first step in normalizing was clustering the data elements by entity type. The data elements that remain with the entity type after normalization comprise the root table.

Foreign keys represent another logical pathway. A foreign key is a data element that is also a primary data element in another table. It is possible for a single relation to be "recursive," to have a nonkey data element that is also part of the primary key. For instance,

STUDENT. INSTRUCTOR. ALUMNI (SIA-NUMBER, ...
{ADVISOR}-SIA-NUMBER, ...)

Each student has one advisor who is an instructor. The prefix {ADVISOR} indicates the unique identification number of the instructor advisor; to obtain the unique instructor attributes you would use the {ADVISOR}-SIA-NUMBER as a foreign access key.

The objective of this activity is twofold:

1. To identify all foreign keys
2. To identify meaningful foreign keys for this application

Secondary Keys (indices)

The primary key identified by the normalization process usually represents the computer access method and is often an arbitrarily assigned unique number (i.e., Student-number). Human beings prefer names and usually want to access by name as opposed to "meaningless" (to the person) number. The analyst must augment the static model by indicating the user-desired secondary access keys.[7]

Logical Records

Larry Constantine and Ed Yourdon in their classic book[8] on structured design demonstrated the necessity for each module to have access only to the data required by that module. The same requirement extends to logical database calls; each call should retrieve only the data elements that are actually required. Furthermore, this information is vital to the next activity.

Statistical Information

The physical database designer needs at least the following statistical information in order to have any chance of designing a user-responsive physical database:

1. Volume of each relation (current plus estimated growth)
2. Volatility of each relation (anticipated number of inserts, updates, deletes, plus estimated growth)

---

[7]Primary keys identify a single record; a secondary key can identify from zero to n records.

[8]Ed Yourdon and Larry L. Constantine, *Structured Design*, Yourdon Press, Inc., New York, 1975.

3. Asymmetrical distribution (i.e., do 10% of the relation occurrences have 90% of the volatility?)
4. Anticipated number of secondary key queries plus estimated growth
5. Anticipated logical path transversals plus estimated growth
6. Priority of user-defined transactions

Defining logical path transactions requires that the analyst specify each user requirement (on-line or batch) in the terms of the required data elements. The required data elements form the logical record. Placement of the data elements of the logical record within the logical database specifies the logical pathways; the quantity of each data element required determines the logical path transversal.

PHYSICAL DATABASE

First-Cut Executable Physical Model

The static logical database, after being augmented by foreign keys, secondary keys, and statistical information, becomes the dynamic logical database. This represents the basic input to the physical database designer.

The first step is to derive an executable physical model (analogous to having a program "accepted" by a compiler as syntactically correct). All DBMSs fall into one of the following general categories:

1. Tree (hierarchical)
2. Plex (network)
3. Inverted
4. Relational

Each DBMS has its own rules for acceptable (executable) physical models. Chapter 21 provides rules for converting the dynamic logical database to physical.

Response Timing of Logical Transactions

The first physical database will probably be unacceptable because transaction response times will exceed user-required time frames. The objective of this activity is to time *each* user logical transaction as defined by the logical record activity. System programmers can provide average disc access time and average CPU time to generate and execute DBMS calls, etc.

The major component of any response time is the disc I/O time (this will undoubtably change when large nonmechanical memories become economically feasible). Therefore, the critical algorithm is to count the number of disc accesses required to provide the logical records for each user transaction. Any calculated response time that exceeds the user maximum time frame is forwarded to the next activity.

Skewing Physical Model to Achieve User Response Requirements

The first-cut physical model will probably have too many disc accesses to achieve the user response time. The database designer will have to modify the physical database to reduce the disc accesses. Some possibilities include:

> Combining physical records
> Inserting redundant data
> Establishing physical indices
> Adding additional chains
> Adding additional pathways

The possibilities are discussed in Chapter 23.

Eliminating Programmer Navigation

Programmer navigation is the term used to describe the knowledge of the physical database structure that an application programmer *must have* in order to program the user application. The amount of knowledge required is dependent on the specific DBMS. It can include:

> Knowing the access key or method
> Knowing exactly where the DBMS ''current pointer'' is
> Knowing whether owners (parents, masters) are automatic or manual
> Knowing whether members (details) are optional
> Currency
> Etc.

Currency is critical. It requires the application programmer to know *exactly* the precise effects that any update has within the database. Further, it requires the application programmer to specify the appropriate locking to prevent misapplication of concurrent updates.

A significant hidden cost of programmer navigation is the need to modify application programs if the database physical structure changes. A simple database change can cause significant modifications to application programs.

The objective of this design philosophy is to eliminate programmer navigation by using logical records. Cullinet's IDMS currently has a logical record facility (LRF) that eliminates programmer navigation via LRF. Chapter 24 contains extensive discussions.

SUMMARY

The objective of this design philosophy is to define a consistent approach subdivided into manageable activities that begin with the user request and end with an acceptable physical database. Subobjectives include:

All user information available within acceptable user time frame
All user information correct
Elimination of redundant data
Elimination of detrimental data dependencies
Providing a stable logical database that is portable between physical DBMS'
Data independence
Elimination of programmer navigation

An alternative method of expressing the above is the elimination of GIGO!

2

Design Philosophy Rationale

The design philosophy advocated by this book requires significant work by skilled data processing professionals. The management question should be: *Are the results worth the cost?*

Cost justification of data processing tools is difficult because most data processing departments do *not* maintain adequate cost or historical data (e.g., cost estimates for new applications are usually developed from scratch rather than related to previous similar projects).

Various authorities have quoted some general statistics, such as:

A programmer produces one to two debugged instructions per hour.

The cost of that debugged instruction is $10 to $50.[1]

Fifty to ninety percent of DP budgets is spent on maintaining those debugged instructions.[2]

User backlog is measured in *decades* or *centuries* because of low productivity and the unavailability of programmers for new development.

Cost justification for eliminating or reducing published errors to users is even more difficult to estimate. The first problem is the probability of occurrence; the second problem is the cost of the occurrence. For instance:

[1]Hewlett-Packard, ad in *Computerworld,* April 16, 1984.

[2]Girish Parish estimated that annual US maintenance cost exceeds $10,000,000,000 in *Infosystems* January, 1985.

What is the probability of a bug in a tax program causing an error in a tax return, and what is the cost of the accounting department in manually recasting the tax return?

What is the cost for a user to maintain separate manual records because they do not trust the computer reports?

What is the cost of turning down a customer order because the reported credit information was incorrect or the inventory was incorrect?

The rationale offered in this chapter is based on the foregoing *general* principles.

DATA CORRECTNESS

Data correctness means that each user receives a correct or acceptable[3] answer for every transaction. This requires that all transactions be:

Applied correctly regardless of concurrency

Discrete without effecting data not privy to the transaction.

Correct data reduces the probability of a published error, which causes a significant cost to correct.

DATA SECURITY

Data security involves protecting the data from both accidental and deliberate (sabotage) modification; it also includes protecting the privacy of the data.

Data destroyed can cause serious published errors; data stolen can provide competition with a competitive edge. Privacy invasion can cause serious legal problems.

MINIMAL COVER

Minimal cover is the buzzword used to describe the result of reducing the user data to the absolute minimum required by the user application. The process is normalization as described in Chapter 8. The benefits are:

Eliminating redundant data (which aids in data correctness and in reducing wasteful secondary storage)

Providing users with tables (flat files) that are user verifiable

---

[3]There are many instances where a user performing a browsing inquiry does not require absolutely correct data but data *accurate* to some previous time mark.

USER VIEWS

The objective of database management systems is to provide concurrent access by multiple users to the same data universe. Each user has a unique need to insert, see, modify, or delete data. This methodology collects each user view to establish appropriate data security and privacy rules.

STABLE PORTABLE LOGICAL DATABASE

The logical database developed by this design represents a stable view of a particular user application. Each application logical database represents a subset of a subject database or a corporate database. Each new application can be inserted into the original logical database, thereby developing a corporate database piece by piece.

The logical database is independent of both hardware and the physical database. Therefore, it can be "ported" between DBMSs whenever the requirement arises. It also provides analysts with data elements and relationships that can reduce future application development time.

RESPONSIVE PHYSICAL DATABASE

An unresponsive physical database causes:

> User frustration
> Ignoring or sabotaging the computer
> Maintaining separate manual records
> Mistakes in user processing

This methodology stresses timing and refining and timing and refining and so on until the best responsive physical database is achieved. Normally, not all user transactions can be processed within the user-required time frame. The user should be made aware of the options and permitted to choose the least evil. The user will then be provided with the best possible physical database within the current physical environment. It is still possible that the user will be frustrated, but at least the user will know why and will have participated in the decision.

DATA INDEPENDENCE

Data independence is normally defined in the degree of freedom that the application programs have from changes in the actual structure of the data. Ideally, data structure changes should affect only those programs that use the data. Unfortunately, the most prevalent business application language, Cobol, requires at least recompilation of every program that *references* the changed data element. It is common in Cobol to incorporate within the Data Division the entire record regardless of whether the particular program *uses* the data element. The solution is to use logical records which provide each program with only the data elements that it requires. This provides two important benefits:

1. Programs do not have to be recompiled *merely* because they referenced a data element.
2. The elimination of the possibility that a program will erroneously modify a data element that it should not (the Cobol corresponding phrase is a notorious example).

APPLICATION INDEPENDENCE

The goal of storing a single data element *once* requires the building of a corporate database. This means that *several* applications will be referring to the same physical record containing the data elements. Changes to the physical record should not affect any application unless that application uses the modified data element within the physical record. Again, the solution is the logical record.

ELIMINATION OF PROGRAMMER NAVIGATION

Corruption of the physical database is a serious problem when it occurs. Corruption means that the database has been modified in such a fashion that accurate and predictable results cannot be guaranteed (sometimes the database will not even function). Infrequently (because the major DBMS vendors have had time to stabilize their database), the DBMS causes corruption (losing pointers, breaking chains, etc.). The major cause is programmer navigation; the knowledge that the application program requires of the physical structure of the database. Inappropriate inserts and deletes, disconnects or connects, not using or misinterpreting currency, etc., are the principal corruption causes. Recovery usually means:

Shutting down the database (i.e., users cannot access their data)

Determining when the original corruption occurred

Reloading the database as it was before the corruption (assuming, of course, that you can find it)

Correcting the program

Reapplying the transactions (hopefully, automatically from the log file—otherwise, manually)

Shutdowns of *weeks* have been reported. Again, the solution is logical records.

LOGICAL RECORDS

The preceding three sections have indicated that logical records are the panacea to many ills afflicting databases. They are. So what is a logical record? A logical record is a *single user view*. Each user transaction requires *specific* data elements. The logical record is composed of those specific data elements. If application programmers need only specify the logical records in their programs, then you have achieved:

> *Data independence:* Only those programs that *use* the changed data element need be modified (maybe—see the next section).
>
> *Application independence:* Changes to physical structure do not affect application programs.
>
> *Elimination of programmer navigation:* The application programmer does not need *any* knowledge of the physical structure.

As W. C. Fields stated, there is no such thing as a free lunch. Somebody must code the physical accesses that acquire the data elements that the application programmer requires. That somebody is the physical database designer. Only he/she has the required knowledge of the physical database. An additional benefit is that the physical database designer can design *and* code the optimum path for each user transaction. At this writing, Cullinet has introduced a Logical Record Facility in IDMS to assist physical database designers in providing logical record accesses to application programmers.

FOURTH-GENERATION LANGUAGES

Fourth-generation languages are generally defined as nonprocedural. Procedural languages include Cobol, PL/I, Fortran, RPG, etc. They are procedural because they require certain procedures to be followed to have a syntactically acceptable program. For instance, Cobol requires:

> Identification division
> Environment division
> Data division and usually a working storage section
> Procedure division
> Optionally, a linkage section for calls

Cobol is a "wordy" language. It requires many pages[4] of definition before the programmer can even begin to write the logic. A nonprocedural language requires only that the *logic* be specified in an "English-like" syntax with data elements identification being re-

---

[4]The number of coded pages can be substantially reduced by using Copylibs.

solved by the DBMS (usually by a data dictionary). Meaningful user results can often be obtained quickly (and often by the user) by using "free-form" inquiry languages (SQL, RAMIS, NOMAD, QUERY, etc.). However, for an inquiry language to be effective, all data elements must be stored once. (Otherwise, how would the user or the inquiry language know which data element to use?)

REAL DOLLAR SAVINGS

The preceding sections in this chapter have discussed savings that are difficult to quantify in real dollars. There is one saving that is quantifiable—the cost of storing redundant data on physical devices (discs, tape, etc.). Each redundant byte costs real dollars. The questions are: How much redundancy? and At what cost?

Eric H. Joyall in the *Database Newsletter*[5] estimated that there is up to 75% redundant data storage and that many "facts of interest" are stored 10 times. *Computerworld* has estimated that IBM has shipped approximately ninety thousand 3380 disk drives at about $90,000 each. The formula 90,000 $\times$ $90,000 $\times$ 0.75 indicates that IBM customers have spent *six billion* dollars on redundant data storage. If your company has ten 3380 disc drives and a conservative 25% redundancy factor is used, the real dollar savings would be $225,000.

SUMMARY

Management should *adopt and advocate* this philosophy because:

Each user will receive a correct result *every* time he/she accesses his/her data.

Each data element will be protected from misuse.

Each data element will be stored once.

Each user can access only his/her data.

The database is portable and responsive.

It reduces maintenance by:

      Providing data independence

      Providing application independence

      Eliminating programmer navigation

It permits the effective use of fourth-generation languages.

It reduces *actual* storage costs.

[5]See Appendix D for address.

3

Defining the Application Boundary

DEFINITION

Users have a general idea of which of their functions should be automated. This idea is based on the users' perception of what a computer can do to assist in performing their functions. The objective of this activity is to preliminarily define those functions that will be automated. The recommended graphic is the entity diagram.

ENTITY DIAGRAM

Virtually every methodologist recommends a very high level diagram to initiate the analysis phase. It is called either *entity* or *context* and comes in two distinct formats.

Graphic

The graphic diagram uses four symbols:

1. A square to denote an *external* entity which is a source and/or destination of data to/from the application
2. A line to denote the flow of specific transaction to/from the application
3. An arrow to denote the direction of the data flow
4. A large circle in the center to denote the application

ENTITY CHART - LOGIC UNIVERSITY - CLASS SCHEDULING

INDENT	EXTERNAL ENTITY	DATAFLOW IN	DATAFLOW OUT	COMMENTS
a	REGISTRAR	STUDENT CHANGES	3 SEMESTER COURSE LISTIG	
b	STUDENT	STUDENT CLASS REQUEST INSTRUCTOR GRADE	STUDENT CLASS SCHEDULE STUDENT CLASS CATALOG STUDENT REPORT CARD	
c	INSTRUCTOR	STUDENT GRADE	PRELIMINARY CLASS SCHEDULE INSTRUCTOR CLASS SCHEDULE INSTRUCTOR RATING	
d	DEAN OF SCHOOL	COURSE CHANGES CURRICULM CHANGES INSTRUCTOR CHANGES	INSTRUCTOR SUMMARY RATING	
e	ALUMNI ASSOCIATION	ALUNMI CHANGES	ALUMNI MAILING LIST	
f	FACILITIES	CLASSROOM CHANGES		
g	STUDENT FACULITY ADVISOR		UNRESOLVED CLASSES	

Library name : ENTITYCH

Figure 3.1   Entity Chart: Logic University Class Scheduling

Chart

The chart uses three columns to denote:

1. External entities
2. Dataflows from the external entities to the application
3. Dataflows from the application to the external entity

The title is the application.

   Which is best? The format most easily understandable to your specific user. Figures 1.2 and 3.1 illustrate both forms for Logic University.

USER VERIFICATION

The completed entity diagram is reviewed with the user to ascertain that:

   All external entities have been identified.
   All major dataflows, including direction of flow, have been identified.

AUTOMATED TOOLS

There are numerous graphic tools that can easily draw the graphic entity diagram. At this writing only one tool—DFDP by ADPAC[1]—uses the entity diagram as the beginning point of analysis and which the computer uses for verifying subsequent diagrams.

SUMMARY

The entity diagram is used by analysts to communicate to users their impression of the general scope of the users' applications. The users verify and correct the entity diagram to reflect their views.

[1]DFDP—Diagraphics for Data Processing.

4

Data Collection

DEFINITION

The toolkits defined later in this chapter are often represented as ways to define the general logic required to fulfill the user requirements. In so doing, they *must collect* the data required to satisfy the logic. This chapter and this book concentrate on the data collection aspects of the toolkits.

NEW APPLICATIONS

A wise person has written: "There is nothing new under the sun." It is difficult to envision a *business application* that has not already been programmed by somebody somewhere. This theorem has prompted an explosive growth in vendor-supplied business application software. Why design and program an accounts receivable/payable, MRP (material requirement planning), payroll, etc., application when somebody else (vendor) can provide the application at an apparently lower cost? It is usually easier to define (or redefine) an existing *automated* solution than start from scratch. However, it is often not possible to progress from an existing system because:

It does not exist in *your* corporate environment.
It is too difficult to use your existing automated system because:
It is poorly and/or undocumented (as many existing automated systems are).
The coding is undecipherable by anybody.

A major change has occurred in the corporate goals and objectives.

Vendor packages are too expensive and/or not purchasable by your organization.

In any of the cases above, you have a "new" application. New applications should use the entity context diagram as input into an analysis diagramming toolkit. Analysis diagramming toolkits are broadly divided into (1) functional decomposition and (2) data decomposition.

Functional Decomposition

Functional decomposition is the graphic process of decomposing the logic required for the user application to its ultimate detail. The most popular—but not the only—functional

Figure 4.1A Logical Level 0 DFD: Logic University (Gane/Sarson; ADPAC; McAuto)

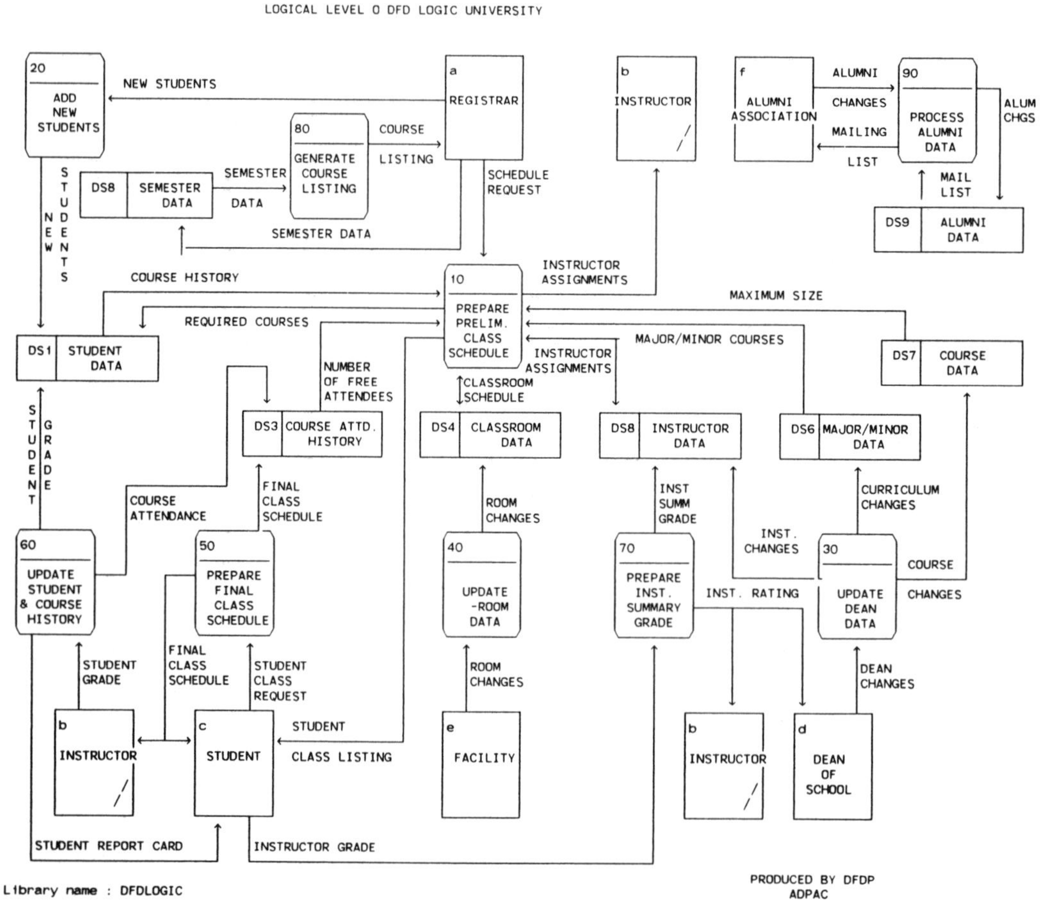

LOGICAL LEVEL 0 DFD LOGIC UNIVERSITY

Library name : DFDLOGIC

PRODUCED BY DFDP
ADPAC

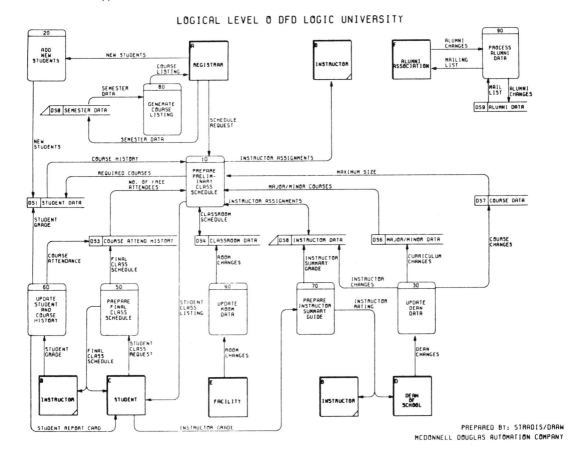

Figure 4.1B

decomposition toolkits are those of (1) Gane/Sarson (2) Sadt, and (3) Yourdon.

Gane/Sarson   Chris Gane and Trish Sarson wrote their classic book on functional de-composition in 1977. It is affectionately known by its aficionados as the "Black Mon-ster" since its covers were printed on black paper (the official title is *Structured System Analysis and Design*). The Gane/Sarson dataflow diagram uses four symbols:

1. A "double" square to denote external entities
2. A line and arrowhead to denote a dataflow and its direction
3. A "rounded rectangle" to denote a function (process, transform)
4. An "open rectangle" to denote a data store (a "place" where the application logic-ally stores the data for future use)

The Gane/Sarson approach basically recommends three levels of diagrams:

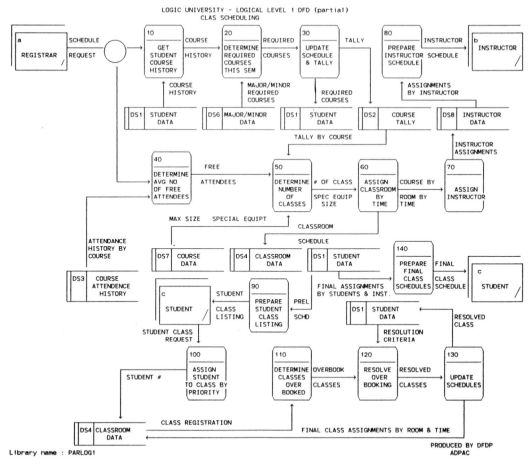

Figure 4.2A Logic University: Logical Level 1 (Partial), Class Scheduling (Gane/Sarson; ADPAC; McAuto)

Level 0: Displays the major function of the application.

Level 1: Decomposes each major function into its subordinate functional processes.

Level 2: "Explodes" each subordinate functional process into detailed transforms (it is possible to go "lower" if a subordinate process is still too complicated).

The basic procedure is to decompose each function that is represented by a rounded rectangle into its subordinate functions until each final rounded rectangle can be represented by one page (8½ by 11 inches) of structured English.[1] The steps include:

---

[1]Structured English is a precise form of English derived from structured coding standards for defining functional logic. One page (approximately 50 instructions) is considered by many authorities as the maximum for a functional module.

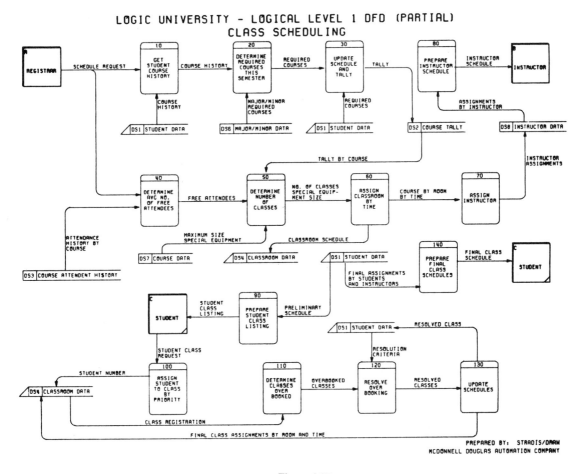

Figure 4.2B

1. Converting the entity context diagram into a level 0 by decomposing "the application" into its major functions:

   a. Each incoming dataflow on the entity context diagram terminates at a function (rounded rectangle) that briefly describes the application processing.

   b. Each outgoing dataflow begins at a function that briefly describes the application processing.

2. Decomposing each function in the level 0 into its "normal"[2] subfunctions. A suggested guideline is that each "standard"[2] level 1 rounded rectangle have three or fewer dataflows in *and* out.

---

[2]The "normal" level 1 function does not show exception dataflows. A function that distributes or performs as a "mailbox" can have more than three dataflows.

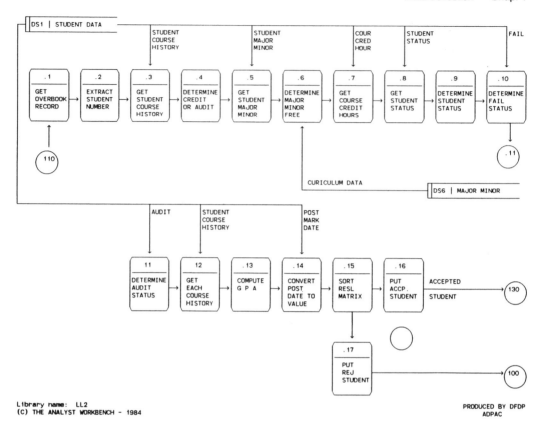

Figure 4.3 Logical Level 2: 120 Resolve Overbooked Classes (Gane/Sarson; ADPAC; McAuto)

3. Exploding each level 1 normal subfunction into its detailed subfunctions.

Figures 4.1 to 4.3 represent the Gane/Sarson diagram progression for Logic University. Figure 4.10 shows the data elements collected from level 1.

Further description of Gane/Sarson and the other toolkits are available in the reference manuals listed in the Bibliography. This book concentrates on the data collection aspects of each toolkit.

Yourdon   Larry Constantine, Tom De Marco, and Ed Yourdon have written several books describing the Yourdon approach. The Yourdon dataflow diagram also uses four symbols:

1. A square to denote external entities
2. A line and arrowhead to denote a dataflow and its directions.

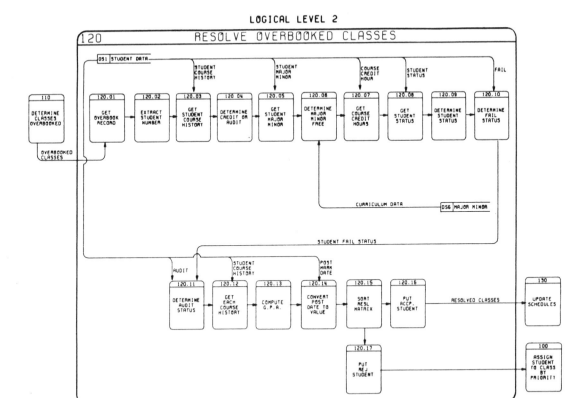

Figure 4.3B

3. A circle to denote a function
4. One or two straight lines to denote a data store

The Yourdon approach decomposes each function until it is described by a "mini-spec." The mini-spec is again one page of structured English. An additional constraint is that each diagram should contain seven or fewer functions (circles).

The steps involved are analogous to those of Gane/Sarson. Figures 4.4 to 4.7 represent the Yourdon diagram progression for Logic University.

Data Decomposition

Data decomposition is the graphic process of decomposing data beginning with the *output* until all input required for the output has been defined. Data decomposition is not extensively used in North America. In England Jackson is used, and in Europe, Warnier. Ken

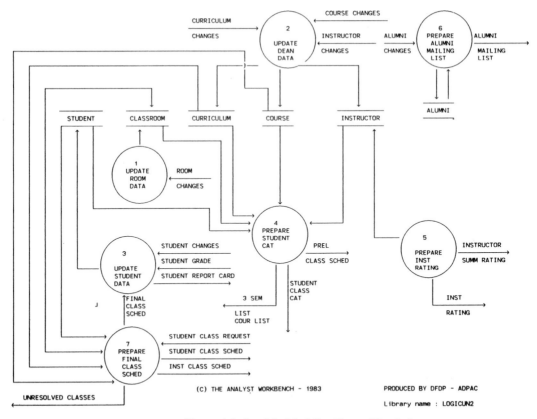

Figure 4.4 Level 0: Scheduling Classes (Yourdon)

Figure 4.5 Level 1: Prepare Final Class Schedule (Yourdon)

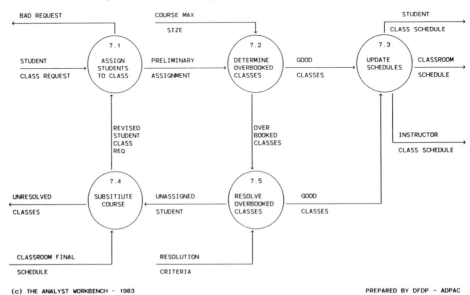

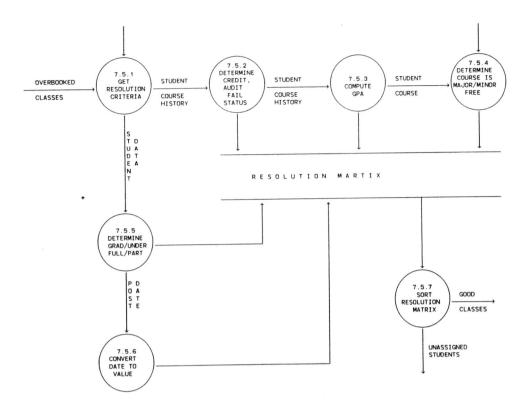

GPA = GRADE POINT AVERAGE

Figure 4.6 Level 2: Resolve Overbooked Classes (Yourdon)

Figure 4.7 Jackson: Student Report Card

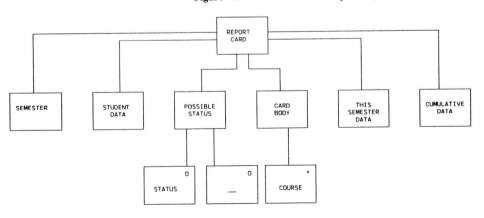

PRODUCED BY DFDP
ADPAC

Orr has modified Warnier and introduced it to Canada and the United States as Warnier/ Orr.

Jackson   Jackson uses one symbol (square) to denote a data grouping and two possible figures within the square:

     o, Alternative data grouping (choice)

     *, Repetitive

The top square of a Jackson diagram represents the complete output, with each lower level representing the hierarchical decomposition of the upper level. The lowest level in any hierarchical leg represents a data element. Figure 4.7 is a Jackson diagram for a student report card. Figure 4.8 is the facsimile student report card.

Warnier/Orr   The Warnier/Orr approach uses one symbol (a bracket) to denote a data grouping and three figures:

     (m,n), Repetition (m = lower limit; n = upper limit)

     ?, Alteration—if

     +, Alteration—ifelse

Figure 4.8   Student Report Card (Sample)

STUDENT REPORT CARD

SEMESTER

STUDENT NAME		STUDENT NUMBER	
ADDRESS		CURRICLUM SCHOOL	
CITY/STATE		STATUS	

COURSE NUMBER	COURSE TITLE	INSTRUCTOR NAME	GRADE	CREDIT HOURS
			AVERAGE	
	THIS SEMESTER			
	COMULATIVE			

Library name: SRC

The text to the left of the first bracket represents the complete output, with each bracket representing the hierarchical decomposition of the leftmost bracket. Any data without a bracket to its right is a data element (Orr refers to this as an atomic element). Figure 4.9 is a Warnier/Orr diagram for a student report card.

Automated Tools

The following mainframe automated tools are available:[3]

Figure 4.9 Warnier/Orr: Student Report Card

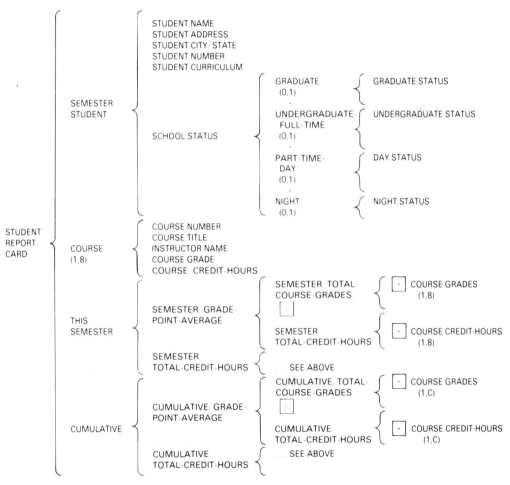

Courtesy of Ken Orr & Associates

[3]DFDP (Diagraphics for Data Processing), ADPAC Corp.; STRADIS-DRAW, McDonnell-Douglas Automation Co.; PACT, 3D Systems; PDF, Michael Jackson Systems Limited; STRUCTURE(S)®, Ken Orr & Associates. Addresses are provided in Appendix D.

```
DSI    STUDENT DATA

       K/RG      Data Element Name      Comment

       P         student-number
                 student-name
                 student-status           graduate/undergraduate, fulltime/
                                          parttime, day/night, etc.
                 student-home-address
                 student-home-phone
                 student-date-graduation-expected
                 student-date-enrollment
                 student.instructor-number-{advisor}
                                          {} = role (see Chapter 10
                                              for explanation)
                 student.curriculum-school-name
                                          the school that "owns" the
                                          student's first major
         *       student.course-history
                     student.course.semester-taken
                     student.course-number-taken
                     student.course-title
                     student.course-hours-credit taken
                     student.course-hours-credit-earned
                     student.course-grade-earned
         *       student.major            0, 1, or 2 majors allowed
         *       student.minor            0, 1, or 2 minors allowed
         *       student-degree-previous
                     student-degree-type-previous
                     student-date-graduation-previous


DS2      STUDENT SCHEDULE

         P       student-number
         P       student.classroom-number-attending
         P       student-dayofweek-attending
         P       student-time-start-attending
                 student-time-end-attending
                 student.instructor-name
                                          name of instructor teaching class

DS3      COURSE ATTENDANCE (ATTD.) HISTORY

         P       course-number
         P       course.semester-taken
                 course.student-tally-taken
                                          tally of all students taking course
                                          in the specified semester
                 course.student-tally-major-taken
                                          tally of all students taking course
                                          for major
                 course.student-tally-minor-taken
                                          tally of all students taking course
                                          for minor
                 course.student-tally-free-taken
                                          tally of all students taking course
                                          for free (optional) credit
```

Figure 4.10   Data Elements Collected by Data Store from Gane/Sarson Logical
Level 1 of Logic University

DS4   CLASSROOM DATA

P   classroom-number
    classroom-capacity
*   classroom-dayofweek
        classroom-dayofweek
        classroom-time-start
        classroom-time-end
        classroom.course-number
        classroom.course-title
        classroom.instructor-number
        classroom.instructor-name
**   classroom.student-number
            student numbers for students taking
            course from specified instructor
            in specified classroom on specified
            day at specified start time
          classroom.student-name
*   classroom.equipment-special
        classroom.equipment-type-special

DS5   INSTRUCTOR DATA

P   instructor-number
    instructor-name
    instructor-statue   full/associate/assistant/graduate
    instructor-home-address
    instructor-home-phone
    instructor-date-teach-start
    instructor-date-tenure
    instructor.curriculum-school-name
            the school that "owns" the
            instructor
*   instructor.course-history
        instructor.course.semester-taught
        instructor.course-number-taught
        instructor.course-title
        instructor.course-grade-summary-earned
            a mathematical average of all grades
            given by all students taking the
            specified course from the specified
            instructor in the specified
            semester
*   instructor-degree-previous
        instructor-degree-previous
        instructor-date-graduation-previous

DS6   MAJOR/MINOR DATA

P   major:minor.curriculum-school-name
            the school that "owns" the
            major:minor
P   major:minor-name
P   major:minor-type
    major:minor-hours-graduation-required
*   major:minor.course-requirements
        major:minor.course-requirements
        major:minor.course-title

Figure 4.10 Con't.

DS7   COURSE DATA

    P   course-number
          course-title
          course.curriculum-school-name
          course-hours-credit-minimum
                    the minimum credit hours that a
                    student can take the specified
                    course for
          course-hours-credit-maximum
          course-classize-minimum
                    the minimum number of students that
                    must enroll otherwise the specified
                    course is canceled for the current
                    semester
          course-classize-maximum
                    the maximum number of students that
                    can be taught in a class session
                    regardless of the classroom size
          course-hours-duration
                    the hours that a session of the
                    specified course requires (i.e., a
                    course session with a start time of
                    8:30 AM and an end time of 11:00 AM
                    has a duration of 2 1/2 hours)
   *   course-prerequisite
            course-number-{prerequisite}
   *   course.equipment-special
            course-equipment-type-special

DS8   SEMESTER

    P semester
          semester-date-start
          semester-date-end

DS9   ALUMNI DATA

    P   alumni-number
          alumni-name
          alumni-home-address
          alumni-home-phone
          alumni-employer-name
          alumni-employer-address
          alumni-contribution-year-current
          alumni-contribution-summary
   *   alumni-degree-previous
            alumni-degree-type-previous
            alumni-data-graduation-previous

NOTES:

    K = Key: P = a data element that forms the entire or part of a
               primary key. A primary key with multiple data elements
               is a concatenated (multiple) primary key.

    * = repeating group: a group of data elements that occur
                      "n" (0 to many) times per single occurrence
                      of the table.

    ** = a repeating group within a repeating group.

Figure 4.10 Con't.

The data elements that are part of the repeating group are indented
under the repeating group name (it is possible—as in
student.major and student.minor that there are no data elements
within the repeating group).

Created by the intersection of two entity types (such as
student.course-history).

: = a preliminary guess that data element is part of a
super/subtype entity type (such as major:minor).

Figure 4.10   Con't.

Gane/Sarson:	DFDP,	Stradis-Draw
Yourdon:	DFDP	
Jackson:	DFDP,	PACT, PDF
Warnier/Orr:	DFDP,	Structures

EXISTING PROGRAMS

Existing programs must contain the data universe for the current system. They can be used
as the initial source of data for the new application. The generic steps involved in an IBM
Cobol environment are given below.

Program Inventory

Identification of *all* programs (daily, weekly, monthly, quarterly, annual, "on demand,"
etc.) that comprise the application under review is required, with the only accurate source
being in the JCL. Therefore, the first step is to identify the complete set of JCL for the
application. Usually, the complete set of JCL can be determined by:

Standard prefix (suffix) of the program identification and/or
Operational run books

Each program executed by a JCL EXEC statement must be placed in the program inventory. Each program in the program inventory must be examined for CALL statements.
Each program CALLed must be placed in the program inventory and in turn be examined
for CALL statements. Eventually, all programs involved in the application, including utilities, non-Cobol, etc., will be listed in the program inventory.

The program inventory is used for:

Creating a List of Unique Data Element Names

Unique data elements[4] are extracted from the Data Division (including File, Working-
Storage, Linkage, and Report Sections) and literals defined in the Procedure Division.
The metadata[5] extracted should include:

[4]A data element is any elementary field with a PIC clause.
[5]Metadata is data about data.

Data element name
Logical length[6]
PIC clause

The complete text should be sorted in alphanumeric (major) logical length (minor) sequence. The sorted list of data elements is used for:

Data Purification

Most old Cobol programs suffer from a proliferation of homonyms, aliases, and synonyms. Numerous studies have indicated that there are 20 "other" names for each real data element. The problem is to identify and eliminate (or catalog) the other names.

Homonyms   A homonym is the same data element name for two or more different data elements. Homonyms must be resolved; otherwise, inconsistent results will be generated because the computer will access the wrong data elements. Homonyms can be identified when the same data element name has multiple logical lengths.

Aliases   Aliases are multiple data element names for a single data element. Aliases should be kept to a minimum but there will probably be a few:

User name
Programming language name
Database administrator name
Etc.

The identification of aliases requires an analyst knowledgeable of the data and automated tools to perform the voluminous clerical operations required. The identification of aliases (and synonyms) has been called *data name rationalization*. An extensive discussion is provided on pages 236-255.

Synonyms   Synonyms are multiple physical representations for a single data element. Synonyms, like aliases, should be kept to a minimum, but there will probably be a few:

Storage format
CRT display format
Report format
Etc.

---

[6]Logical length is the number of characters required to store a data element value *exclusive* of decimal, currency, and editing symbols. Specifically, the logical length of an elementary field is the number of A, B, X, Z, 9, * symbols in the PIC clause; the logical length of a literal is the number of characters between the quotation marks (alpha) or the number of digits (numeric).

Synonyms are identified by the data name rationalization process.

Automated Tools   There are various software tools that perform some of the functions listed above (see Appendix D for addresses); for example,

> SCAN 370 (Group Operations)
> Data Dictionary Composer (Composer Technology Corp.)

However, at this writing only one product, PM/SS (ADPAC Corp.) incorporates all the functions necessary to perform data name rationalization.

SUMMARY

"Diagrams" are used to collect the data universe for new applications; existing Cobol programs are analyzed to provide the current data universe. Data elements collected from Cobol programs must be purified of homonyms, synonyms, and aliases to be useful.

5

Data Verification

DEFINITION

The data elements collected by the techniques described in Chapter 4 represent the preliminary universe of data elements for the specific application. The objective of data verification is to refine the preliminary universe so that it contains only those data elements that are required *and* updated.

ALL INPUT DATA ELEMENTS ARE USED

The first logical step is to verify that all data elements are in fact used either directly for output or to derive output. Unused data elements:

Waste human resources to input
Waste computer time to edit and store
Waste computer storage
Etc.

The actual steps are dependent on the tool utilized.

Functional Decomposition

Data stores are repositories of data flowing within the application. Each dataflow entering a data store contains data that is logically being created and/or maintained; each dataflow exiting a data store uses the data contained within. It is axiomatic that:

> All data entered is maintained.
>
> All data entered is used for output.

Figure 5.1 is a check form for validating data stores; Figure 5.2 is a completed form for the student data store. Essentially, the data store validation forms list data elements in the left with columns for create (C), maintain (M), and used for output (O).

DATA STORE _____

ID	DATA ELEMENT	*	CREATE	MAINTAIN	OUTPUT

COMMENTS:

Page __ of __

Library name: DS1A

Figure 5.1 Data Store Check Form (Sample)

DATA STORE DS1 Student Data

ID	DATA ELEMENT	*	CREATE	MAINTAIN	OUTPUT
		D A T A F L O W S			
1	STUDENT-NUMBER		150	150	10, 120, 190
2	STUDENT-NAME		150	150	10, 120, 190
3	STUDENT COURSE-HISTORY	*	160	C1	10
4	COURSE-NUMBER		160	C1	10, 190
5	COURSE-TITLE		160	C1	10, 190
6	COURSE-GRADE		160	C1	10, 190
7	COURSE CREDIT-HOURS		160	C1	10, 190
8	COURSE HOURS-TAKEN		160, C2	C1	10
9	STUDENT-MAJOR	*	150	150	120
10	STUDENT-MINOR	*	150	150	120
11	STUDENT-STATUS		150	150	120
12	STUDENT-COMULATIVE CREDIT-HOURS		C3	C1	120, 190
13	STUDENT-COMULATIVE GRADE-POINT-AVG		C3	C1	120, 190
14	STUDENT POSTMARK-DATE		C4	C4	120

COMMENTS: (* = repeating groups)

C1 level 2 DFD must show how to correct erroneous data.

C2 COURSE-CREDIT-HOURS = COURSE-HOURS-TAKEN if student
   passes course, else COURSE-CREDIT-HOURS = zero.

C3 Derivable level 2 DFD must show calculation.

Library name: DS1B
Page 1 of 2

Figure 5.2 Data Store Check Form for DSI Student Data

Data Element	C	M	O
Student-name	×	×	×
Student-major	×		×
Student-previous-degree			×

Student-name is logically correct since there is at least one dataflow that creates, maintains, and outputs it. Student-major is incorrect since once the student-major is entered it can never be changed. Student-previous-degree is used somewhere but never entered. The errors represent dataflow "bugs" and must be corrected.

Process boxes represent data transformation. All output data elements must be derivable from the input elements. If the algorithm for X is

DATA STORE   DS1 Student Data

ID	DATA ELEMENT	*	DATAFLOWS		
			CREATE	MAINTAIN	OUTPUT
15	STUDENT HOME-ADDRESS		150	150	190
16	STUDENT-EXPECTED GRAUDATION-DATE		150	150	C5
17	STUDENT ENROLLMENT-DATE		150	150	C5
18	STUDENT PREVIOUS-DEGREE	*	150	150	C5
19	DEGREE-TYPE		150	150	C5
20	GRAUDATION-DATE		150	150	C5
21	STUDENT CURRICULUM-SCHOOL		150	150	120
22	SEMESTER		C6	C1	190
23	STUDENT-CREDIT-HRS THIS-SEMESTER		C3	C1	190
24	STUDENT-GRADE-POINT AVG-THIS-SEMESTER		C3	C1	190

COMMENTS:

C4   level 1 DFD must be revised to collect this data elements
     from process box 95.

C5   user believes these data elements are required for future.

C6   semester should be made part of STUDENT-COURSE-HISTORY
     repating group.

Page 2 of 2
library name: DS1C   **Figure 5.2** Con't.

$$X = A + B * C / D$$

then A, B, C, and D must be input. This check is in addition to the data store checks. Figure 5.3 is a process box validation form. Again, data elements are listed in the left with appropriate columns.

Figure 5.2 displays a major problem (!) for data element 9 and minor problems (?) for items 3 and 8.

Student-cumulative-gradepoint-average (9) cannot be derived from the input. Either a course-history group including grade and credit-hours needs to be input, or the student-cumulative-gradepoint-average-to-date data element must be input.

Note: If a group containing credit-hours is entered, data element 4 (student-course-hours-to-date) can be derived by summing the individual credit-hours.

	Data Element	I	O	Pᵃ	D	Algorithm
1.	Student-number	×	×			
2.	Student-name	×	×			
3.	Student-address	×	(?)			
4.	Student-course-hour-to-date	×		×		
5.	Student-grade-by-course-this-semester	×	×	×		
6.	Student-credit-hours-earned-by-course-this-semester	×	×	×		
7.	Student-cumulative-credit-hours		×		×	4 plus sum of 6
8.	Student-cumulative-gradepoint-average-this-semester		(?)		×	Sum of 5 divided by sum of 6
9.	Student-cumulative-gradepoint-average				(!)	*Cannot be derived*

ᵃData element used as a *Parameter* in an algorithm.

PROCESS BOX _____

ID	DATA ELEMENT	*	IN	OUT	PARM	DEV	ALGORITHM

COMMENTS:

Figure 5.3 Process Box Check Form (Sample)

Student-address (3) is entered but never used. Why?

Student-cumulative-gradepoint-average-this-semester (8) is calculated with the required data elements but is not output. Why?

As stated in Chapter 1, this design cycle stresses maximum consistency checking at the earliest point in the design cycle to significantly reduce the correction cost and time. Data is the most important attribute of any application. It must be correct. Rectifying the error here means changing some paper forms; correcting later could mean redoing the physical database. Figure 5.4 is a completed form for process box 120 from the Gane/Sarson level 1 of Logic University (Figure 4.2).

Data Decomposition

Data decomposition (Jackson, Warnier/Orr) is self-checking in that each starts with output working backward to identify the necessary parameters. Any data at the lowest level

PROCESS BOX   120 Resolve Overbooking

ID	DATA ELEMENT	*	IN	OUT	PARM	DEV	ALGORITHM
a	COURSE-NUMBER		110	130	X		
b	COURSE-MAX-SIZE		110		X		
c	STUDENTS-ASSIGNED-TO-COURSE-SESSION	*	110		X		used as key for DS1 student data
d	STUDENT-COURSE-HISTORY	*	DS1		C1		
e	STUDENT-MAJOR	*	DS1		X		used to determine if course is for student major
f	STUDENT-MINOR	*	DS1		X		used to determine if course is for student minor
g	STUDENT-STATUS		DS1		X		graduate/unergraudate full/part
h	POSTMARK-DATE-OF-REQUEST		DS1		X		final tie breaker before "COIN FLIP"
i	STUDENT-ACTUALY-ASGND TO-COURSE-SESSION	*		130		X	see page 1 of appendix for priority scheme
j	STUDENTS-BUMPED-FROM COURSE-SESSION	*		C2		X	see page 1 of appendix

COMMENTS:

C1   used to determine CREDIT/AUDIT STATUS; COURSE-CREDIT-HOURS FAIL/AUDIT STATUS; CUMULATIVE CREDIT HOURS & GPA.

C2   considered to be exception dataflow and not shown on level 1, must be shown on level 2.

Library name: PROB2   Page 1 of 1

Figure 5.4   Process Box Check Form for 120 Resolve Overbooking

(Jackson) or without a bracket to the right (Warnier/Orr) is a data element (atomic). Any other data is derivable.

"FORGOTTEN DATA ELEMENTS" (USER VERIFICATION)

There is a raging debate between the decomposition theoreticians as to which toolkit collects data better. Essentially the two points are:

1. How do the analysts know that they have collected all the output documents (data decomposition)?
2. How do the analysts know that they have collected all the input (functional decomposition)?

Who is right (or more correct)? My opinion is that neither is correct as long as they rely on a data processing analyst to perform the data collection activity. Data collection, verification, normalization, etc., requires intimate knowledge of the data, knowledge that only a user working with the data on a day-to-day basis can acquire. My preferred solution is that users perform the data activities with data processing providing technical assistance. I suspect (without any empirical proof) that most users would prefer data decomposition since they would not have to concern themselves with functional processes. I also suspect that Warnier/Orr would be preferred since it does not appear to be as "computerese" as Jackson. In any case, the user should perform the data activities.

This practitioner realizes that most analysis is done by and will continue to be done by programmers promoted to analysts. Programmers usually do not talk to users; analysts must. The major benefit of any toolkit or methodology is that it stresses user communication. The user must verify the correctness of the data. The analyst must communicate to the user in an as user friendly a mode as possible. The "company" toolkit will work if (and only if) the user has been trained to understand the basic rudiments and philosophy of the toolkit. An alternative is the table. Users relate to tables. They create, use, and maintain tables in their work environment. Therefore, tables are a natural communication tool. Figure 5.5 is a table of data in Logic University.

COURSE DATA TABLE

COURSE NUMBER	COURSE TITLE	CURR SCHOOL	MIN CRE	MAX CRE	MIN SIZE	MAX SIZE	DUR HRS
0169	Boolean Logic	MATH	3	5	5	20	3
0170	Relation Algebra	MATH	4	6	5	15	4
0171	Relation Calculus	MATH	5	7	5	10	5
. . .							

Library name: CDT

Figure 5.5   Course Data Table

EXISTING COBOL PROGRAMS

The data purification described in Chapter 4 created a unique list of data elements cited in Cobol programs. The next steps are to determine that all data elements are used and which ones are derivable. A "where used" analysis of the Procedure Division will reveal those data elements that are unused (no statement explicitly or implicitly uses the data element). The "where used" analysis should also show the derivable data elements, i.e.,

```
      ADD A TO B
  COMPUTE A = B X C
 DIVIDE A BY B GIVING C
   MULTIPLY A BY B
  SUBTRACT A FROM B
      MOVE A TO B
         etc.
```

Of course, the final list must be user verified!

AUTOMATED TOOLS

All the automated tools mentioned previously are available. However, at this writing, only the ADPAC tools provide consistency checking for Gane/Sarson and Yourdon. These checks include:

All dataflows on a higher-level diagram are represented on lower-level diagrams.[1]

All new dataflows on a lower-level diagram are either exception dataflows or "single structure" dataflows.[2]

All input data elements maintained and used.

All output data elements entered and maintained.

SUMMARY

It is essential that the user verify the correctness of each and every data element. A mistake here is guaranteed to cause significant grief when found—and it is usually found *after* the physical database has been designed.

[1]Yourdon refers to this check as "balancing."
[2]It is possible to split a dataflow that contains multiple structures into single-structure dataflows, i.e.,

```
                         CUSTOMER-ORDER
                         ------------->
 CUSTOMER-MAIL    =       CUSTOMER-CHECK
 ------------->          ------------->
                         CUSTOMER-INQUIRY
                         --------------->
```

[1]Yourdon refers to this check as "balancing."
[2]It is possible to split a dataflow that contains multiple structures into single-structure dataflows, i.e.,

6

Entity Type Analysis

DEFINITION

Entity type[1] analysis is the identification of those "things" that require storage of independent information. The thing can be people:

STUDENT	INSTRUCTOR	ALUMNI

or facility:

CLASSROOM	OFFICE	LIBRARY

or concept:

COURSE	CURRICULUM	MAJOR

or government:

CITY	PROVINCE	COUNTRY

or. . . . The key attribute is the requirement that independent information must be maintained. Mixing of entity types causes corrupt databases.

---

[1]Many authors use only the word "entity" to identify what this book calls entity type. I use *entity type* to define the class, i.e., course, and *entity* to define a single occurrence of the class, i.e., Computer Science 101. Entity set is a term sometimes used to define the class.

44

IDENTIFICATION

The identification of entity types is again dependent on the tools being used.

Entity (context) diagram

The entity (context) diagram displays external entities (sources or destinations of the data for the application). Normally, external entities are entity types. Each external entity should be tentatively identified as an entity type. The Logic University entity diagram (Figure 1.2) has the following external entities, which will be tentatively identified as *entity types*:

REGISTRAR	DEAN-OF-SCHOOL	STUDENT
ALUMNI-ASSOC	STUDENT-FACULTY-ADVISOR	
FACILITIES	INSTRUCTOR	

"DATA" DIAGRAMS

Functional decomposition (Gane/Sarson, Yourdon) uses a "rectangle" to identify a logical data store. The data store holds information logically required for later use by the application. The information being held must be an attribute of some entity type. Therefore, analysis of the data stores should reveal the entity types. In fact, analysis of the data store *names* should be sufficient. All methodologists recommend honest, complete, and meaningful[2] names. Therefore, the honest, complete, and meaningful data store name should disclose which entity type data is being held.

The complete level 1 Gane/Sarson diagram (Figure 4.2 is partial) has the following data stores:

STUDENT-DATA	MAJOR-MINOR-DATA	STUDENT-SCHEDULE (not on partial)
COURSE-TALLY	COURSE-ATTND-HIST	COURSE-DATA
CLASSROOM-DATA	INSTRUCTOR-DATA	SEMESTER (not on partial)
ALUMNI-DATA (not on partial)		

A cross correlation between the entity (context) diagram indicates the following matches:

STUDENT   ALUMNI   INSTRUCTOR

The above, then, are the major preliminary entity types. Registrar, dean-of-school, student-faculty-advisor, and facilities are entity types but not for the class scheduling ap-

---

[2]The author believes that each name should be honest, complete, and meaningful to the user rather than to data processing.

plication because the application does not need to maintain independent information about them. The lack of any data store on the level 1 justifies their elimination.[3]

On the other hand, major-minor, course, classroom, and semester must be added to the preliminary entity type list since the level 1 does have data stores containing information relating to them. Therefore, the preliminary list of entity types for the class scheduling application of Logic University are:

STUDENT	ALUMNI	INSTRUCTOR
MAJOR-MINOR	COURSE	CLASSROOM
SEMESTER		

Data decomposition (Jackson, Warnier/Orr) has no equivalence of data stores. The entity type analysis must be performed on the decomposition of the output documents. Most Warnier/Orr diagrams have the following generic format:

$$\text{DOCUMENT} \left\{ \begin{array}{l} \text{HEADER} \\ \text{DETAIL} \\ \text{SUMMARY} \end{array} \right.$$

The header section usually contains information being maintained for entity types. For instance,

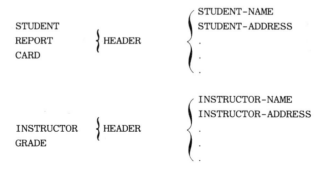

It should be clear that both the name of the document (STUDENT REPORT CARD) and the header information will identify entity types. A similar technique works for Jackson.

EXISTING PROGRAMS

Virtually all existing business programs use the concept of master/transaction records. The name of the master record (STUDENT master) or an analysis of its data element will identify the entity types.

---

[3]At this point we are only building an *application* logical database. The class scheduling logical database should be incorporated into a ''subject'' database or into an organization database. Entity relation models and total logical databases are outside the scope of this book.

AUTOMATED TOOLS

Existing automated tools are of little use in identifying entity types. DFDP and WHERE (ADPAC) can provide lists of external entities, data stores, level 0 names, master record names, etc. The lists are helpful as cross checks to determine that all relevant "things" have been considered. However, it takes a human analyst to translate people-taking-courses to STUDENT, or analyze a master record identified as MR1762 (master record number 17 developed in 1962) as INSTRUCTOR.

THE SUBTLE TRAP

A subtle trap awaits the unwary analyst who performs only a cursory or superficial entity type analysis. That subtle trap is allowing entity occurrences to pose as entity types. This chapter identified

STUDENT   ALUMNI   INSTRUCTOR

as preliminary entity types. Additional analysis should reveal that a graduate STUDENT who graduated from Logic University was also an ALUMNI and if he/she was also earning money by teaching was also an INSTRUCTOR. The objective of logical database design is the elimination of redundant data. Maintaining three separate "entity types" would create a logical database that stored redundant data (name, address, phone, . . .) in three places. Chapter 10 provides rules for detecting entity occurrences, but further design is simplified if entity occurrences are detected before clustering.

SUMMARY

Entity type analysis investigates all relevant documents to determine those things about which the application must maintain independent information and combines entity occurrences into a general entity type. This simplifies the task of normalization by permitting automatic clustering of data elements to entity types and reduces the possibility of mixing entity types within a single relation (mixing entity types causes corrupt databases).

7

Data Clustering

DEFINITION

Clustering is the assignment of attributes (data elements) to their respective entity types. Each attribute defines something about the entity type. For instance, the entity type of student has attributes of

NAME	BIRTH-DATE	ADDRESS
SEX	MAJOR	MINOR

and many more. This is the first step before normalization.

GLOBAL ASSIGNMENT BY ENTITY TYPE

Many (and probably most) analysts who perform normalization individually assign each attribute to "something" (if up-front entity type analysis has not been performed, the attribute may be assigned to a relationship instead of an entity type). The problem of individual assignment is the tendency to spend inordinate amounts of time, sweat, and labor in deciding where to place the attribute. A benefit of normalization is the final assignment of attributes to the correct table. Why spend subjective time in doing (probably not as well) something that can be performed by a series of unsubjective algorithms? My recommendation is to globally assign attributes to entity types based on simple rules for each tool type.

48

Data Stores

Assign all data elements (attributes) to the entity type identified in the data store name (if more than one entity type, then assign to *first*; i.e., if data store name is STUDENT.COURSE-HISTORY, then assign to STUDENT).

At Logic University:

Data Store Name	Assigned To:
STUDENT-data	STUDENT
MAJOR-MINOR-data	MAJOR-MINOR
STUDENT-schedule	STUDENT
COURSE-tally	COURSE
COURSE-attnd-hist	COURSE
COURSE-data	COURSE
CLASSROOM-data	CLASSROOM
INSTRUCTOR-data	INSTRUCTOR
SEMESTER	SEMESTER
ALUMNI-data	ALUMNI

Figure 7.1 is a list of data elements clustered by entity type.

```
DISPLAY


     NN    NN WW    WW LL      GGGGGG  UU    UU NN    NN
     NNN   NN WW    WW LL      GGGGGGGG UU    UU NNN   NN
     NNNN  NN WW    WW LL      GG    GG UU    UU NNNN  NN
     NNNNN NN WW WW WW LL      GG       UU    UU NNNNN NN
     NN NNNNN WW WW WW LL      GG  GGGG UU    UU NN NNNNN
     NN  NNNN WWW   WWW LL     GG    GG UU    UU NN   NNNN
     NN   NNN WW    WW LLLLLLL GGGGGGGG UUUUUUUU NN    NNN
     NN    NN W     W LLLLLLL  GGGGGG   UUUU    NN    NN

 SEQ     DISPLAY OF  NWLGUN   FROM LIBRARY: ADP.PM.A200.PMLIB
NUMBER  1...5...10...15...20...25...30...35...40...45...50...55...60...6
    1              STUDENT          STUDENT
    2                               S-NUMBER
    3                               S-NAME
    4                               S-STATUS
    5                               S-HOME-ADDRESS
    6                               S-HOME-PHONE
    7                               S-GRADUATION-EXPECTED-DATE
    8                               S_I-NUMBER<ADVISOR>
    9                               S_C-HISTORY
   10                               S_C_T-TAKEN
   11                               S_C-NUMBER-TAKEN
   12                               S_C-TITLE
   13                               S_C-HOURS-CREDIT-TAKEN
   14                               S_C-HOURS-CREDIT-EARNED
   15                               S_C-GRADE-EARNED
```

Figure 7.1 List of Data Elements Clustered by Entity Type

16		S_M<MAJOR>
17		S_M<MINOR>
18		S-DEGREE-PREVIOUS
19		S-DEGREE-TYPE-PREVIOUS
20		S-GRADUATION-PREVIOUS-DATE
21		S_R-NUMBER-ATTENDING
22		S-DAYOFWEEK-ATTENDING
23		S-TIME-START-ATTENDING
24		S-TIME-END-ATTENDING
25		S_I-NAME<TEACHING>
26		S_H-NAME
27	COURSE	COURSE
28		C-NUMBER
29		C-TITLE
30		C_H-NAME-CURRICULUM
31		C-HOURS-CREDIT-MINIMUM
32		C-HOURS-CREDIT-MAXIMUM
33		C-CLASSSIZE-MINIMUM
34		C-CLASSSIZE-MAXIMUM
35		C-HOURS-DURATION
36		C-PREREQUISITE
37		C-NUMBER<PREREQUISITE>
38		C_E-SPECIAL
39		C_E-EQUIPMENT-TYPE-SPECIAL
40		C_T-TAKEN
41		C_S-TALLY-TAKEN
42		C_S-TALLY-MAJOR-TAKEN
43		C_S-TALLY-MINOR-TAKEN
44		C_S-TALLY-FREE-TAKEN
45	CLASSROM	CLASSROOM
46		R-NUMBER
47		R-CAPACITY
48		R-DAYOFWEEK
49		R-TIME-START-ATTENDING
50		R-TIME-END-ATTENDING
51		R_C-NUMBER
52		R_C-TITLE
53		R_I-NUMBER
54		R_I-NAME
55		STUDENTS-REGISTERED
56		R_S-NUMBER
57		R_S-NAME
58		R_E-SPECIAL
59		R_E-TYPE-SPECIAL
60	INSTRCT	INSTRUCTOR
61		I-NUMBER
62		I-NAME
63		I-STATUS
64		I-HOME-ADDRESS
65		I-HOME-PHONE
66		I-DATE-TEACH-START
67		I-DATE-TENURE
68		I_H-NAME
69		I_C-HISTORY
70		I_C_T-TAUGHT
71		I_C-NUMBER-TAUGHT
72		I_C-TITLE
73		I_C-GRADE-SUMMARY-EARNED
74		I-DEGREE-PREVIOUS
75		I-GRADUATION-PREVIOUS-DATE

Figure 7.1 Con't.

76	MAJIMIN	MAJOR-MINOR
77		M_H-NAME-CURRICULUM
78		M-NAME
79		M-TYPE
80		M-HOURS-GRADUATION-REQUIRED
81		M_C-REQUIREMENTS
82		M_C-NUMBER
83	SEMESTER	SEMESTER
84		T-NAME
85		T-DATE-START
86		T-DATE-END
87	ALUMNI	ALUMNI
88		A-NUMBER
89		A-NAME
90		A-HOME-ADRESS
91		A-HOME-PHONE
92		A-EMPLOYER-NAME
93		A-EMPLOYER-ADDRESS
94		A-CONTRIBUTION-YEAR-CURRENT
95		A-CONTRIBUTION-SUMMARY
96		A-DEGREE-PREVIOUS
97		A-DEGREE-TYPE-PREVIOUS
98		A-DEGREE-GRADUATION-PREVIOUS

Figure 7.1   Con't.

Universal

Ken Orr defines basic information about entity types as universals. Assign all data elements (attributes) to the "right" of the universal to the entity type represented by the universal as per the rules for data stores.

Jackson

Assign all data elements (attributes) in a single chart to the entity type represented by the header box as per the rules for data stores.

Existing Programs—General

Assign all data elements (attributes) located *anywhere* within the program to the entity type represented by the first master record.

Existing Programs—Cobol

Applying the generic rule to Cobol requires that all data elements in the Data Division, including Working-Storage, Linkage, and Report *plus* that the data elements represented by the literals in the Procedure Division be assigned to the entity type represented by the first master record. Strictly speaking, only data with Picture clauses (or literals) should be assigned. Group names are not essential but I recommend that they also be assigned—if the names are reasonably meaningful—to facilitate the naming of new tables.

AUTOMATED TOOLS

DFDP (ADPAC) permits interactive assignment of data elements by data store, universal, or Jackson chart. WHERE (ADPAC) permits global assignment of all data within a program to an entity type specified by an analyst.

SUMMARY

Global clustering of data elements (attributes) to entity types by the rules of this chapter saves analytical time. The result is an unnormalized list of attributes that *probably* belong to the assigned entity type. Normalization—properly applied, of course—will determine the correct placement.

8

Normalization

DEFINITION

Normalization is the term applied to a set of rules derived by Ted Codd of IBM from set theory to reduce *any* universe of data to its minimal cover. Minimal cover is defined as the *smallest* amount of data necessary to satisfy the application requirements. The process includes the creation of tables (flat files), eliminating derivable data elements, and determining that all data elements are ''fully functionally dependent'' on their respective keys.

CODD RELATIONAL NOTATION

Most authors use the notation development by Ted Codd. The system is

$$\text{TABLE-NAME} \quad (\underline{K1}, \underline{K2}, . \quad . \quad ., DE1, DE2, DE3, . \quad . \quad .)$$

where   K = a data element designated as the primary *key* or part thereof. Keys are underlined and placed at the beginning. The sequence of the keys has no meaning. The purpose of the primary key is to uniquely identify a *single* occurrence of the table.

DE = data element; a column heading in the table.

For example, Student.course-history in Codd notation is

```
STUDENT.COURSE-HISTORY (student-number, course number, semester,
                        course-title, course-grade,
                        course-credit-hours-earned)
```

which in tabular format is

STUDENT NUMBER	COURSE NUMBER	SEMESTER	COURSE TITLE	COURSE GRADE	COURSE HOURS
1	13	FAL 8	MATH I	FAIL	0
1	14	FAL 8	ENGL I	PASS	3
1	13	SPG 7	MATH I	PASS	3
2	13	FAL 8	MATH I	PASS	3
.	.	.			

Each data element (including the data elements forming the primary key) within the parentheses is a column in the table. Each occurrence of the table is a row. The primary key identifies a *single row* in the table.

Student-number by itself cannot be the primary key because it would not identify a single row. Student-number plus course-number would also not work because a student could take the same course more than once. In the example above Student 1 took course 13 twice because he/she failed the course in FAL 8 and passed it in SPG 7. Therefore, semester must be added to student-number and course-number to form the primary key. The implicit assumption is that a student *cannot* take the same course more than once in the *same* semester.

This book retains a vertical format in the figures because they were produced by the DESIGN software tool developed by ADPAC. The system is

```
TABLE-NAME
P    K1
P    K2
     . . .
         DE1
         DE2
         DE3
       . . .
```

where P is a prefix indicating a data element that forms part or add of the primary key.

FIRST NORMAL FORM

Atre has defined first normal form (1NF) "as transforming data stores into two-dimensional tables. All that is usually required at this step is the removal of repeating groups." Data stores are the "rectangles" in dataflow diagrams (see Figures 4.1 to 4.6).

They represent data elements that are "at rest" in the application defined by the dataflow diagram and *must* contain the entire universe of data.

A repeating group is a set of data elements that can occur from *zero* to *n* times per occurrence of the data store. Student.course-history is a repeating group within the student data store because it can occur zero times (entering freshmen) to many times as the student progresses through Logic University. The X prefix in the vertical format represents data elements within a repeating group. The occurs clause in Cobol represents a repeating group.

The steps in performing 1NF are:

1. Identifying the primary key of each data store
2. Identifying the repeating groups in each data store
3. Removing the repeating groups thereby establishing new tables
4. Identifying the primary key of the new table

Primary Key Identification

As stated before, the primary key must uniquely identify a single occurrence. Most computer systems assign an arbitrary unique number as the primary key:

        Student-NUMBER   instructor-NUMBER
        course-NUMBER   room-NUMBER
                    etc.

All data at Logic University except semester have unique arbitrary numbers. Semester has a unique alphanumeric name:

            FAL 8   SPG 7   etc.

Candidate Keys   It is possible in performing the primary key analysis that more than one set of data elements can comprise the primary key. Each set is designated as a candidate key. The analyst must choose the "best" set using intuitive judgment. The candidate key selected as primary is underlined in Codd notation and prefixed with a P in vertical notation. The other candidate keys have "dotted" underlines in Codd and Cn prefixes in vertical, where n = candidate key number (1, 2, etc.).

In the previous student.course-history example it is possible that course-title could be used instead of course-number to form the primary key. Course-title could be used if it is a "well-structured" name; i.e., each name is unique and always spelled the same way. For instance, MATHbI is unique only if it always refers to the same course and is always spelled the same way. bMATHbI, MATHbbI, bMATHIb, bbMTHIb would *not* work (b = blank).

Assuming that course-title is well structured, the format of student.course-history is

```
Student.course-history (student-number, course-number, semester,
course-credit-hours-earned.)            course-title, course-grade,
                         . . . . . . . . . . . .
```

```
          STUDENT. COURSE-HISTORY
          PC student-number
          P  course-number
          PC semester
           C    course-title
                course-grade
                course-credit-hours-earned
```

Let's add student-name to student.course-history. Could student-name be substituted for student-number as a key? Again, it would have to be well structured. It is certainly possible to force a person's name always to be spelled exactly identically, but can a person's name ever be unique? Last name would never work (Jones, Smith, etc.). Last name and first name would narrow the choices, but how many Tom Jones are there? Adding the middle name would restrict the choices even more but would *not* guarantee uniqueness. Consequently, it is almost impossible to use a person's name as a primary key. If you still have doubts, consult your local phone book.

Candidate keys are used in second normal form (2NF).

Concatenated Keys   A primary key composed of two or more unique data elements is concatenated (multiple). Concatenated keys are used in 2NF.

Compound Keys   A compound key is composed of two or more data elements of which at least one is "meaningless." For example, assume that student-number is really two data elements:

1. Curriculum-school, which is a two-digit number that uniquely identifies each school.
2. Student-number-within-curriculum-school, which is a sequentially assigned number. (*Note:* This type of data element is often called an odometer or counter.)

If there are 99 curriculum-schools, there could be 99 students with a student-number of 0169. Student-number by itself is meaningless unless it is attached to a qualifier (curriculum school). The symbol for a compound key is +:

```
Curriculum-school + student-number
or
          P  curriculum-school
          +  student-number
```

Compound keys are used in 4NF. Naturally, a table row can be identified by a mixture of compound and concatenated keys.

Repeating Group Identification

An analyst must decide if there is a one-to-many relationship (1:*M*) between the primary key of a data store and any of its data elements. For instance, there is only *one* student-name, date-of-birth, sex, etc., per student-number. These are one-to-one relationships (1:1). However, student.course-history is a 1:*M* because there can be many[1] occurrences per student-number. The syntax for identifying repeating groups in the vertical format is to place the symbolic name next to the repeating group name and to prefix each data element within the repeating group with an X (see Figure 8.1).

 Occasionally, a repeating group can be just a repeating data element. Major and minor are examples in the student entity type since each student can have one or *two* majors and one or *two* minors. Repeating data elements are treated as repeating groups.

 An alternative approach for handling a "limited" repeating group is to split the repeating groups into separate data elements which have a 1:1 relationship with the primary key. For example,

> Major could be split into Major-1 and Major-2.
>
> Minor could be split into Minor-1 and Minor-2.

The approach above restricts the flexibility of the logical database and fails if the repeating group becomes "unlimited." For example, airlines used to have only *two* fare classes—first and other. A logical database could have been constructed as follows:

```
P    Route
     First-class-fare
     Other-class-fare
     .
     .
     .
```

How many fare classes do airlines offer now? What would be the consequences to the logical database? Worse, what would be the consequences if the physical database had been implemented using the same construct? The moral is to split *all* repeating groups even if you truly believe there can only be *two* and no more than two occurrences per primary key.

 Figure 8.1 is a list of entity types with primary keys and repeating groups identified.

---

[1]*Many* is defined as zero to *n*.

DISPLAY

```
NN     NN WW     WW LL        GGGGGG    0000      0000
NNN    NN WW     WW LL        GGGGGGGG  00  00    00  00
NNNN   NN WW     WW LL        GG    GG 00     00 00     00
NNNNN NN WW WW WW WW LL       GG        00     00 00    00
NN NNNNN WW WW WW WW LL       GG  GGGG 00     00 00     00
NN  NNNN WWW    WWW LL        GG    GG 00     00 00     00
NN   NNN WW     WW LLLLLLL GGGGGGG  00  00    00  00
NN    NN W      W LLLLLLL  GGGGGG    0000      0000
```

```
SEQ        DISPLAY OF  NWLG00    FROM LIBRARY: ADP.PM.A200.PMLIB
NUMBER   10...15...20...25...30...35...40...45...50...55...60...65...70..
  1       STUDENT               STUDENT
  2                           P S-NUMBER
  3                             S-NAME
  4                             S-STATUS
  5                             S-HOME-ADDRESS
  6                             S-HOME-PHONE
  7                             S-GRADUATION-EXPECTED-DATE
  8                             S_I-NUMBER<ADVISOR>
  9                             S_C-HISTORY                    S_C-HIST
 10                            XS_C_T-TAKEN
 11                            XS_C-NUMBER-TAKEN
 12                            XS_C-TITLE
 13                            XS_C-HOURS-CREDIT-TAKEN
 14                            XS_C-HOURS-CREDIT-EARNED
 15                            XS_C-GRADE-EARNED
 16                             S_M<MAJOR>                     S_M-MAJR
 17                             S_M<MINOR>                     S_M-MINR
 18                             S-DEGREE-PREVIOUS              S_DEG-PV
 19                            XS-DEGREE-TYPE-PREVIOUS
 20                            XS-GRADUATION-PREVIOUS-DATE
 21                             S_R-NUMBER-ATTENDING           S_R-#-AT
 22                            XS-DAYOFWEEK-ATTENDING
 23                            XS-TIME-START-ATTENDING
 24                            XS-TIME-END-ATTENDING
 25                            XS_I-NAME<TEACHING>
 26                             S_H-NAME
 27       COURSE                COURSE
 28                           P C-NUMBER
 29                             C-TITLE
 30                             C_H-NAME-CURRICULUM
 31                             C-HOURS-CREDIT-MINIMUM
 32                             C-HOURS-CREDIT-MAXIMUM
 33                             C-CLASSSIZE-MINIMUM
 34                             C-CLASSSIZE-MAXIMUM
 35                             C-HOURS-DURATION
 36                             C-PREREQUSITE                  C-PREREQ
 37                            XC-NUMBER<PREREQUISITE>
 38                             C_E-SPECIAL                    C_E-SPEC
 39                            XC_E-EQUIPMENT-TYPE-SPECIAL
 40                             C_T-TAKEN                      C_T-TAKN
 41                            XC_S-TALLY-TAKEN
 42                            XC_S-TALLY-MAJOR-TAKEN
 43                            XC_S-TALLY-MINOR-TAKEN
 44                            XC_S-TALLY-FREE-TAKEN
 45       CLASSROM              CLASSROOM
 46                           P R-NUMBER
 47                             R-CAPACITY
 48                             R-DAYOFWEEK                    RDAYOFWK
 49                            XR-TIME-START-ATTENDING
 50                            XR-TIME-END-ATTENDING
```

Figure 8.1 Partial List of Entity Types with Primary Keys and Repeating Groups Identified

51		XR_C-NUMBER	
52		XR_C-TITLE	
53		XR_I-NUMBER	
54		XR_I-NAME	
55		XSTUDENTS-REGISTERED	
56		XR_S-NUMBER	
57		XR_S-NAME	
58		R_E-SPECIAL	R_E-SPEC
59		XR_E-TYPE-SPECIAL	
60	INSTRCT	INSTRUCTOR	
61		P I-NUMBER	
62		I-NAME	
63		I-STATUS	
64		I-HOME-ADDRESS	
65		I-HOME-PHONE	
66		I-DATE-TEACH-START	
67		I-DATE-TENURE	
68		I_H-NAME	
69		I_C-HISTORY	I_C-HIST
70		XI_C_T-TAUGHT	
71		XI_C-NUMBER-TAUGHT	
72		XI_C-TITLE	
73		XI_C-GRADE-SUMMARY-EARNED	
74		I-DEGREE-PREVIOUS	I-DEG-PV
75		XI-GRADUATION-PREVIOUS-DATE	
76	MAJIMIN	MAJOR-MINOR	
77		P M_H-NAME-CURRICULUM	
78		M-NAME	
79		M-TYPE	
80		M-HOURS-GRADUATION-REQUIRED	
81		M_C-REQUIREMENTS	M_C-REQR
82		XM_C-NUMBER	
83	SEMESTER	SEMESTER	
84		P T-NAME	
85		T-DATE-START	
86		T-DATE-END	
87	ALUMNI	ALUMNI	
88		P A-NUMBER	
89		A-NAME	
90		A-HOME-ADRESS	
91		A-HOME-PHONE	
92		A-EMPLOYER-NAME	
93		A-EMPLOYER-ADDRESS	
94		A-CONTRIBUTION-YEAR-CURRENT	
95		A-CONTRIBUTION-SUMMARY	
96		A-DEGREE-PREVIOUS	A-DEG-PV
97		XA-DEGREE-TYPE-PREVIOUS	
98		XA-DEGREE-GRADUATION-PREVIOUS	

DISPLAY END: NWLG00

Figure 8.1 Con't.

Removing Repeating Group to New Table

Once a repeating group is identified it is removed from the entity type root table and placed into its own table. The name of the new table should be honest, complete, and meaningful. It is composed from

The repeating group name, and/or

The entity type that it is part of, and/or

Any entity type which has contributed

Data elements (attributes) to the repeating group

Assume that the repeating group name of student.course-history was *only* history. Naming the new table history would be incomplete (what kind of history). Adding the entity type name of student helps (student-history), but are we maintaining attendance history or course history? A review of the data elements reveals that the entity type course has contributed data elements (course-number and course-title); therefore, course should be part of the table name. The honest, complete, and meaningful table name is

```
Student.course.semester-history
```

Student is first because the repeating group was part of the student entity type. Course is second because it is an entity type that contributed more data elements (course-number and course-title) than semester. Semester is third because it is an entity type that contributed the fewest data elements (semester). The period (·) between student.course and course.semester indicates that this is a relation*SHIP* table. It is a relationship table because it combines data elements from the intersection of separate occurrences of multiple entity types. A row in the student.course.semester-history table could *not* exist *unless* a specific student took a specific course in a specific semester. In particular, course-grade and course-credit-hours-earned could *not* exist without the intersection of student, course, and semester. These data elements are often called *intersection* or *junction data.*

Bringing Down the Original Primary Key   The first column in the new table is the primary key of the entity type from which the repeating group was removed. This is necessary to "tie back" the repeating group to its "owner." If student-number was not part of the student.course.semester-history table, how would you know which student had taken the course? Therefore, the table starts with

```
Student-Number     followed by all the data elements in the
                   repeating group
```

Identifying Primary Key for New Relation   The primary key brought down from the entity type can *never* uniquely identify a row in the new table. As discussed previously, student-number and course-number are insufficient because a student can take a course more than once (audit, fail, pass). Therefore, semester must be added to complete the *concatenated* primary key of

```
student-number, course-number, semester.
```

Figure 8.2 is the complete 1NF for Logic University.

FIRST NORMAL FORM

RPT LINE	USER CODES	PARENT IDENT	SUBORD IDENT	DATA NAME
1--------	11-----	21------	31--------------------------
1	A	STUDENT		STUDENT
2	A			P S-NUMBER
3	A			S-NAME
4	A			S-STATUS
5	A			S-HOME-ADDRESS
6	A			S-HOME-PHONE
7	A			S-GRADUATION-EXPECTED-DATE
8	A			S_I-NUMBER<ADVISOR>
9	A			S_H-NAME
10	A	STUDENT	S_C-HIST	STUDENT.S_C-HISTORY
11	A			P S-NUMBER
12	A			P S_C_T-TAKEN
13	A			P S_C-NUMBER-TAKEN
14	A			S_C-TITLE
15	A			S_C-HOURS-CREDIT-TAKEN
16	A			S_C-HOURS-CREDIT-EARNED
17	A			S_C-GRADE-EARNED
18	A	STUDENT	S_M-MAJR	STUDENT.S_M<MAJOR>
19	A			P S-NUMBER
20	A			P S_M<MAJOR>
21	A	STUDENT	S_M-MINR	STUDENT.S_M<MINOR>
22	A			P S-NUMBER
23	A			P S_M<MINOR>
24	A	STUDENT	S_DEG-PV	STUDENT.S-DEGREE-PREVIOUS
25	A			P S-NUMBER
26	A			P S-DEGREE-TYPE-PREVIOUS
27	A			S-GRADUATION-PREVIOUS-DATE
28	A	STUDENT	S_R-#-AT	STUDENT.S_R-NUMBER-ATTENDING
29	A			P S-NUMBER
30	A			P S-TIME-START-ATTENDING
31	A			P S-DAYOFWEEK-ATTENDING
32	A			S-TIME-END-ATTENDING
33	A			S_I-NAME<TEACHING>
34	B	COURSE		COURSE
35	B			P C-NUMBER
36	B			C-TITLE
37	B			C_H-NAME-CURRICULUM
38	B			C-HOURS-CREDIT-MINIMUM
39	B			C-HOURS-CREDIT-MAXIMUM
40	B			C-CLASSSIZE-MINIMUM
41	B			C-CLASSSIZE-MAXIMUM
42	B			C-HOURS-DURATION
43	B	COURSE	C-PREREQ	COURSE.C-PREREQUSITE
44	B			P C-NUMBER
45	B			P C-NUMBER<PREREQUISITE>
46	B	COURSE	C_E-SPEC	COURSE.C_E-SPECIAL
47	B			P C-NUMBER
48	B			P C_E-EQUIPMENT-TYPE-SPECIAL
49	B	COURSE	C_T-TAKN	COURSE.C_T-TAKEN
50	B			P C-NUMBER
51	B			P C_T-GIVEN
52	B			C_S-TALLY-TAKEN
53	B			C_S-TALLY-MAJOR-TAKEN
54	B			C_S-TALLY-MINOR-TAKEN
55	B			C_S-TALLY-FREE-TAKEN
56	C	CLASSROM		CLASSROOM
57	C			P R-NUMBER
58	C			R-CAPACITY
59	C	CLASSROM	RDAYOFWK	CLASSROOM.R-DAYOFWEEK

Figure 8.2 First Normal Form

```
FIRST NORMAL FORM
  RPT    USER     PARENT      SUBORD      DATA
  LINE   CODES    IDENT       IDENT       NAME
         1--------- 11-----   21------    31--------------------------
    60   C                                  P R-NUMBER
    61   C                                  P R-DAYOFWK
    62   C                                  P R-TIME-START-ATTENDING
    63   C                                    R-TIME-END-ATTENDING
    64   C                                    R_C-NUMBER
    65   C                                    R_C-TITLE
    66   C                                    R_I-NUMBER
    67   C                                    R_I-NAME
PM@NOR-32 CLASSROOM.R-DAYOFWEEK.STUDENTS-REGISTERED
PM@NOR-32 NAME WILL EXCEED 30 CHARS, ELEMENT NAME USED
--------------------
    68   C        RDAYOFWK    STDNREST      STUDENTS-REGISTERED
    69   C                                  P R-NUMBER
    70   C                                  P R-DAYOFWK
    71   C                                  P R-TIME-START-ATTENDING
    72   C                                    R_S-NUMBER
    73   C                                    R_S-NAME
    74   C        CLASSROM    R_E-SPEC      CLASSROOM.R_E-SPECIAL
    75   C                                  P R-NUMBER
    76   C                                  P R_E-TYPE-SPECIAL
    77   D        INSTRCT                   INSTRUCTOR
    78   D                                  P I-NUMBER
    79   D                                    I-NAME
    80   D                                    I-STATUS
    81   D                                    I-HOME-ADDRESS
    82   D                                    I-HOME-PHONE
    83   D                                    I-DATE-TEACH-START
    84   D                                    I-DATE-TENURE
    85   D                                    I_H-NAME
    86   D        INSTRCT     I_C-HIST      INSTRUCTOR.I_C-HISTORY
    87   D                                  P I-NUMBER
    88   D                                  P I_C_T-TAUGHT
    89   D                                  P I_C-NUMBER-TAUGHT
    90   D                                    I_C-TITLE
    91   D                                    I_C-GRADE-SUMMARY-EARNED
    92   D        INSTRCT     I-DEG-PV      INSTRUCTOR.I-DEGREE-PREVIOUS
    93   D                                  P I-NUMBER
    94   D                                  P I-GRADUATION-PREVIOUS-DATE
    95   E        MAJIMIN                   MAJOR-MINOR
    96   E                                  P M_H-NAME-CURRICULUM
    97   E                                  P M_C-NUMBER
    98   E                                    M-NAME
    99   E                                    M-TYPE
   100   E                                    M-HOURS-GRADUATION-REQUIRED
   101   E        MAJIMIN     M_C-REQR      MAJOR-MINOR.M_C-REQUIREMENTS
   102   E                                  P M_H-NAME-CURRICULUM
   103   E                                    M_C-NUMBER
   104   F        SEMESTER                  SEMESTER
   105   F                                  P T-NAME
   106   F                                    T-DATE-START
   107   F                                    T-DATE-END
   108   G        ALUMNI                    ALUMNI
   109   G                                  P A-NUMBER
   110   G                                    A-NAME
   111   G                                    A-HOME-ADRESS
   112   G                                    A-HOME-PHONE
   113   G                                    A-EMPLOYER-NAME
   114   G                                    A-EMPLOYER-ADDRESS
   115   G                                    A-CONTRIBUTION-YEAR-CURRENT
   116   G                                    A-CONTRIBUTION-SUMMARY
```

Figure 8.2 Con't.

```
FIRST NORMAL FORM

   RPT    USER     PARENT      SUBORD      DATA
   LINE   CODES    IDENT       IDENT       NAME
          1--------- 11-----    21------    31--------------------------
   117    G         ALUMNI      A-DEG-PV    ALUMNI.A-DEGREE-PREVIOUS
   118    G                   P A-NUMBER
   119    G                   P A-DEGREE-TYPE-PREVIOUS
   120    G                     A-DEGREE-GRADUATION-PREVIOUS

   PM@NOR-M04  NWLG02   REPLACED IN PMLIB AS AN   RLIST    SEE   NWLG02
   --------------------
```

Figure 8.2 Con't.

SECOND NORMAL FORM

Definition

The objective of second normal form (2NF) is to ascertain that all nonkey data elements are fully functionally dependent on *all* of the data elements that form the primary key. Another definition is that each nonkey data element must be completely dependent on each data element of the primary key, the whole key, and nothing but the key, so help you Ted Codd. The procedure is:

1. Check each nonkey to each individual key element to determine if there is a 1:1 relationship.
2. If a 1:1 relationship exists, remove that nonkey data element *and* its key data elements to a separate table.
3. If a 1:1 relationship does not exist, that nonkey data element is fully functionally dependent on the intersection of at least two of the primary key data elements—the question is, which one?

The following table will be processed through second normal form:

```
STUD   COUR   SEM    STUD   COUR   COUR   CRED
NUMB   NUMB   ___    NAME   NAME   GRDE   HRS        ___ = key data element

0013   0169   SPG7   ERIC   MAT1   AUD    0
0013   0169   FAL8   ERIC   MAT1   87     3
0013   0182   FAL8   ERIC   ENG1   90     3
0026   0338   FAL8   LISA   LIT1   99     3
0026   0333   FAL8   LISA   CHM1   92     5
```

The first nonkey is student-name. Does it have a 1:1 relationship to student-number? (yes) Does t have a 1:1 relationship to course-number? (no) Does it have a 1:1 relationship to semester? (no) Therefore, the student-name should be removed to a separate table:

```
student-name (student-number, student-name)
```

with a table name of "student-name" and a primary key of student-number and a nonkey data element of student-name.

The second nonkey is course-name. Does it have a 1:1 relationship to student-number? (no) Does it have a 1:1 relationship to course-number? (yes) Does it have a 1:1 relationship to semester? (no) Therefore, the course-title should be removed to a separate table.

Venn Diagrams

The third nonkey is course-grade. Does it have a 1:1 relationship to student-number? (no—a student can have many grades) Does it have a 1:1 relationship to course-number? (no—a course can have many grades issued to many students) Does it have a 1:1 relationship to semester? (no—each semester has many courses, which in turn have many grades for many students) Therefore, course-grade must be dependent on the intersection of at least two of the three primary key data elements. Venn diagrams will be used to define the intersection.

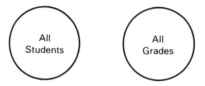

The two Venn diagrams above represent the set of all students and the set of all grades issued to all students. For each student there is a subset of grades associated with the specific student. For student 0169, the Venn diagram would be:

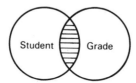

The shaded intersection represents the specific subset of grades associated with (or belonging to) the specific student 0169. Therefore, a specific student-number is necessary to define a subset of grades. Would adding the set of course-number to the Venn diagram above reduce the intersection?

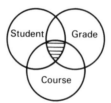

Yes. Therefore, a specific course-number is necessary to refine (reduce to a smaller intersection) the Venn diagram. The next question is: Has the intersection been reduced to a single occurrence? A superficial investigation would say yes (a student can only take a course once). Wrong. Although it is unusual, it is possible for a student to take the same course more than once; i.e., the student could audit, fail, incomplete, and pass the same course.

Therefore, the next question is: Would adding the set of semester reduce the Venn diagram to a single occurrence? (yes—it does make the reasonable assumption that a student cannot take the same course more than once in the same semester) The completed Venn diagram is

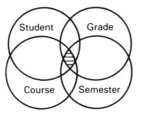

The reader may believe that I have stacked the comparison sequence to make 2NF work. The answer is no. Any comparison sequence works and yields the same result. For instance, if the comparison sequence was inverted:

```
Semester, course-number, student-number
```

and course-grade was the nonkey data element being analyzed, the initial Venn diagram would be

A specific semester would cause an intersection with all course-grades that yields the subset of course-grades issued during that specific semester, as illustrated below.

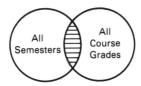

Semester is necessary to refine the intersection. Does a specific course-number refine the intersection? (yes—it defines the intersection of all course-grades issued for that specific course in that specific semester) Course-number is therefore required.

At this point, it should be clear that the intersection can contain *n* values and we are looking for a single value. Does a specific student-number refine the intersection to a single occurrence? (yes—a specific student can only take a specific course *once* in a specific semester)

The moral is that any comparison sequence works.

The last nonkey data element is credit-hours. Again a superficial review might indicate that there is a 1:1 relationship between course-number and credit-hours (a specific course can only be taken for specific credit-hours). However, if you reread the priority scheme of Appendix A (description of Logic University), it implies that a student has the right to choose the number of credit-hours for each specific course. For instance:

A student can take a course for the normal credit-hours of 3.

A student can add a thesis and take the course for 4 credit-hours.

A student can add a workshop and take the course for 5 credit-hours.

Under this interpretation of credit-hours, is credit-hours fully functionally dependent on student-number, course-number, and semester? (yes—you need the specific student-number and specific course-number and specific semester to refine the intersection to a single occurrence) Try Venn diagrams if you disagree or are uncertain.

The table that was processed through 2NF was simple (three key data elements and four nonkey data elements) and the rules for 2NF are also simple. The hard part is knowing and understanding the user interpretation and the user use of the data. The person performing 2NF must know the *data intimately* or have access to such a user person. Data processing technicians normally *cannot* perform 2NF—even if they know the rules—because they *do not* know the data. It is *absolutely imperative* that the person performing 2NF know (as in the original biblical sense) or know and *communicate* with the person who does. Figure 8.3 is a "decision table" to assist analysts in performing 2NF.

Venn Diagrams Revisited

Venn diagrams are a graphic method of determining full functional dependency. They can also be used initially as a replacement for asking the 1 : 1 relationship question. For example, you could draw a diagram for all students and for all student names. The use of the student-number would refine the intersection to a single occurrence and determine that student-name was fully functionally dependent only on student-number (a 1:1 relationship).

Do you need Venn diagrams? Not really. The analyst must acquire the habit of asking the question:

Does a specific value in this key data element *or* combination of data elements return a single value in the nonkey data element under analysis?

Using this approach, the analysis of the table would be:

```
DISPLAY

NN    NN WW    WW LL       GGGGGG   222222   AAAA    DDDDD   TTTTTTT
NNN   NN WW    WW LL     GGGGGGGG 22222222 AAAAAA   DDDDDD   TTTTTTT
NNNN  NN WW    WW LL     GG   GG 22     22 AAA  AAA DD    DD   TT
NNNNN NN WW WW WW LL     GG         22     22 AA    AA DD    DD   TT
NN NNNNN WW WW WW LL     GG  GGGG   222    AAAAAAAA DD    DD   TT
NN  NNNN WWW  WWW LL     GG   GG   222     AAAAAAAA DD    DD   TT
NN   NNN WW    WW LLLLLLLL GGGGGGGG 22222222 AA    AA DDDDDD   TT
NN    NN W     W LLLLLLLL GGGGG   22222222 AA    AA DDDDD    TT

   SEQ      DISPLAY OF  NWLG2ADT  FROM LIBRARY: ADP.PM.A200.PMLIB
  NUMBER   1...5...10...15...20...25...30...35...40...45...50...55...60...65...70..
     1       1 RELATION: STUDENT.S_C-HISTORY              STUDENT.S_C-HIST
     2       2 ---------------------------:---:------------------------------
     3       3            KEY ITEM          :Y/N:          NON-KEY ITEM
     4       4 ---------------------------:---:------------------------------
     5       5 S-NUMBER                    : N : S_C-TITLE
     6       6 S_C_T-TAKEN                 : N :
     7       7 S_C-NUMBER-TAKEN            : Y :
     8     NAME=S_C-TITLE                  ID=S_C-TIT
     9       9 S-NUMBER                    : Y : S_C-HOURS-CREDIT-TAKEN
    10      10 S_C_T-TAKEN                 : Y :
    11      11 S_C-NUMBER-TAKEN            : Y :
    12     NAME=                           ID=
    13      13 S-NUMBER                    : Y : S_C-HOURS-CREDIT-EARNED
    14      14 S_C_T-TAKEN                 : Y :
    15      15 S_C-NUMBER-TAKEN            : Y :
    16     NAME=                           ID=
    17      17 S-NUMBER                    : Y : S_C-GRADE-EARNED
    18      18 S_C_T-TAKEN                 : Y :
    19      19 S_C-NUMBER-TAKEN            : Y :
    20     NAME=                           ID=

DISPLAY END:  NWLG2ADT
```

Figure 8.3 Second-Normal-Form Decision Table

1. Does a specific student-number return a single student-name? (yes—therefore re-move to a separate table)

2. Does a specific student-number return a single course-title (no—a student can take many courses)

3. Does a specific course-number return a single course-title? (yes—therefore remove to a separate table)

4. Does a specific student-number return a single course-grade? (no—a student re-ceives as many grades as she/he has courses) However, a specific student-number returns only the course-grades that belong to the specific student.

5. Does a specific student-number + a specific course-number return a single course-grade? (no—a student can take the same course more than once)

6. Does a specific student-number + a specific course-number + a specific semester return a single course-grade? (yes—therefore, course-grade is fully functionally de-pendent on student-number, course-number, and semester)

The analysis of credit-hours is the same for course-grade (assuming the user interpretation that a student can select the credit-hours).

Creating New Tables

The pure rule is that you create a new table for any nonkey data element(s) that are not fully functionally dependent on the entire key with the new table containing the fully functional dependent keys and the nonkey data elements. It often happens that the new table is an "absorbable" subset of an existing table. Figure 8.4 is a listing of 2NF. Note that a table created by 2NF was

course-history.title (course-number, title)

There is a process after normalization entitled "optimization" (Chapter 9 contains specific details). The main purpose of optimization is to combine tables that have identical keys. A cursory inspection of Figure 8.4 reveals that the course table has a primary key of course-number. Also, the course table contains a nonkey data element identical to the new table nonkey element. My recommendation is to eliminate the new table since nonkey data elements are already available in another table having the *same* primary key. The rationale is that the bulk of normalization is a clerical process in realigning the tables. Why carry a table through normalization if you know that you are going to eliminate it in a later process?

```
SECOND NORMAL FORM

  RPT    USER      PARENT       SUBORD        DATA
  LINE   CODES     IDENT        IDENT         NAME
       1---------  11-----    21------      31--------------------------
     1   A         STUDENT                    STUDENT
     2   A                               P    S-NUMBER
     3   A                                    S-NAME
     4   A                                    S-STATUS
     5   A                                    S-HOME-ADDRESS
     6   A                                    S-HOME-PHONE
     7   A                                    S-GRADUATION-EXPECTED-DATE
     8   A                                    S_I-NUMBER<ADVISOR>
     9   A                                    S_H-NAME
    10   A         STUDENT      S_C-HIST      STUDENT.S_C-HISTORY
    11   A                               P    S-NUMBER
    12   A                               P    S_C_T-TAKEN
    13   A                               P    S_C-NUMBER-TAKEN
    14   A                                    S_C-HOURS-CREDIT-TAKEN
    15   A                                    S_C-HOURS-CREDIT-EARNED
    16   A                                    S_C-GRADE-EARNED
    17   A         S_C-TIT                    S_C-TITLE
    18   A                               P    S_C-NUMBER-TAKEN
    19   A                                    S_C-TITLE
    20   A         STUDENT      S_M-MAJR      STUDENT.S_M<MAJOR>
    21   A                               P    S-NUMBER
    22   A                               P    S_M<MAJOR>
    23   A         STUDENT      S_M-MINR      STUDENT.S_M<MINOR>
    24   A                               P    S-NUMBER
    25   A                               P    S_M<MINOR>
    26   A         STUDENT      S_DEG-PV      STUDENT.S-DEGREE-PREVIOUS
    27   A                               P    S-NUMBER
    28   A                               P    S-DEGREE-TYPE-PREVIOUS
```

Figure 8.4 Second Normal Form

SECOND NORMAL FORM

RPT LINE	USER CODES	PARENT IDENT	SUBORD IDENT		DATA NAME
	1---------	11-----	21------		31-------------------------------
29	A				S-GRADUATION-PREVIOUS-DATE
30	A	STUDENT	S_R-#-AT		STUDENT.S_R-NUMBER-ATTENDING
31	A			P	S-NUMBER
32	A			P	S-TIME-START-ATTENDING
33	A			P	S-DAYOFWEEK-ATTENDING
34	A				S-TIME-END-ATTENDING
35	A				S_I-NAME<TEACHING>
36	B	COURSE			COURSE
37	B			P	C-NUMBER
38	B				C-TITLE
39	B				C_H-NAME-CURRICULUM
40	B				C-HOURS-CREDIT-MINIMUM
41	B				C-HOURS-CREDIT-MAXIMUM
42	B				C-CLASSSIZE-MINIMUM
43	B				C-CLASSSIZE-MAXIMUM
44	B				C-HOURS-DURATION
45	B	COURSE	C-PREREQ		COURSE.C-PREREQUSITE
46	B			P	C-NUMBER
47	B			P	C-NUMBER<PREREQUISITE>
48	B	COURSE	C_E-SPEC		COURSE.C_E-SPECIAL
49	B			P	C-NUMBER
50	B			P	C_E-EQUIPMENT-TYPE-SPECIAL
51	B	COURSE	C_T-TAKN		COURSE.C_T-TAKEN
52	B			P	C-NUMBER
53	B			P	C_T-GIVEN
54	B				C_S-TALLY-TAKEN
55	B				C_S-TALLY-MAJOR-TAKEN
56	B				C_S-TALLY-MINOR-TAKEN
57	B				C_S-TALLY-FREE-TAKEN
58	C	CLASSROM			CLASSROOM
59	C			P	R-NUMBER
60	C				R-CAPACITY
61	C	CLASSROM	RDAYOFWK		CLASSROOM.R-DAYOFWEEK
62	C			P	R-NUMBER
63	C			P	R-DAYOFWK
64	C			P	R-TIME-START-ATTENDING
65	C				R-TIME-END-ATTENDING
66	C				R_C-NUMBER
67	C				R_C-TITLE
68	C				R_I-NUMBER
69	C				R_I-NAME
70	C	RDAYOFWK	STDNREST		R_C-NUMBER.STUDENTS-REGISTERED
71	C			P	R-NUMBER
72	C			P	R-DAYOFWK
73	C			P	R-TIME-START-ATTENDING
74	C				R_S-NUMBER
75	C				R_S-NAME
76	C	CLASSROM	R_E-SPEC		CLASSROOM.R_E-SPECIAL
77	C			P	R-NUMBER
78	C			P	R_E-TYPE-SPECIAL
79	D	INSTRCT			INSTRUCTOR
80	D			P	I-NUMBER
81	D				I-NAME
82	D				I-STATUS
83	D				I-HOME-ADDRESS
84	D				I-HOME-PHONE
85	D				I-DATE-TEACH-START
86	D				I-DATE-TENURE
87	D				I_H-NAME

Figure 8.4 Con't.

SECOND NORMAL FORM

RPT LINE	USER CODES	PARENT IDENT	SUBORD IDENT	DATA NAME
	1--------	11-----	21------	31--------------------------
88	D	INSTRCT	I_C-HIST	INSTRUCTOR.I_C-HISTORY
89	D			P I-NUMBER
90	D			P I_C_T-TAUGHT
91	D			P I_C-NUMBER-TAUGHT
92	D			I_C-TITLE
93	D			I_C-GRADE-SUMMARY-EARNED
94	D	INSTRCT	I-DEG-PV	INSTRUCTOR.I-DEGREE-PREVIOUS
95	D			P I-NUMBER
96	D			P I-GRADUATION-PREVIOUS-DATE
97	E	MAJIMIN		MAJOR-MINOR
98	E			P M_H-NAME-CURRICULUM
99	E			P M_C-NUMBER
100	E			M-NAME
101	E			M-TYPE
102	E			M-HOURS-GRADUATION-REQUIRED
103	E	MAJIMIN	M_C-REQR	MAJOR-MINOR.M_C-REQUIREMENTS
104	E			P M_H-NAME-CURRICULUM
105	E			M_C-NUMBER
106	F	SEMESTER		SEMESTER
107	F			P T-NAME
108	F			T-DATE-START
109	F			T-DATE-END
110	G	ALUMNI		ALUMNI
111	G			P A-NUMBER
112	G			A-NAME
113	G			A-HOME-ADRESS
114	G			A-HOME-PHONE
115	G			A-EMPLOYER-NAME
116	G			A-EMPLOYER-ADDRESS
117	G			A-CONTRIBUTION-YEAR-CURRENT
118	G			A-CONTRIBUTION-SUMMARY
119	G	ALUMNI	A-DEG-PV	ALUMNI.A-DEGREE-PREVIOUS
120	G			P A-NUMBER
121	G			P A-DEGREE-TYPE-PREVIOUS
122	G			A-DEGREE-GRADUATION-PREVIOUS

PM@TAB-M04   NWLG03   REPLACED IN PMLIB AS AN   DTABLE   SEE   NWLG03

Figure 8.4 Con't.

The Nasty Problem of Timestamping

Up to this point, we have blithely ignored the problem of timestamping. The definition of timestamping is the recording of a suitable time frame (second, minute, hour, day, date, week, month, quarter, year, decade, century, or whatever) to record when a value in a specific data element changed. Virtually any data element—regardless of how stable—can change value. Let's reevaluate student-name. Up to this point, we have stated that there is a 1:1 relationship between student-number and student-name. Is there? What happens if the student gets married or legally changes his/her name? Since marriage or legal change is a real possibility, it must be reconciled by the analyst. The first question that must be asked is:

Does the *user* care?

If the user does not care, then timestamping for the particular data element is not necessary. In the case of the student-name, the user would be willing to use whatever is the latest name of the student. If the user states that student-name changes are important and must be recorded, the analyst has a new problem:

Would semester be sufficient?

Probably not. A student could marry and divorce in the same semester (recent statistics state that most divorces happen in the first year). Therefore, the analyst would have to create a new table *and* a new data element (timestamp) to record the effective date of each change in the value of the student-name.

How about course-title? It is certainly possible that the dean responsible for the course could change its name. Does the dean care if the original name of the course was Math 101 and now is Basic Math? If the dean does not, timestamping is not required. If the dean does, timestamping is required. Would semester suffice as a timestamp? Probably. It is unlikely that the dean would change the course-title during a semester. In this case, the analyst would have to set up a new table:

```
course-title (course-number, semester, course-title)
```

The timestamping considerations discussed previously only emphasize the need for the analyst to know absolutely and positively and without doubt how the user interprets and uses the data.

Candidate Keys

The previous discussion considered the actual primary key defined by the analyst. It is possible that other candidate keys exist. As defined previously, a candidate key data element is a data element that could have been used within, or as the primary key. The analysts—using their knowledge of the user area—subjectively choose other data elements to form the primary key. However, in 2NF the analyst must compare all nonkey data elements to both actual primary key data elements and the candidate key data elements. The comparison and action rules are the same for candidate keys.

Candidate Keys: Primary Keys

Is a candidate key data element a key or a nonkey? Yes. Candidate key data elements are treated as nonkey data elements to the primary key data elements and as key data elements to the remaining nonkey data elements. To avoid confusion and later difficulties, this practitioner recommends that candidate key data elements be resolved first, thereby leaving only fully functionally dependent candidate key data elements for later comparison with the "true" nonkey data elements.

Compound Keys

At this point, we have limited the discussion of key data elements to "stand-alone" or "meaningful" data elements (i.e., each key data element had an independent meaning). As defined previously, a compound key consists (typically) of a meaningful data element plus an odometer (counter) data element. The odometer data element has no specific meaning unless attached to its meaningful partner. At Logic University the student and the instructor data elements are really two fields:

```
curriculum-school-number + odometer
```

For instance, the number 01-0169 really means that this is the 169th student (or instructor) within curriculum school 01. If Logic University had 99 curriculum schools, there could be 99 students or instructors with an odometer of 0169. The compound key modifies the comparison sequence:

> Each nonkey (including candidate key) data element must be compared *first* against the meaningful data element to determine if there is a 1:1 relationship; if not, it is compared against the entire compound key for a 1:1 relationship.

For instance, student-name does not have a 1:1 relationship with just curriculum-school but it does with curriculum-school + student-odometer. However, curriculum-school-name does have a 1:1 relationship with just curriculum-school-number. Therefore, curriculum-school-name should be removed to a separate table or eliminated because it is absorbable.

Summary

It is the author's opinion that 2NF is the most important "form." It requires the greatest knowledge on the part of the analyst of the data relationships and interpretations. To perform 2NF the analysts must know their data. To perform 2NF requires:

1. Compare each nonkey data element to each specific key data element.[2] If a 1:1 relationship exists, remove to a separate table. Compare the new table to existing tables to determine if the new table is an absorbable table. If the table is absorbable, eliminate the table.
2. If the nonkey data element does not have a 1:1 relationship with any key data element, refine the nonkey data element until a single value will be returned by the combination of data elements.[2]
3. If all the key data elements[2] are required, do nothing.

---

[2]Includes key data elements and fully functionally dependent candidate key data elements.

4. If all the key data elements[2] are not required, create a new table containing only the fully functional key data elements + the fully functional nonkey data elements.

5. As before, compare the new table to existing tables and eliminate any tables that are absorbable.

THIRD NORMAL FORM

Definition

The objective of third normal form (3NF) is to remove transitive dependencies. A data element is transitively dependent on another data element (or data elements) if its value can be derived *or* calculated from that data element.

Derivable Data Elements

In 2NF the comparison sequence is nonkey data elements in a single table versus the key data elements in the *same* table. In 3NF the comparison sequence is all nonkey data elements in *any* table versus all other nonkey data elements in *any* other table. Derivable data elements typically exist in the same table. For instance, if the student.course.semester-history table is expanded to

> Student.course.semester-history(student-number, course- number,
> semester, course-grade, course-credit-hours, (and)
> instructor-number, instructor-name)

instructor-name would *not* be removed because it is fully functionally dependent on the student-number AND the course-number AND semester (a specific student can only take a specific course in a specific semester from a specific instructor (Logic University does not use multiple instructors per course session). It should be obvious—hopefully[3]—that instructor-name can be derived from instructor-number (a 1:1 relationship exist between instructor-number and instructor-name). The 2NF comparison sequence of nonkey to key did not provide the opportunity to compare instructor-name to instructor-number; 3NF does.

Another method for finding derivable data elements is to sort all nonkey data elements alphabetically and look for matches. Since an objective of normalization is to eliminate redundant nonkey data elements, there should be zero matches after 3NF. The sort and match technique above assumes that a data element naming standard is used AND enforced. A software tool probably could not determine that instructor-name and name-of-instructor were identical; a person probably could not determine that instructor-name and name-of-pedagogue were identical. Naming standards are discussed in greater detail in Chapter 19.

---

[2]Includes key data elements and fully functionally dependent candidate key data elements.
[3]With apologies to Edwin Newman.

Removing Derivable Data Elements to New Tables   Derivable data elements are removed to a new table consisting of the data element(s) that the data elements are derivable from as key(s)—this is analogous to 2NF. Therefore, instructor-name would be removed to the following new table:

Instructor-name(<u>instructor-number</u>, instructor-name)

Consistent with the recommendations in 2NF, all newly created tables should be compared with existing tables to determine if the newly created table is absorbable. A cursory review of the existing tables reveals that the instructor table contains the same primary key (instructor-number). Therefore, the new table should be absorbed (eliminated).

Some derivable data elements are not present in other existing tables. In this case, the new table is not absorbable and must be retained. This *usually means* that the original entity type analysis was *incorrect*.

Nonkey data elements are attributes of entity types. Any derivable nonkey data element discovered in 3NF must be an attribute of an entity type. If the entity type exists in the current tables, the data element and its table are absorbable; if not absorbable, an entity type is probably *missing*.

The alumni table contains as nonkey data elements:

employer-name and employer-address

Is employer-address derivable from employer-name? The first question—as discussed previously—Is the employer-name "well structured"? If yes, does a specific employer-name have only one address? (probably not) Does the employer-name have a specific address? (probably) Is the employer an entity type, i.e., does Logic University wish to maintain independent information about alumni employers? (probably—since some employers may have some form of matching funds for alumni contributions). Consequently, there should be an entity type *root* table of alumni-employer consisting of

Alumni-employer (<u>employer-number</u>, employer-name, employer-matching-
contribution-policy)

What happens to employer-address? Since it can be a 1:*M* relationship, a new table would be needed:

Employer-address (<u>employer-number</u>, <u>employer-address</u>)

The analysis above should again prove the necessity of the person performing the analysis to *know and know and know* the data.

Calculable Data Elements

Calculable data elements are typically the hardest to find in 3NF. A calculable data element is an element whose value at *any* time can be computed from one or more other data elements in any table. For instance, if A = B*C, the value of A or B or C can be calculated from the other two.

In the 2NF printout of Logic University (Figure 8.4) there is the following table:

```
course.semester (course-number, semester-number, tally-of-students,
    number-of-major-attendees, number-of-minor-attendees,
    number-of-free-attendees)
```

Tally-of-students = number-of-major-attendees + number-of-minor-attendees + number-of-free-attendees. It should be clear that the commutative rule of mathematics permits any one of the four data elements to be calculated from the other three. Therefore, one of the four data elements can be identified as calculable. Which one? That is the judgment of the analyst who knows how the user wants to use the information. For instance:

> If tally-of-students is most important to the user, "tally" should be kept and either "major" or "minor" or "free" should be identified as calculable.
>
> If number-of-major-attendees is most important, "major" should be kept and "tally" or "minor" or "free" should be identified as calculable.

However, the discussion above is academic. All four data elements (and therefore the table) are computable.

> Student.course.semester-history table contains data on all the courses that all the students have taken.
>
> Student-major and Student-minor tables contain data about each student's majors and minors.
>
> Major and Minor tables contain data about which courses are required for each major and for each minor.

It is therefore possible to determine and tally each course as "major," "minor," or "free." "Tally" therefore equals "major" + "minor" + "free." Relational algebra operands (described in Chapter 16) can be used to verify the derivability of the Course-tally table.

Another calculable data element is the course-end-time, where

```
Course-end-time = the time that a particular session of the
                  specific course "lets out"
```

Course-end-time therefore can be calculated by adding course-duration-in-hours (course table) to course-start-time (classroom-day-of-week table). It would also be possible to identify course-duration-in-hours as calculable.

```
course-duration-in-hours = course-end-time-
                           course-start-time
```

and

course-start-time =   course-end-time -
                            course-duration-in-hours

Which data element is identified as calculable is again the analyst's decision based on intimate knowledge of the users' needs.

Removing Calculable Data Elements   Unlike *derivable* data elements, calculable data elements are *never* moved to a new table. The reason is the value contained in the calculable data element can always be computed from data elements remaining in the tables. Does this mean that calculable data elements are banished to the "bit bucket"?[4] No, the algorithm for calculating the data element is placed in the data dictionary. This permits involved persons—particularly the physical database designer—to access a central repository of metadata[5] about the *total* user requirements.

Roger Learmonth, principal of the London-based database consulting firm of LBMS,[6] recommends that calculable data elements be flagged in the logical database (algorithm placed in data dictionary). His rationale is that it is easier for the physical database designer to eliminate flagged data elements from the physical database than to insert them from the data dictionary. I agree if the data dictionary access is manual; I disagree if a software tool can provide a listing of all calculable data elements. In any case, a standard should be adopted by each organization for the actual processing of calculable data elements.

Figure 8.5 is a decision table for assisting analysts in performing 3NF. Figure 8.6 is 3NF for Logic University.

Summary

3NF is both the easiest and the most difficult of the "forms." This contradictory sentence can be explained by reviewing the procedures involved;

1. Examine all nonkey data elements to all other nonkey data elements.
2. Remove to a new table and/or eliminate any data elements whose value can be derived and/or computed from other remaining nonkey data elements.

The 3NF rule is easy; the clerical examination of all nonkey data elements to all other nonkey data elements is clerically difficult. Consider a real-world database of 2000 or 3000 data elements; consider the comparisons required is a factorial of the number of data elements (2000 or 3000). Many organizations that believe in normalization perform only a cursory 3NF if it must be done manually. Automated tools are discussed later in this chapter.

----

[4]Bit bucket is an "old" DP term for data (bits) that have disappeared. The term originated from the "chad" box that held the "holes" punched from tab cards or paper tape.

[5]Metadata is data about data.

[6]Learmonth & Burchett Management Systems (see Appendix D for address).

```
THIRD NORMAL FORM

 1 ENTITY: A
 2 -----------------------------:---:-----------------------------------
 3          NON-KEY ITEM        :Y/N:          NON-KEY ITEM
 4 -----------------------------:---:-----------------------------------
 5 S-NAME                       :   : S-STATUS
 6                              :   : S-HOME-ADDRESS
 7                              :   : S-HOME-PHONE
 8                              :   : S-GRADUATION-EXPECTED-DATE
 9                              :   : S_I-NUMBER<ADVISOR>
10                              :   : S_H-NAME
11                              :   : S_C-HOURS-CREDIT-TAKEN
12                              :   : S_C-HOURS-CREDIT-EARNED
13                              :   : S_C-GRADE-EARNED
14                              :   : S_C-TITLE
15                              :   : S-GRADUATION-PREVIOUS-DATE
16                              :   : S-TIME-END-ATTENDING
17                              :   : S_I-NAME<TEACHING>
18 -----------------------------:---:-----------------------------------
19 S-STATUS                     :   : S-NAME
20                              :   : S-HOME-ADDRESS
21                              :   : S-HOME-PHONE
22                              :   : S-GRADUATION-EXPECTED-DATE
23                              :   : S_I-NUMBER<ADVISOR>
24                              :   : S_H-NAME
25                              :   : S_C-HOURS-CREDIT-TAKEN
26                              :   : S_C-HOURS-CREDIT-EARNED
27                              :   : S_C-GRADE-EARNED
28                              :   : S_C-TITLE
29                              :   : S-GRADUATION-PREVIOUS-DATE
30                              :   : S-TIME-END-ATTENDING
31                              :   : S_I-NAME<TEACHING>
32 -----------------------------:---:-----------------------------------
33 S-HOME-ADDRESS               :   : S-NAME
34                              :   : S-STATUS
35                              :   : S-HOME-PHONE
36                              :   : S-GRADUATION-EXPECTED-DATE
37                              :   : S_I-NUMBER<ADVISOR>
38                              :   : S_H-NAME
39                              :   : S_C-HOURS-CREDIT-TAKEN
40                              :   : S_C-HOURS-CREDIT-EARNED
41                              :   : S_C-GRADE-EARNED
42                              :   : S_C-TITLE
43                              :   : S-GRADUATION-PREVIOUS-DATE
44                              :   : S-TIME-END-ATTENDING
45                              :   : S_I-NAME<TEACHING>
46 -----------------------------:---:-----------------------------------
47 S-HOME-PHONE                 :   : S-NAME
48                              :   : S-STATUS
49                              :   : S-HOME-ADDRESS
50                              :   : S-GRADUATION-EXPECTED-DATE
51                              :   : S_I-NUMBER<ADVISOR>
52                              :   : S_H-NAME
53                              :   : S_C-HOURS-CREDIT-TAKEN
54                              :   : S_C-HOURS-CREDIT-EARNED
```

Figure 8.5 Third-Normal-Form Decision Table

THIRD NORMAL FORM

RPT LINE	USER CODES	PARENT IDENT	SUBORD IDENT	DATA NAME
	1---------	11-----	21------	31----------------------------
1	A	STUDENT		STUDENT
2	A			P S-NUMBER
3	A			S-NAME
4	A			S-STATUS
5	A			S-HOME-ADDRESS
6	A			S-HOME-PHONE
7	A			S-GRADUATION-EXPECTED-DATE
8	A			S_I-NUMBER<ADVISOR>
9	A			S_H-NAME
10	A	STUDENT	S_C-HIST	STUDENT.S_C-HISTORY
11	A			P S-NUMBER
12	A			P S_C_T-TAKEN
13	A			P S_C-NUMBER-TAKEN
14	A			S_C-HOURS-CREDIT-TAKEN
15	A			S_C-HOURS-CREDIT-EARNED
16	A			S_C-GRADE-EARNED
17	A	S_C-TIT		S_C-TITLE
18	A			P S_C-NUMBER-TAKEN
19	A			S_C-TITLE
20	A	STUDENT	S_M-MAJR	STUDENT.S_M<MAJOR>
21	A			P S-NUMBER
22	A			P S_M<MAJOR>
23	A	STUDENT	S_M-MINR	STUDENT.S_M<MINOR>
24	A			P S-NUMBER
25	A			P S_M<MINOR>
26	A	STUDENT	S_DEG-PV	STUDENT.S-DEGREE-PREVIOUS
27	A			P S-NUMBER
28	A			P S-DEGREE-TYPE-PREVIOUS
29	A			S-GRADUATION-PREVIOUS-DATE
30	A	STUDENT	S_R-#-AT	STUDENT.S_R-NUMBER-ATTENDING
31	A			P S-NUMBER
32	A			P S-TIME-START-ATTENDING
33	A			P S-DAYOFWEEK-ATTENDING
34	A			S_I-NAME<TEACHING>
35	B	COURSE		COURSE
36	B			P C-NUMBER
37	B			C-TITLE
38	B			C_H-NAME-CURRICULUM
39	B			C-HOURS-CREDIT-MINIMUM
40	B			C-HOURS-CREDIT-MAXIMUM
41	B			C-CLASSSIZE-MINIMUM
42	B			C-CLASSSIZE-MAXIMUM
43	B			C-HOURS-DURATION
44	B	COURSE	C-PREREQ	COURSE.C-PREREQUSITE
45	B			P C-NUMBER
46	B			P C-NUMBER<PREREQUISITE>
47	B	COURSE	C_E-SPEC	COURSE.C_E-SPECIAL
48	B			P C-NUMBER
49	B			P C_E-EQUIPMENT-TYPE-SPECIAL
50	B	COURSE	C_T-TAKN	COURSE.C_T-TAKEN
51	B			P C-NUMBER
52	B			P C_T-GIVEN
53	C	CLASSROM		CLASSROOM
54	C			P R-NUMBER
55	C			R-CAPACITY
56	C	CLASSROM	RDAYOFWK	CLASSROOM.R-DAYOFWEEK
57	C			P R-NUMBER
58	C			P R-DAYOFWK
59	C			P R-TIME-START-ATTENDING

Figure 8.6 Third Normal Form

THIRD NORMAL FORM

RPT LINE	USER CODES	PARENT IDENT	SUBORD IDENT	DATA NAME
	1---------	11-----	21------	31--------------------------
60	C			R-TIME-END-ATTENDING
61	C			R_C-NUMBER
62	C			R_C-TITLE
63	C			R_I-NUMBER
64	C	RDAYOFWK	STDNREST	R_C-NUMBER.STUDENTS-REGISTERED
65	C			P R-NUMBER
66	C			P R-DAYOFWK
67	C			P R-TIME-START-ATTENDING
68	C			R_S-NUMBER
69	C	CLASSROM	R_E-SPEC	CLASSROOM.R_E-SPECIAL
70	C			P R-NUMBER
71	C			P R_E-TYPE-SPECIAL
72	D	INSTRCT		INSTRUCTOR
73	D			P I-NUMBER
74	D			I-NAME
75	D			I-STATUS
76	D			I-HOME-ADDRESS
77	D			I-HOME-PHONE
78	D			I-DATE-TEACH-START
79	D			I-DATE-TENURE
80	D			I_H-NAME
81	D	INSTRCT	I_C-HIST	INSTRUCTOR.I_C-HISTORY
82	D			P I-NUMBER
83	D			P I_C_T-TAUGHT
84	D			P I_C-NUMBER-TAUGHT
85	D			I_C-TITLE
86	D			I_C-GRADE-SUMMARY-EARNED
87	D	INSTRCT	I-DEG-PV	INSTRUCTOR.I-DEGREE-PREVIOUS
88	D			P I-NUMBER
89	D			P I-GRADUATION-PREVIOUS-DATE
90	E	MAJIMIN		MAJOR-MINOR
91	E			P M_H-NAME-CURRICULUM
92	E			P M_C-NUMBER
93	E			M-NAME
94	E			M-TYPE
95	E			M-HOURS-GRADUATION-REQUIRED
96	E	MAJIMIN	M_C-REQR	MAJOR-MINOR.M_C-REQUIREMENTS
97	E			P M_H-NAME-CURRICULUM
98	E			M_C-NUMBER
99	F	SEMESTER		SEMESTER
100	F			P T-NAME
101	F			T-DATE-START
102	F			T-DATE-END
103	G	ALUMNI		ALUMNI
104	G			P A-NUMBER
105	G			A-NAME
106	G			A-HOME-ADRESS
107	G			A-HOME-PHONE
108	G			A-EMPLOYER-NAME
109	G			A-EMPLOYER-ADDRESS
110	G			A-CONTRIBUTION-YEAR-CURRENT
111	G			A-CONTRIBUTION-SUMMARY
112	G	ALUMNI	A-DEG-PV	ALUMNI.A-DEGREE-PREVIOUS
113	G			P A-NUMBER
114	G			P A-DEGREE-TYPE-PREVIOUS
115	G			A-DEGREE-GRADUATION-PREVIOUS

Figure 8.6 Con't.

```
THIRD NORMAL FORM

 RPT
 LINE     ENTITY   DERIVABLE ELEMENT
 ------   ------   --------------------
   1        A      S-TIME-END-ATTENDING
   2        B      C_S-TALLY-TAKEN
   3        B      C_S-TALLY-MAJOR-TAKEN
   4        B      C_S-TALLY-MINOR-TAKEN
   5        B      C_S-TALLY-FREE-TAKEN
   6        C      R_S-NAME
   7        C      R_I-NAME
PM@TAB-M04  NWLG04   REPLACED IN PMLIB AS AN    DTABLE     SEE    NWLG04
--------------------
```

Figure 8.6   Con't.

FOURTH NORMAL FORM

Definition

Rumor has it that Dr. Codd has called fourth normal form (4NF) ''obscure.'' Vetter has stated ''that there is no formal definition for 4NF.'' And if 4NF is obscure and undefinable, what of the higher levels (fifth, sixth, etc.)? What is clear is that the higher levels were developed when normalization moved from theoretical discussions in trade publications to practical use in designing logical databases. Normalization practitioners quickly discovered that their 3NF logical databases still had problems, such as:

> Redundant data
>
> Storage anomolies (delete, insert, and update)

What had gone wrong? Was there a real flaw in 3NF, or had we the practitioners misapplied the forms? There is no black/white answer. 3NF is correct if the forms are *rigorously* applied; unfortunately, the forms are not rigorously defined for nonmathematical practitioners. The net *practical* result is that 3NF is often incorrect and ''higher'' normal forms are required. My definition of 4NF is:

> the elimination of key data element anomolies from 3NF tables.

The key data element anomolies are:

> Key data elements hidden in the table name
>
> Key data elements that are really *groups* consisting of multiple Key data elements
>
> Interkey data element dependencies

Key Data Elements Hidden in the Table Name

It is very possible to hide both nonkey and key data elements in the table name and thereby eliminate them from any of the comparison sequences in 2NF and 3NF. It is also possible to hide the data elements either explicitly or implicitly. The Logic University 3NF (Figure 8.6) contains the following table:

```
student.courses-being-taken (student-number, course-number,. . . .)
```

The honest name of the table is Student.course-being-taken-this-semester . Semester is a data element implicitly hidden in the table name which should be inside the parentheses. Is it a key data element? Reviewing 1NF, a key data element participates in identifying a single occurrence of a table. Can the same student take the same course in different semesters? (yes) Do we therefore need semester as a key data element? (yes) Therefore, semester should be added to the table as a key data element. Do we need to redo 2NF on this table? (yes) This is one of the very real dangers of hidden key data elements in that 2NF must be redone and this may "ripple" and cause 3NF and 4NF to be redone—a great deal of frustrating clerical work.

The reader may have noticed that the new table resembles the Student.Course.semester-history table. It does. In fact, the new table is absorbable in the Student.course.semester-history table. This absorption could not be accomplished without discovering the hidden key implicitly buried in the table name. This would permit *redundant* data to be present in the logical database.

Implicit hidden data elements can be discovered only by a user-knowledgeable analyst reviewing each table name and making that table name honest and complete. Then compare each table name "field" (the name inside a period and/or hyphen) with the existing data element list. Any field that matches an existing data element must be within the table. If it is not, it is a hidden data element that must be placed within the table.

Key Data Elements Hidden Within a Group

Another subtle method of hiding key data elements is permitting a group to masquerade as a data element. Some definitions first:

Group:	a data structure composed of related data elements. Cobol calls this type of data structure a group item. A group item does *not* have a picture clause; all "fields" that have a higher-level number than the group item and have picture clauses are elementary items that "belong" to group item.
Data element:	the smallest unit of data *meaningful* for this user requirement. In Cobol, any "field" that has a picture clause.

The hidden trap in the data element definition is the word "meaningful." Gane and Sarson have defined data element as any "field" that does not need to be decomposed any further even though it *could*. Let's take the familiar telephone number as an example. It could be defined:

```
TELEPHONE-NUMBER     PIC 9(10).
```

or

```
TELEPHONE-NUMBER.
     AREA-CODE        PIC 999.
     EXCHANGE         PIC 999.
     INSTRUMENT       PIC 9(4).
```

or

```
TELEPHONE-NUMBER.
     AREA-CODE.
          AREA-CODE-DIGIT-1      PIC 9.
          AREA-CODE-DIGIT-2      PIC 9.
          AREA-CODE-DIGIT-3      PIC 9.
     EXCHANGE.
          EXCHANGE-DIGIT-1       PIC 9.
          EXCHANGE-DIGIT-2       PIC 9.
          EXCHANGE-DIGIT-3       PIC 9.
     INSTRUMENT.
          INSTRUMENT-DIGIT-1     PIC 9.
          INSTRUMENT-DIGIT-2     PIC 9.
          INSTRUMENT-DIGIT-3     PIC 9.
          INSTRUMENT-DIGIT-4     PIC 9.
```

Either of the first two definitions could be construed to be data "elements" if the user requirements did not require further decomposition. In fact, most users probably would be satisfied with the second definition (area-code, exchange, instrument). Although the user may be satisfied, the analyst MUST probe further to determine if any of the normalization forms would be affected by further decomposition of key data "elements" to their "atomic" components. The 3NF tables of Logic University (Figure 8.6) of student and instructor have a single primary key data "element" of student-number and instructor-number. Occasionally in this book, I have stated that both "numbers" were really groups composed of

```
curriculum-school-number
```

and

```
student(instructor)-number
```

Would decomposing "number" have an effect on 2NF? (yes) Let's decompose "number" into both concatenated and compound keys.

Concatenated Keys

A concatenated key is composed of two or more data elements all of which are meaningful in their own right. This means that there is a 1:1 relationship between curriculum-school-number and curriculum-school-name and there is a 1:1 relationship between student-number and student-name and a 1:1 relationship between instructor-number and instructor-name.

Both the Student and the Instructor tables contain a nonkey data element.

```
curriculum-school-name
```

2NF requires a comparison sequence of nonkey data elements in a single table to the key data elements in that table. With "number" being treated as a data "element," there is a 1:1 relationship between "number" and curriculum-school-name (a student or instructor can only belong to one curriculum-school). Obviously, if "number" is decomposed, curriculum-school-name is only fully funtionally dependent on curriculum-school-number and should be removed to a new table (or more likely be absorbed by an existing table). Does nonremoval cause any problems? (*absolutely*) The first problem is the update anomaly. If there are 10,000 students/instructors in the school of architecture and the name is changed to the school of physical environmental design, then each occurrence (row) of the Student/Instructor tables would have to be examined before the change could be completed. This example requires 10,000 updates instead of *one* if the curriculum-school-name was in a separate table.

The bad problems are the insert and deletion anomalies. This requires a review of *1NF* for each table. Is curriculum-school-number required to participate in identifying a single occurrence of the Student/Instructor tables (i.e., should it be part of the primary key)? (no) The erroneous identification of curriculum-school-number permits the following errors.

> Many universities—and in particular Logic University—allow students to postpone their decision on majors and minors for one or more semesters. Under these conditions, the student does *not* belong to any curriculum-school. Logical databases developed by normalization *and* most physical databases do not permit *null* primary keys. Therefore, *NONE* of the student data could be stored in the database. The database would not know that the student existed. Of course, clever people have a "standard" solution to the null key problem—use a "dummy" curriculum-school-number. Among many problems caused by dummy primary keys is updating the physical database. Most physical database management systems (DBMS) do not permit primary keys to be updated because of the physical storage method used and/or the chaining method used and/or the indexing method used. Consequently, when a student does select a curriculum-school, his/her record would have to be *deleted* and reentered with the new curriculum-school-number. Consider the problems of recovery, security, etc.

The mirror image of the insert anomaly is the delete anomaly:

> Logic University decides to discontinue its school of physical environmental design. The deletion in effect places a null value in the curriculum-school-number. The physical DBMS does not permit null primary keys, and therefore all physical environment design students tables are *deleted*. Depending on the physical DBMS, other student tables, such as Student.course.semester-history, would be placed in the bit bucket (unretrievable) or also deleted.

Although the case above may seem unreal, deletion anomalies unfortunately happen many times in the real world. And when they happen, it usually causes the loss of data that cannot be replaced or only replaced at great cost—assuming that anybody knows that the data is missing.

Compound Keys

A compound key is composed of two or more data elements, of which one data element is meaningless unless attached to another data element. Let's change the student/instructor-number to

```
curriculum-school-number
```

which is unique, plus

```
student(instructor)-number
```

which is an odometer (counter) within curriculum-school-number [i.e., the student(instructor)-number is *not* unique and cannot be used to identify a single occurrence of student/instructor].

Does the storage anomaly still exist? (yes) Curriculum-school-name is only fully functionally dependent on curriculum-school-number and should be removed to its own table (or absorbed). Failure to remove curriculum-school-name would again require searching each row (occurrence) of the Student/Instructors tables to update the name of the curriculum-school whenever the name changes.

Does the insert anomaly still exist? (yes) A student occurrence cannot be stored without knowing the curriculum-school-number. Unfortunately—because it is a compound key—a student occurrence cannot be stored *unless* there is a curriculum-school-number. This *regrettable* situation requires the use of a dummy curriculum-school-number with all its attendant problems. There is the additional problem that when the student does choose a curriculum-school, *both* the dummy curriculum-school-number AND the student-number *must* be changed (student-number is an odometer within each curriculum-school-number).

Does the deletion anomaly still exist? (yes)

Mixing Entity Types

The cause of the storage anomalies is the mixing of entity types in *root* tables [a root table contains specific attributes (data elements) about a *specific* entity type]. An entity type is "something" that an organization wants to maintain specific information (attributes, data elements) about. Mixing two or more entity types—all of which require independent data—in a root table that should only store information about a SINGLE entity type is a *mistake*. The effect of the mistake is the storage anomalies.

The mixing of the entity types at Logic University was hidden by the failure to decompose the "element" of student(instructor)-number to its atomic components.

Moral: Decompose all primary key data "fields" to their atomic components *before* beginning normalization.

After normalization, the atomic components can be combined for user or physical database convenience. The atomic components should be noted in the data dictionary so that future changes to the database can be analyzed in terms of the atomic components.

Compound Keys Revisited

Compound keys should *never* be permitted in database design because of the problems they cause. Unfortunately, compound keys do exist in the world and must be managed. My first suggestion is that a frank discussion be held with the users to ascertain whether the users can change their requirements and use only unique key elements. Users—which may surprise many DP people—can understand the risk of compound keys and will often change their requirements. However, users *must* be informed before they can make a decision.

Sometimes, the users cannot be convinced or cannot make the change. In this case, my recommendations are:

The compound key be highlighted "in red" in every appropriate piece of system documentation

Maintenance (insert, update, delete) of the compound key be restricted to a *single* program

That a single maintenance program be written by a *physical* database designer familiar with the physical database structure

That the maintenance program be given the greatest security possible and *only* be revised by a physical database designer

The recommendations above will help ensure that the compound key does not "explode" and destroy the database.

Interkey Data Element Dependencies

None of the first three normal forms has a comparison sequence of key data elements to key data elements. 4NF takes care of that omission. Logic University does not have any interkey dependencies, so a "demo" table is required:

```
Demo-table(class-start-time,class-end-time,class-duration-in
hours,. .  .  .  .  .  .)
```

where			
	class-start-time	=	starting time of the class session
	class-end-time	=	ending time of the class session
	class-duration-in-hours	=	class-end-time- class-start-time

It is clear from the definitions above that any of the three key data elements could be calculated from the other two key data elements. If they were nonkey data elements, one of the data elements would be eliminated. Are key data elements immune from this procedure? (no) Therefore, the least important key data element to the user should be eliminated.

Does 2NF for the involved table have to be redone? (yes) Let's expand the Demo-table for illustration:

```
Demo-table (class-start-time, class-end-time, class-duration-in-hours,
    day-of-the-week, instructor-name)
```

The analyst performing 2NF on the table above should have noted that instructor-name was fully functionally dependent on

1. Day-of-the-week
2. Start-time or end-time

Let's assume that the analyst removed the instructor-name to the following new table:

```
End-time-instructor-name (day-of-the-week, end-time, instructor-name)
```

If end-time is now eliminated from the database because it is calculable, the database is left with a table that has a *nonexistent* key. This type of error is usually not discovered until physical database load time when values for the nonexistent key cannot be found. The rework required is time consuming, frustrating, and costly.

Interkey dependencies are often masked by being included in a group that has been inserted in the database as an "element" (see previous hidden key discussion). The copyright page of this book contains an ISBN or international standard book number. A table about book data could be constructed as follows:

```
Book-data (ISBN, author, title, list-price)
```

ISBN is treated as an element but it is really composed of four fields separated by hyphens:

1. Country where published
2. Publisher
3. Book identifier
4. Check digit

The "real" table should be

```
Book-data (country-where published, publisher, book-identifier,
    check-digit, author, title, list-price)
```

Check-digit is a "hash"[7] digit calculated by a specific algorithm applied to other digits within the "field." In ISBN, the tenth or check digit is calculated from the first nine digits. The purpose of the check digit is to discover entry and/or transmission errors. An ISBN with a transposed digit should produce a check digit different from the precalculated check digit and should be caught as an error by an edit program. Check digits are definitely necessary for entry and transmission, but why must they be stored in the database? A database of 200,000,000 records would require 200,000,000 bytes of storage just for the check digit.

The reader may ask:

> Wouldn't the calculation required to compute the check digit each time require a great deal of computer time?

The answer now is no. Even the microcomputers on a single chip have MIP (million instructions per second) ratings. If the ISBN check digit required 100 instructions to calculate, a 1-MIP computer could perform approximately 10,000 check digit calculations per second.

In any case, the check digit is calculable and should not be included in the logical database. If it remains in the database, it should be treated as a *nonkey* data element because it has a 1:1 relationship with the other key data elements. If it remains as a key data element, a new table for author, title, and list-price will have to be created because it is not necessary to know the value of the check digit to identify a specific book author and the specific book title and the specific book list-price. Removing author, title, and list-price to a separate table would leave

```
Book-data(country-where-published, publisher, book-identifier
           check-digit)
```

or an all-key table.

All-key Tables

All-key tables are suspect. They are usually caused by incorrect application of the normalization rules. The all-key Book-data table is incorrect because:

1. Check-digit is calculable and therefore should have been eliminated.

or

2. Check-digit should have been converted to a nonkey because of its 1:1 relationship to the other key data elements.

---

[7]Hash is a "meaningless" number computed to provide a control value for error detection.

In any case, the all-key table would disappear by being absorbable into another existing table. Valid all-key tables contain the intersection of two or more entity types involved in a relationship (student takes course; instructor is assigned a course; etc.) but *without* any intersection data (no nonkey data elements). This is a rare circumstance in the real world. Valid all-key tables provide *logical* pathways through the logical database.

Summary

4NF is the "cleanup" form. It is used to catch all the mistakes made in the previous forms. It concentrates on finding key data element anomalies by:

> Investigating each table name to determine if there is a key data element buried (hidden) in the table name
>
> Investigating each key data element and determining if it really is a data element; if not, then decomposing it to its atomic components
>
> Examining each "atomic" key data element and determining if there is any interkey dependency

Discovery of any key data element anomaly *requires* redoing some or *all* of the normalization forms. Time, effort, and money are all wasted. Better to have been more rigorous in the first three normal forms than having to redo them because of errors discovered in 4NF. An anonymous DP person contributed this maxim:

> "Why is there never time to do it right but always time to fix it?"

In the discussion of 4NF, I stated that 3NF is correct if the forms are rigorously applied. 4NF is *unnecessary* if key data element anomalies are resolved during the first three normal forms.

THE PRACTICAL WAY TO PERFORM NORMALIZATION

Normalization begins after the *verified* data elements have been clustered to the identified entity types (see Chapter 7).

INF

1. Identify all sets of data elements that can *uniquely* identify a *single* occurrence of the entity type.
   a. Determine that each key data "element" is actually a data element. If not a data element, decompose it into its atomic components.
   b. Determine if any "key" is a compound key. If a compound key exists, try to eliminate it; otherwise, note it for special attention.

   c. Each set is a "candidate" key. Choose as *the* primary key the candidate key that is of most value to the user. Retain the other sets for 2NF.

2. Identify all prima facie derivable and calculable data elements (see Chapter 5 for techniques). Eliminate or mark all derivable and calculable data elements.

   a. Enter the calculable data element algorithm into the data dictionary. (*Note: Key* and nonkey data elements participate in this step.)

3. Identify all repeating groups (any data structure *or* single data elements) that can occur *n* (zero to "unlimited") times per single occurrence of the entity type.

   a. Remove each repeating group to its own newly created table.

   b. Name each new table with an honest complete name (see first normal form section in this chapter).

      (1) Investigate the new table name to determine if there are any hidden data elements (implicit or explicit). If so, move data element into table.

   c. Bring down the primary key data element(s) from the table from which the repeating group was removed.

   d. Identify all sets of data elements that can *uniquely* identify a *single* occurrence of the new table.

      (1) Remember to decompose all new key data "elements" into their atomic components.

2NF

1. Compare each candidate key data element to each specific primary key data element to determine if there is a 1:1 relationship.

   a. If a 1:1 relationship exists, remove to a new table composed of the 1:1 primary key data element and the candidate key data element.

      (1) Eliminate the new table if it is "absorbable."

   b. If a 1:1 relationship does not exist between the candidate key data element and any single primary key data element, determine which combination of primary key data elements are required to return a single value of the candidate key data element.

      (1) If all primary key data elements are required, do nothing; otherwise, create a new table consisting of the primary key data elements required to return a single value of the candidate key data element and the candidate key data element.

         (a) Eliminate the new table if absorbable.

2. Repeat for each nonkey data element using both the primary key data elements *and* the surviving candidate key data elements.

3NF

This form is *unnecessary.* All derivable and calculable data elements were eliminated or flagged in 1NF. A cursory 3NF can be performed as a check.

4NF

This form is *definitely unnecessary*. The rigorous application of 1NF and 2NF have:

1. Prevented the mixing of entity type data in root tables
2. Prevented primary key data element anomalies

Elimination of 4NF prevents costly rework.

AUTOMATED TOOLS

At this writing four companies have software packages to assist the analyst in performing normalization:

DDI and ADR:	Data Designer
TSI:	Facets
MSP:	Design Manager
HOLLAND:	Information Builder
ADPAC:	Design

Data Designer and Information Builder develop a canonical model of the logical database from 3NF user views.[8] It is the analyst's responsibility to:

1. Identify each user view.
2. Normalize it through 3NF.

Numerous cross-references and information reports are available. See Appendix D for address.

Facets and Design Manager perform normalization from their own internal data dictionaries. It is the analyst's responsibility to completely define each data element and its relationship to all the *other* data elements. Again, numerous cross-reference and informational reports are available. See Appendix D for address.

DESIGN is an interactive software package that performs all the clerical work of normalization. It uses specialized decision tables and simple coding to assist the analyst. Again, numerous cross-reference and informational reports are available. See Appendix D for address.

CAVEAT

The author prefers the DESIGN package from ADPAC. This is not surprising since the author was the designer of DESIGN.

---

[8]A user view is the set of data elements that a specific user requires to perform a specific task.

9

Optimization

DEFINITION

Optimization is the term applied to the process of combining tables with identical primary keys. The process of normalization creates many new tables. Some of these tables are absorbable into existing tables because both tables contain the same set of primary key data elements.

IDENTICAL KEYS

Relational theory stipulates that the sequence of the data elements (key or nonkey) is meaningless, i.e., the columns in the table can be placed in any order without affecting the values or meaning of the rows. It is *conventional* to place key data elements first but that is *not* required. Therefore, the analyst must look for matching *sets* of primary keys. For instance, a table containing A and B and C as key data elements:

Table-1(a, b, c, ...)

is equal to

Table-2(a, c, b, ...)

and equal to

$$\texttt{Table-3}\,(\underline{\texttt{b}},\underline{\texttt{a}},\underline{\texttt{c}},\dots\,)$$

and equal to

$$\texttt{Table-4}\,(\underline{\texttt{b}},\underline{\texttt{c}},\underline{\texttt{a}},\dots\,)$$

and equal to

$$\texttt{Table-5}\,(\underline{\texttt{c}},\underline{\texttt{a}},\underline{\texttt{b}},\dots\,)$$

and equal to

$$\texttt{Table-6}\,(\underline{\texttt{c}},\underline{\texttt{b}},\underline{\texttt{a}},\dots\,)\,.$$

Consequently, the six tables above could be (and should be) combined. The clerical problem escalates with the number of primary key—it is clerically more difficult to look for matching sets of 10 primary keys (very possible in the real world) than for three primary key data elements.

THE FAILURE TO COMBINE

Failure to combine tables invariably places *redundant* data into the database since the combinable tables almost certainly contain identical nonkey data elements. "Pure" 2NF and 3NF of Logic University would have created several tables of

$$\texttt{Student-name}\,(\underline{\texttt{student-number}},\ \texttt{student-name})$$

$$\texttt{Course-title}\,(\underline{\texttt{course-number}},\ \texttt{course-title})$$

$$\texttt{Instructor-name}\,(\underline{\texttt{instructor-number}},\ \texttt{instructor-name})$$

Failure to eliminate any occurrence of these absorbable tables would cause "name" to be redundant. This would cause the database to have anomalies:

> *Insert:* would have to insert "name" in each table
> *Update:* would have to update "name" in each table
> *Delete:* would have to delete "name" from each table

> *Moral:* Optimization is important.

SUBSET/SUPERSET

A common mistake made in optimization is combining tables that contain subsets or supersets of primary key data elements. For instance,

$$\texttt{Table-abc}\,(\underline{A}, \underline{B}, \underline{C}, \ldots)$$

and

$$\texttt{Table-abcd}\,(\underline{A}, \underline{B}, \underline{C}, \underline{D}, \ldots)$$

are not combinable even though they both contain A and B and C as primary key data elements. They are not combinable because Table-abcd contains an additional primary key data element (D). The problem in combining these two tables is that any "unique" data element in Table-abc would only be fully functionally dependent on A and B and C. Combining subsets/supersets *destroys* 2NF. Combining subsets/supersets causes the database to have anomalies.

THE ACTUAL COMBINATION PROCESS

The trick in combining two or more tables is *not* to lose any information. For instance,

$$\texttt{Table-1}\,(\underline{A}, \underline{B}, \underline{C}, D, E, F)$$

and

$$\texttt{Table-2}\,(\underline{A}, \underline{C}, \underline{B}, D, F, G)$$

should be combined into a new table:

$$\texttt{Table-new}\,(\underline{A}, \underline{B}, \underline{C}, D, E, F, G)$$

Note that data element E, which was only in Table-1, and data element G, which was only in Table-2, are both present in Table-new. Combining Table-1 and Table-2 eliminated multiple copies of data elements D and F and preserved the singular data elements E and G.

THE HIDDEN KEY PROBLEM REVISITED

Logic University (Figure 8.6) contains the following two tables:

1. Instructor.courses-can-teach(*instructor-number*, *course-number*)
2. Instructor-courses-can-backup(*instructor-number*, *course-number*)

They both contain the same primary keys (instructor-number and course number) and neither table has any additional keys. Therefore, they are combinable into a single table:

```
Instructor,courses-can-teach-or-backup
(instructor-number,course-number)
```

Unfortunately, this combination has lost the information about whether the specific instructor could teach *or* back up the specific course. What happened? A special kind of data element was *hidden* in the table name. That special data element defines a *role*[1] that the entity type is playing at any specific instant. Therefore, the analyst must examine table names for

Hidden key data elements (implicit or explicit)

Hidden nonkey data elements

Hidden role data elements

The role data element poses special problems. The method previously recommended in 4NF for finding hidden elements in table names was to compare each table name "field" with the existing data element list—does not work since "can-teach" and "can-back-up" are roles (or values) for a data element *not* specified in the data element list. The analyst could very naturally establish the following two tables:

1. Instructor.course-can-teach(instructor-number, course-number, can-teach)
2. Instructor,course-can-backup(instructor-number, course-number, can-back-up)

and combine them into

```
Instructor.course(instructor-number,  course-number,
        can-back-up,can-teach)
```

The new Instructor-course table preserves the data on whether a specific instructor can teach or back-up a specific course. However, it contains extra data. The roles of can-teach and can-back-up are mutually exclusive (an instructor who can-back-up cannot teach; an instructor who can teach does not need to back up). The problem now is that there are roles (values) posing as data elements and they should be combined into a single role data element:

```
Teach-backup-role.
```

The teach-backup-role element should be stored in the data dictionary as a role element with all roles listed separately. As an aside, I would recommend that the roles be defined by 88 levels within Cobol programs.

---

[1]Charles Bachman has been instrumental in developing and defining the role concept in databases.

The final table should be

```
Instructor.course(instructor-number, course-number,
teach-backup-role)
```

This new table fulfills the minimal cover concept of normalization. It is composed of the minimum number of data elements required for the user's application.

AUTOMATED TOOLS

Automated tools would again have a difficult time finding hidden role elements. However, software tools should have little difficulty in finding matching sets of primary key. At this writing, only the ADPAC tool of DESIGN performs this analysis.

10

Generalization

DEFINITION

Generalization is the term used to describe the process of trying to determine if all root tables represent entity types or entities. For review:

> *Entity type:* anything that an organization wishes to maintain independent information about
>
> *Entity:* a single occurrence of an entity type

The scope of the operation is to analyze all root tables. Why? Failure to identify entities causes redundant information to be stored in the database. At this point—after 4NF and optimization—Logic University has the following three root tables: (1) Student, (2) Instructor, and (3) Alumni.

These tables contain similar-sounding data elements:

Name
Home-address
Home-phone
Number
Etc.

Are Students, Instructors, Alumni entity types or entities?

To answer this question requires another question:

> Can a single person be a student *and* an instructor *and* an alumni? Certainly. A GRADUATE STUDENT earning his/her way through Logic University as an INSTRUCTOR is all three simultaneously. If the separate root tables of student and instructor and alumni are maintained, that person's name, number, home address, phone, etc., will be stored in the database redundantly three times. Therefore, any inserts, updates, and deletes have to examine three tables rather than one (the storage anomalies).

REDUCING DATA ELEMENT NAMES TO GENERIC NAMES

The clerical method of identifying entities posing as entity types is to reduce all data elements within the root tables to their generic nouns. This basically means that each data element name is reduced to its noun component by stripping off all prefixes and suffixes. The first step is to look at the generic primary key data elements.

COMBINING RELATIONS WITH IDENTICAL GENERIC KEYS

All entity occurrences of a specific entity type must contain the same primary key data elements. Therefore, the first step is to match the generic keys of the root tables (similar to the optimization process discussed in Chapter 9). A review of Figure 8.6 shows that four root tables have the same generic key of "number": (1) Student, (2) Instructor, (3) Alumni, and (4) Course.

They are candidates for generalization (i.e., combining into a single table). The next step is to compare the generic nonkey data elements in each table for matches.

Student, Instructor, and Alumni have the following matches:

> NAME, ADDRESS, PHONE, SCHOOL

Course has no matches. This clerically eliminates course from combination but the analyst should still ask: Can a course and a student (or the instructor or alumni) be the same thing? Obviously not. Course is not combinable with the other root tables. This does leave student and instructor and alumni as combinable tables. The rules for combining the nonkey data elements in these tables are the same as in optimization (Chapter 9):

> All duplicate data elements are listed only *once* in the new table.

> All singular data elements in any table are placed into the new table.

The two problems remaining are:

1. What is the primary key of the new table?
2. How do we know if a specific instance (row) of the new table is a student and/or instructor and/or alumni?

ROLE IDENTIFICATION

To identify the role is easy; merely insert a role data element that will contain the permissible role values into the new root tables.

DETERMINING THE PRIMARY KEY

It is hoped that your organization has provided a unique number that follows a "person" through his/her life with the organization regardless of the "role" he/she plays at any instance. In this case—which usually does not happen in the real world—the analyst only has to develop an honest, user meaningful, complete name for the combined entity primary key. At Logic University this name could be:

```
Student-instructor-alumni-number
```

or

```
Person involved-with-courses-number
```

or

```
Person-number
```

or . . . There is no clear-cut answer as to which of the above (or any that the reader could think of) is the best (there is no correct answer). The author's recommendations are:

```
Role-role-role-role-...
```

and if that causes a name that is too large, then

```
Entity-type-generic-role
```

I believe that it is more meaningful and easier for all persons involved with the database to use a name that identifies the roles that the entity type can play. Of course, if the entity type can play 10 or 20 or more roles, that name becomes too long and also less understandable. The next recommendation is to use the generic entity type with a suffix of generic role:

Entity type   person
Generic role   involved with courses
                  (student currently taking courses)
                  (instructor currently teaching courses)
                  (alumni took courses)

The name of the new table should be whatever was used for the primary key prefixes. At Logic University

```
Student-instructor-alumni (student-instructor-alumni-number,...)
```

or

```
                    Person-involved-with-courses
                    (person-involved-with-course-number,...)
```

NONUNIQUE ROLE KEYS

The real world is rarely kind to the analyst. Logic University would have undoubtedly assigned unique *role* numbers to students and instructors and alumni. If Mr. Murphy had his way, the numbers would be duplicated over the three roles so that Eric could be

Student   0013
Instructor   0169
Alumni   1369

and Lisa could be

Student   0169
Instructor   1369
Alumni   0013

Consequently, there is no single "number" that uniquely identifies a specific occurrence of the Student-Instructor-Alumni table. What now?

Each Role Always Occurs

If *every* person involved with courses at Logic University had to be a *student and instructor and alumni,* the problem is relatively simple. Assign the most popular role key—at Logic University this is probably the student role key—as the primary key and make the other role keys *nonkey* data elements in the root table (there is a 1:1 relationship between a specific student-number and a specific instructor-number and a specific alumni-number). Unfortunately, at Logic University, a person can be any combination of student, instructor, or alumni.

Each Role Does Not Always Occur

The "standard DP" solution would probably be to assign another unique number:

```
New-student-instructor-alumni-number
```

This permits each of the role data elements to be nonkey and still remain in the root relation because of the 1:1 relationship with the new-student-instructor-alumni-number. The solution above is valid but it has the disadvantage of requiring extra storage for the new primary key data element.

Another "logical" solution would be to make all three role data elements into primary key data elements. This would "logically" require null values for nonoccurrence. This violates relational theory and is not normally physically implementable because DBMSs usually require a "real" value and cannot work with nulls.

A solution for unacceptable null values is to use dummy values. Substitute all zeros (or Cobol low values or high values) for the null values. This makes the DBMSs happy but still violates the spirit of normalization by using dummy values (see discussion in Chapter 8 under 4NF concatenated keys).

A relationally acceptable method is to permit each role value to be an *alternate* primary key. My graphic for this is to use underscores above *and* below the key data elements:

```
Student-instructor-alumni(student-number,  instructor-number,

alumni-number,...)
```

This is permissible in logical database design but generally unacceptable in physical databases.

SHOULD GENERALIZATION BE PERFORMED?

The author believes it should always be done, even recognizing that physical design considerations may require splitting the new combined root table apart. The operative words are: *may require splitting*. This book has recommended that the person designing the logical database be familiar with the data and *not* familiar with physical database design. In this case, not performing generalization is allowing the logical database design to dictate physical database design, which is wrong. The logical database designer should do logical; the physical database designer should do physical. Some additional reasons:

Generalization fulfills the normalization theory of minimal cover by not storing any redundant nonkey data elements.

Resultant logical database is more flexible and portable. A DBMS that permits alternate primary keys may become available.

Compaction/expansion algorithms may provide the ability to combine divergent entities with little or no loss of storage and little sacrifice of processing speed.

SUMMARY

Reduce all data elements in root tables to generic nouns. Determine if any root tables have a matching *set* of generic primary key data elements.

> If yes   then determine if there is a similarity of nonkey data
>   elements.
>> If yes   then determine if the root tables could be entity
>>   occurrences of a "higher" entity type.
>>> If yes   then combine.

After combining nonkey data elements into a new single-root table, insert role data element into the table to store the role values that each specific occurrence (row) can play.

Next, determine new primary key. If *all* role values identify the *same* entity, rename the primary key to either

```
Role-role-role-...
```

or

```
Entity-type-generic-role
```

If *all* role values do *not* identify the *same* entity, establish each nonunique role value as an alternate primary key. Change table name to the prefixes used in the primary key.

AUTOMATED TOOLS

The ADPAC DESIGN tool—at this writing—is the only tool the author knows of that strips off prefixes and suffixes and provides the analyst with generic root table matches.

11

Blueprint for Devising the Logical Database

The act of generalization has produced my version of *final* normal form (FNF). The rigorous application of the normalization process has produced a logical database in Codd or ADPAC notation that fulfills all the requirements of relational theory *and* produces a practical blueprint for physical database design. A synopsis of steps is listed below.

1. Collect data elements via one of the following:
   a. Functional decomposition diagrams, or
   b. Data decomposition diagrams, or
   c. Existing systems.
2. Verify data elements by:
   a. Datastore and process box analysis, or
   b. Universal and atomic element analysis, or
   c. Homonym, synonym, and alias analysis.
3. Identify entity types by analyzing:
   a. Context diagram, or
   b. Datastores, or
   c. Output document name and/or header information, or
   d. Existing master records.
4. Cluster *all* data in the "figure" (datastore, output document, master record, etc.) to the entity type identified by the "figure."

5. Identify calculable or derivable data elements:
 a. Place calculation algorithms into data dictionary.
 b. Remove calculable and derivable data elements.
6. Create a sorted list of all data elements.
7. Identify the primary key of the entity types.
8. Identify the repeating groups within the entity types.
9. Remove each repeating group to its own table.
10. Create an honest complete name for each table.
11. Match each field within the table name against the sorted list of data elements:
 a. If name is on sorted list, it must be *within* table also.
 b. If name is *not* on sorted list, determine if field represents a role value.
 c. If a role value, insert role data element into table.
12. Bring down the primary key of the table from which the repeating group was removed.
13. Identify the other data elements in the new table necessary to identify a single occurrence of the new table.
14. Continue the repeating group process for repeating groups within repeating groups until all repeating groups have been placed into their own table.
15. Determine if each nonkey data element is fully functionally dependent on *all* the key data elements that identify the table of which the nonkey is part (use Venn diagrams if necessary);
 a. Remove any nonfully functionally dependent nonkey data elements to their own table.
 b. The primary key of the new table is those key data elements on which the nonkey data element is fully functionally dependent.
16. Determine if the new table is absorbable into an existing table; if absorbable, eliminate the new table.
17. Make a cursory check to determine if there are any derivable or calculable data element left; if so, eliminate or create new table if not absorbable.
18. Combine any tables that have identical sets of primary key data elements.
19. Strip the root tables to their generic data elements. If the same generic keys and a plurality of matching generic nonkeys, combine.

THE LOGICAL DATABASE IS NOW COMPLETE.

12

Graphic Models

DEFINITION

It is reputed that Confucius stated that a picture is worth a thousand words. Most database people want to work with a graphic presentation rather than Codd relational notation because it is in fact easier to visualize by looking at pictures rather than a sequence of nouns. Consequently, a graphic model is a true and accurate pictorial model of a database (logical or physical).

TYPES

There are three different types of graphic models generally used to pictorialize relational notation: (1) bubble, (2) canonical, and (3) Database Task Group (DBTG—Bachman).

Bubble

The bubble graphic model uses ellipses (bubbles) to portray each *attribute* (data element), with related attributes being connected by lines. The relationship between connected attributes is indicated by the number and direction of arrowheads.

An attribute is "owned" if the arrowhead is touching the bubble or pointing toward it; it is owned by the bubble that originated the line. A single arrowhead ($>$) means a $1:1$ relationship; a double arrowhead ($>>$) means a $1:M$ relationship.

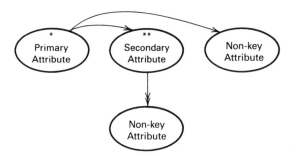

Figure 12.1 Bubble Chart

An attribute that owns a 1:1 relationship is a *primary key*; an attribute that owns a 1:*M* relationship is a *secondary key* (it is possible for a single attribute to be both a primary and a secondary key). An attribute that owns nothing is a *nonkey attribute*. Figure 12.1 illustrates the basic syntax.

Canonical

The canonical model looks very similiar to the vertical format of the normalization figures used in this book. The relationships between the various tables is indicated by solid lines drawn on the left side of the model, again with the number of and the direction of the arrowheads indicating the type of relationship. As with bubble models, the arrowhead points to the owned table; a > is a 1:1 and a >> is a 1:*M*. Figure 12.2 indicates the basic syntax.

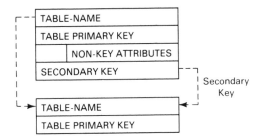

Figure 12.2 Canonical Model

Database Task Group (DBTG—Bachman)

In the late 1960s, the Cobol CODASYL group established a separate task group (DBTG) to propose and establish standards for database management system (DBMS). The chairperson of the committee was Charles Bachman, who at that time was developing a DBMS for General Electric. At this writing, the task group has proposed standards, but they have not yet been accepted. The DBTG DBMS is a plex (network) model and is graphically portrayed by a DBTG model. It is often called a Bachman model because

| OWNER TABLE NAME |
| PRIMARY KEY |
| FOREIGN KEY |
| SECONDARY KEY |

| MEMBER TABLE NAME |
| PRIMARY KEY |
| FOREIGN KEY |
| SECONDARY KEY |

Figure 12.3 DBTG (Bachman) Model

Bachman was the chairperson. IDMS (Cullinet) and IDS II (Honeywell) use a physical DBTG diagram to graphically portray the actual physical database. Figure 12.3 illustrates the basic syntax for the *logical* DBTG model.

CONVERTING RELATIONAL NOTATION TO A GRAPHIC MODEL

Bubble

Place the primary key of the root table[1] in the first bubble (separate concatenated data elements with a plus (+) sign). Place all the nonkey data elements into separate bubbles. Connect all the bubbles with a line from the primary bubble to the nonkey bubbles with arrowheads pointing to the nonkey bubbles. Because all the tables have been normalized, there are *no* double arrowheads (multivalued dependency—$1:M$) on the first bubble chart. Place an asterisk (*) in the primary bubble to identify it as a bubble containing the primary key. Figure 12.4 is a bubble chart for the instructor table of Logic University.

   The instructor.summary table was created during normalization because an instructor can have many summary grades (i.e., a repeating group or $1:M$). To link the instructor table to the instructor.summary table requires that a new primary bubble for the instructor.summary table be drawn below the primary bubble of the instructor table. The two primary bubbles are linked with a line and a *double-headed* arrowhead pointing to the instructor.summary table (a single instructor can have many summary grades). The primary key of the instructor.summary primary bubble is course-number + semester. The primary key data element of instructor-number is *not* repeated because it is implied from the linkage of the two primary bubbles. Add a double asterisk (**) to the instructor primary key to show that it is both a primary and a secondary key. Add a single * to the instructor.summary table to identify it as a primary key. Place all nonkey attributes of the instructor.summary table in separate bubbles connected with single arrowhead lines. Figure 12.5 is the composite bubble chart. Other members of the instructor set are processed similarly. There is no approved graphic for compound keys. The author recommends an exclamation point (!) because of the dangers that compound keys pose.

---

[1]Root tables are created by the initial clustering of data elements (attributes) to an identified entity type. Root tables are owners, with the tables derived through normalization as members.

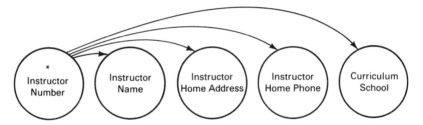

Figure 12.4   Bubble Chart of Instructor Table

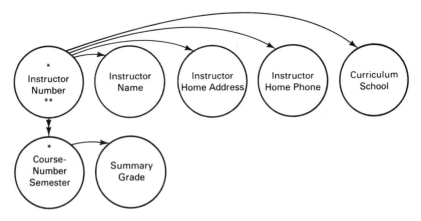

Figure 12.5   Composite Bubble Chart

Canonical

The best way for me to illustrate the building of a canonical model is to place Figure 12.6 (third normal form of Logic University) on the next page. The first entry in the first rectangle is the name of the table and corresponds to the first entry in the vertical listing of FNF:

```
student          student
student.crshist  student-course-history
student.major    student-major
etc.
```

The primary key is placed in the second rectangle with concatenated keys separated by a plus (+) sign (again, I recommend an ! for compound keys). All nonkey data elements are placed into separate rectangles, with each rectangle indented under the table name rectangle and primary key rectangle. Set members are connected by lines from the owner (root) table rectangle to the member table name rectangle. Again, a double-headed arrowhead is used to indicate a 1:*M* dependency. There are no secondary keys at this point. Figure 12.7 shows the canonical models provided by Database Design, Inc.

THIRD NORMAL FORM

RPT LINE	USER CODES	PARENT IDENT	SUBORD IDENT		DATA NAME
	1---------	11-----	21------		31----------------------------
1	A	STUDENT			STUDENT
2	A			P	S-NUMBER
3	A				S-NAME
4	A				S-STATUS
5	A				S-HOME-ADDRESS
6	A				S-HOME-PHONE
7	A				S-GRADUATION-EXPECTED-DATE
8	A				S_I-NUMBER<ADVISOR>
9	A				S_H-NAME
10	A	STUDENT	S_C-HIST		STUDENT.S_C-HISTORY
11	A			P	S-NUMBER
12	A			P	S_C_T-TAKEN
13	A			P	S_C-NUMBER-TAKEN
14	A				S_C-HOURS-CREDIT-TAKEN
15	A				S_C-HOURS-CREDIT-EARNED
16	A				S_C-GRADE-EARNED
17	A	S_C-TIT			S_C-TITLE
18	A			P	S_C-NUMBER-TAKEN
19	A				S_C-TITLE
20	A	STUDENT	S_M-MAJR		STUDENT.S_M<MAJOR>
21	A			P	S-NUMBER
22	A			P	S_M<MAJOR>
23	A	STUDENT	S_M-MINR		STUDENT.S_M<MINOR>
24	A			P	S-NUMBER
25	A			P	S_M<MINOR>
26	A	STUDENT	S_DEG-PV		STUDENT.S-DEGREE-PREVIOUS
27	A			P	S-NUMBER
28	A			P	S-DEGREE-TYPE-PREVIOUS
29	A				S-GRADUATION-PREVIOUS-DATE
30	A	STUDENT	S_R-#-AT		STUDENT.S_R-NUMBER-ATTENDING
31	A			P	S-NUMBER
32	A			P	S-TIME-START-ATTENDING
33	A			P	S-DAYOFWEEK-ATTENDING
34	A				S_I-NAME<TEACHING>
35	B	COURSE			COURSE
36	B			P	C-NUMBER
37	B				C-TITLE
38	B				C_H-NAME-CURRICULUM
39	B				C-HOURS-CREDIT-MINIMUM
40	B				C-HOURS-CREDIT-MAXIMUM
41	B				C-CLASSSIZE-MINIMUM
42	B				C-CLASSSIZE-MAXIMUM
43	B				C-HOURS-DURATION
44	B	COURSE	C-PREREQ		COURSE.C-PREREQUSITE
45	B			P	C-NUMBER
46	B			P	C-NUMBER<PREREQUISITE>
47	B	COURSE	C_E-SPEC		COURSE.C_E-SPECIAL
48	B			P	C-NUMBER
49	B			P	C_E-EQUIPMENT-TYPE-SPECIAL
50	B	COURSE	C_T-TAKN		COURSE.C_T-TAKEN
51	B			P	C-NUMBER
52	B			P	C_T-GIVEN
53	C	CLASSROM			CLASSROOM
54	C			P	R-NUMBER
55	C				R-CAPACITY
56	C	CLASSROM	RDAYOFWK		CLASSROOM.R-DAYOFWEEK
57	C			P	R-NUMBER
58	C			P	R-DAYOFWK

Figure 12.6 Third Normal Form

THIRD NORMAL FORM

RPT LINE	USER CODES	PARENT IDENT	SUBORD IDENT		DATA NAME
	1---------	11-----	21------		31--------------------------
59	C			P	R-TIME-START-ATTENDING
60	C				R-TIME-END-ATTENDING
61	C				R_C-NUMBER
62	C				R_C-TITLE
63	C				R_I-NUMBER
64	C	RDAYOFWK	STDNREST		R_C-NUMBER.STUDENTS-REGISTERED
65	C			P	R-NUMBER
66	C			P	R-DAYOFWK
67	C			P	R-TIME-START-ATTENDING
68	C				R_S-NUMBER
69	C	CLASSROM	R_E-SPEC		CLASSROOM.R_E-SPECIAL
70	C			P	R-NUMBER
71	C			P	R_E-TYPE-SPECIAL
72	D	INSTRCT			INSTRUCTOR
73	D			P	I-NUMBER
74	D				I-NAME
75	D				I-STATUS
76	D				I-HOME-ADDRESS
77	D				I-HOME-PHONE
78	D				I-DATE-TEACH-START
79	D				I-DATE-TENURE
80	D				I_H-NAME
81	D	INSTRCT	I_C-HIST		INSTRUCTOR.I_C-HISTORY
82	D			P	I-NUMBER
83	D			P	I_C_T-TAUGHT
84	D			P	I_C-NUMBER-TAUGHT
85	D				I_C-TITLE
86	D				I_C-GRADE-SUMMARY-EARNED
87	D	INSTRCT	I-DEG-PV		INSTRUCTOR.I-DEGREE-PREVIOUS
88	D			P	I-NUMBER
89	D			P	I-GRADUATION-PREVIOUS-DATE
90	E	MAJIMIN			MAJOR-MINOR
91	E			P	M_H-NAME-CURRICULUM
92	E			P	M_C-NUMBER
93	E				M-NAME
94	E				M-TYPE
95	E				M-HOURS-GRADUATION-REQUIRED
96	E	MAJIMIN	M_C-REQR		MAJOR-MINOR.M_C-REQUIREMENTS
97	E			P	M_H-NAME-CURRICULUM
98	E				M_C-NUMBER
99	F	SEMESTER			SEMESTER
100	F			P	T-NAME
101	F				T-DATE-START
102	F				T-DATE-END
103	G	ALUMNI			ALUMNI
104	G			P	A-NUMBER
105	G				A-NAME
106	G				A-HOME-ADRESS
107	G				A-HOME-PHONE
108	G				A-EMPLOYER-NAME
109	G				A-EMPLOYER-ADDRESS
110	G				A-CONTRIBUTION-YEAR-CURRENT
111	G				A-CONTRIBUTION-SUMMARY
112	G	ALUMNI	A-DEG-PV		ALUMNI.A-DEGREE-PREVIOUS
113	G			P	A-NUMBER
114	G			P	A-DEGREE-TYPE-PREVIOUS
115	G				A-DEGREE-GRADUATION-PREVIOUS

Figure 12.6 Con't.

```
THIRD NORMAL FORM

RPT
LINE    ENTITY   DERIVABLE ELEMENT
------  ------   --------------------
  1       A      S-TIME-END-ATTENDING
  2       B      C_S-TALLY-TAKEN
  3       B      C_S-TALLY-MAJOR-TAKEN
  4       B      C_S-TALLY-MINOR-TAKEN
  5       B      C_S-TALLY-FREE-TAKEN
  6       C      R_S-NAME
  7       C      R_I-NAME
PM@TAB-M04  NWLG04   REPLACED IN PMLIB AS AN   DTABLE    SEE  NWLG04
--------------------
```

Figure 12.6 Con't.

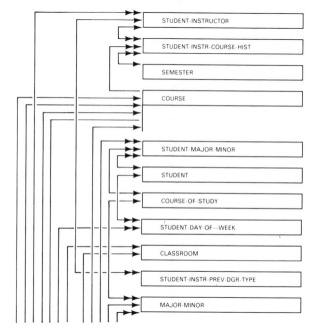

Figure 12.7 Canonical Model of Logic University

Database Task Group (DBTG—Bachman)

The construction of a DBTG diagram from 3NF (third normal form) or FNF (final normal form) is trivial. The DBTG rectangle is divided into four areas:

1. Table name
2. Primary key
3. Foreign key
4. Secondary key

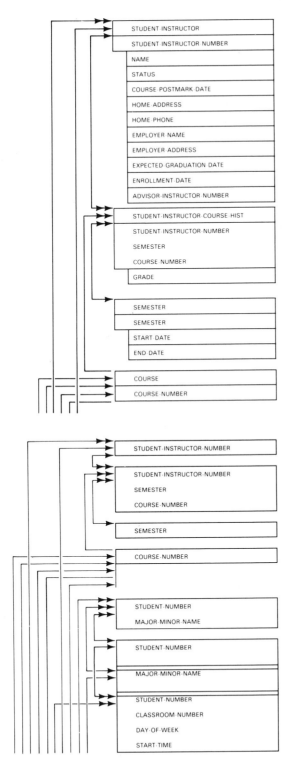

Figure 12.7 Con't.

DYNAMIC DATA CHART

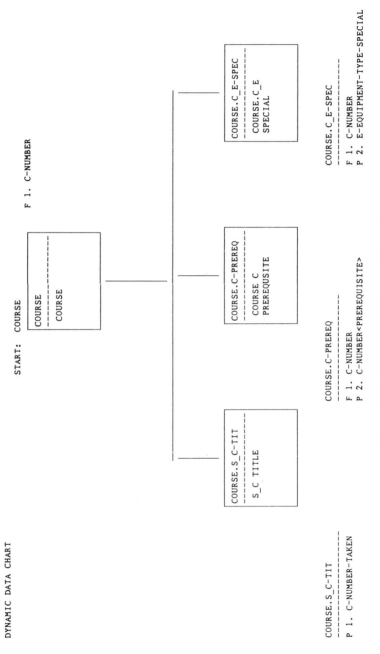

START: COURSE   F 1. C-NUMBER

COURSE.S_C-TIT

S_C TITLE

COURSE.C-PREREQ

COURSE C
PREREQUISITE

COURSE.C_E-SPEC

COURSE.C_E
SPECIAL

COURSE.S_C-TIT

P 1. C-NUMBER-TAKEN

COURSE.C-PREREQ

F 1. C-NUMBER
P 2. C-NUMBER<PREREQUISITE>

COURSE.C_E-SPEC

F 1. C-NUMBER
P 2. E-EQUIPMENT-TYPE-SPECIAL

Figure 12.8   Partial DBTG Diagram of Course Set

The table name is the entry to the left of the first parenthesis [)] in Codd notation or the first entry in the ADPAC notation. The primary keys are underlined in Codd and prefixed by a P in ADPAC. The inclusion of multiple attributes in the primary key portion *implicitly* identifies a concatenated key. This permits the plus (+) sign to be "carried over" as the graphic for a compound key. At this juncture, there are no foreign or secondary keys. The owner (root) table is placed on the "first" level and is connected to its member tables on the "second" level by lines with a *single* arrowhead. In DBTG diagrams, the arrowhead indicates *ownership* and *does not* indicate single or multivalued dependencies as in bubble and canonical models. It is assumed that members have a 1 : *M* relationship with their owners (else why would they be members?). Figure 12.8 is a partial DBTG diagram for the course set. Figure 12.9 is the DBTG diagram for the Logic University application logical database.

```
                  T A B L E    O F    C O N T E N T S
           PAGE  RELATION  DATA NAME
           ----  --------  -----------------------------
              1  ST-IN-AL  STUDENT-INSTRUCTOR-ALUMNI
              1  S_C-HIST  STUDENT.S_C-HISTORY
              1  S_M-MAJR  STUDENT.S_M<MAJOR>
              1  S_M-MINR  STUDENT.S_M<MINOR>
              1  S_DEG-PV  SA-DEGREE-PREVIOUS
              1  S_R-#-AT  STUDENT.S_R-NUMBER-ATTENDING
              1  I_C-HIST  INSTRUCTOR.I_C-HISTORY
              2  I-DEG-PV  INSTRUCTOR.I-DEGREE-PREVIOUS
              3  COURSE    COURSE
              3  S_C-TIT   S_C-TITLE
              3  C-PREREQ  COURSE.C-PREREQUSITE
              3  C_E-SPEC  COURSE.C_E-SPECIAL
              4  CLASSROM  CLASSROOM
              4  RDAYOFWK  CLASSROOM.R-DAYOFWEEK
              4  R_E-SPEC  CLASSROOM.R_E-SPECIAL
              5  MAJIMIN   MAJOR-MINOR
              5  M_C-REQR  MAJOR-MINOR.M_C-REQUIREMENTS
              6  SEMESTER  SEMESTER

WHERE USED
CROSS REFERENCE OF RELATION DATA NAME
RELATION DATA NAME                    SYMBOLIC      DATA CHART PAGE NUMBER
----------------------------          --------      -----------------------

CLASSROOM                             CLASSROM      4
CLASSROOM.R DAYOFWEEK                  RDAYOFWK      4
CLASSROOM.R_E SPECIAL                  R_E-SPEC      4
COURSE                                COURSE        3
COURSE.C PREREQUSITE                  C-PREREQ      3
COURSE.C_E SPECIAL                    C_E-SPEC      3
INSTRUCTOR.I DEGREE PREVIOUS          I-DEG-PV      2
INSTRUCTOR.I_C HISTORY                I_C-HIST      1
MAJOR MINOR                           MAJIMIN       5
MAJOR MINOR.M_C REQUIREMENTS          M_C-REQR      5
S_C TITLE                             S_C-TIT       3
SA DEGREE PREVIOUS                    S_DEG-PV      1
SEMESTER                              SEMESTER      6
STUDENT INSTRUCTOR ALUMNI             ST-IN-AL      1
STUDENT.S_C HISTORY                   S_C-HIST      1
STUDENT.S_M<MAJOR>                    S_M-MAJR      1
STUDENT.S_M<MINOR>                    S_M-MINR      1
STUDENT.S_R NUMBER ATTENDING          S_R-#-AT      1
```

Figure 12.9 DBTG Diagram of Logic University

```
WHERE USED
CROSS REFERENCE OF RELATION SYMBOLIC NAME
SYMBOLIC  RELATION DATA NAME                           DATA CHART PAGE NUMBER
--------  ------------------------------               ----------------------


C-PREREQ   COURSE.C PREREQUSITE                          3
C_E-SPEC   COURSE.C_E SPECIAL                            3
CLASSROM   CLASSROOM                                     4
COURSE     COURSE                                        3
I-DEG-PV   INSTRUCTOR.I DEGREE PREVIOUS                  2
I_C-HIST   INSTRUCTOR.I_C HISTORY                        1
M_C-REQR   MAJOR MINOR.M_C REQUIREMENTS                  5
MAJIMIN    MAJOR MINOR                                   5
R_E-SPEC   CLASSROOM.R_E SPECIAL                         4
RDAYOFWK   CLASSROOM.R DAYOFWEEK                          4
S_C-HIST   STUDENT.S_C HISTORY                           1
S_C-TIT    S_C TITLE                                     3
S_DEG-PV   SA DEGREE PREVIOUS                            1
S_M-MAJR   STUDENT.S_M<MAJOR>                            1
S_M-MINR   STUDENT.S_M<MINOR>                            1
S_R-#-AT   STUDENT.S_R NUMBER ATTENDING                 1
SEMESTER   SEMESTER                                      6
ST-IN-AL   STUDENT INSTRUCTOR ALUMNI                     1
```

```
WHERE USED
CROSS REFERENCE OF DATA NAME
DATA NAME                                              DATA CHART PAGE NUMBER
-----------------------------                          ----------------------


C-NUMBER                                               3    3    3    5
C-NUMBER<PREREQUISITE>                                 3
C-NUMBER-TAKEN                                         3    1
C-NUMBER-TAUGHT                                        1
E-EQUIPMENT-TYPE-SPECIAL                               3
E-TYPE-SPECIAL                                         4
H-NAME-CURRICULUM                                      5    5
I-GRADUATION-PREVIOUS-DATE                             2
I-NUMBER                                               1    2
M<MAJOR>                                               1
M<MINOR>                                               1
R-DAYOFWK                                              4
R-NUMBER                                               4    4    4
R-TIME-START-ATTENDING                                 4
S-DAYOFWEEK-ATTENDING                                  1
S-NUMBER                                               1    1    1    1
S-TIME-START-ATTENDING                                 1
SA-DEGREE-TYPE-PREVIOUS                                1
SA-NUMBER                                              1
SIA-NUMBER                                             1
T-NAME                                                 6
T-TAKEN                                                1
T-TAUGHT                                               1
```

Figure 12.9 Con't.

DYNAMIC DATA CHART

START: ST-IN-AL   P 1. SIA-NUMBER

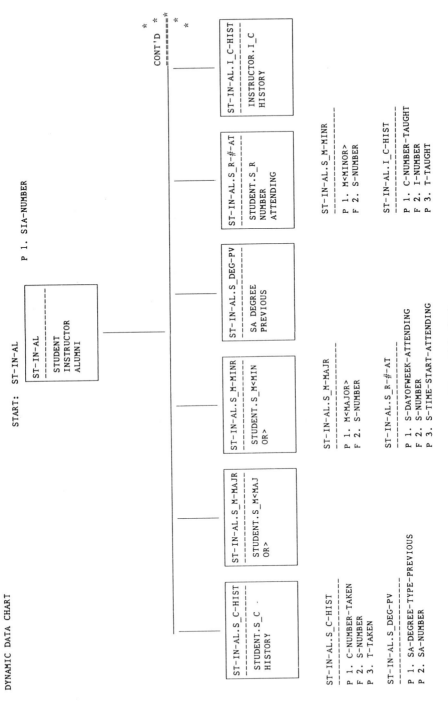

Figure 12.9 Con't.

DYNAMIC DATA CHART

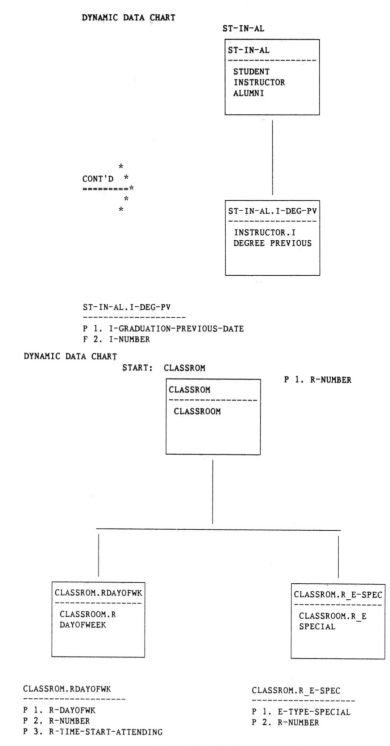

```
                                        ST-IN-AL

                                   ST-IN-AL
                                   ------------------
                                   STUDENT
                                   INSTRUCTOR
                                   ALUMNI




                    *
           CONT'D   *
           =========*
                    *
                    *               ST-IN-AL.I-DEG-PV
                                    ------------------
                                    INSTRUCTOR.I
                                    DEGREE PREVIOUS




           ST-IN-AL.I-DEG-PV
           --------------------
           P 1. I-GRADUATION-PREVIOUS-DATE
           F 2. I-NUMBER
```

DYNAMIC DATA CHART

```
                START:  CLASSROM
                                                P 1. R-NUMBER
                          CLASSROM
                          ------------------
                          CLASSROOM




           CLASSROM.RDAYOFWK                    CLASSROM.R_E-SPEC
           ------------------                   ------------------
           CLASSROOM.R                          CLASSROOM.R_E
           DAYOFWEEK                            SPECIAL




     CLASSROM.RDAYOFWK                     CLASSROM.R_E-SPEC
     --------------------                  --------------------
     P 1. R-DAYOFWK                        P 1. E-TYPE-SPECIAL
     P 2. R-NUMBER                         P 2. R-NUMBER
     P 3. R-TIME-START-ATTENDING
```

Figure 12.9 Con't.

```
DYNAMIC DATA CHART
              START:  MAJIMIN
                      ┌──────────────────┐          F 1. C-NUMBER
                      │ MAJIMIN          │          F 2. H-NAME-CURRICULUM
                      │ ─────────────────│
                      │ MAJOR MINOR      │
                      │                  │
                      │                  │
                      │                  │
                      └─────────┬────────┘
                                │
                                │
                                │
                                │
                                │
                      ┌─────────┴────────┐
                      │ MAJIMIN.M_C-REQR │
                      │ ─────────────────│
                      │ MAJOR MINOR.M_C  │
                      │ REQUIREMENTS     │
                      │                  │
                      └──────────────────┘


MAJIMIN.M_C-REQR
────────────────────
F 1. H-NAME-CURRICULUM
```

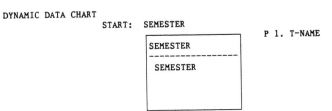

```
DYNAMIC DATA CHART
            START:  SEMESTER
                    ┌──────────────────┐        P 1. T-NAME
                    │ SEMESTER         │
                    │ ─────────────────│
                    │ SEMESTER         │
                    │                  │
                    │                  │
                    └──────────────────┘
```

Figure 12.9 Con't.

AUTOMATED TOOLS

There are—to the best of my knowledge—no software packages that automatically produce bubble charts from relational notation. Data Designer (Database Design, Inc.) takes
bubble charts that have been decomposed into simple coded statements and automatically
produces a canonical model. DESIGN (ADPAC) takes ADPAC notation and automatically produces a DBTG model.

13

Foreign Keys

DEFINITION

A foreign key is an attribute in a table that provides a logical pathway to another entity set because that attribute is part of or the entire primary key of a table in another entity set. The foreign key attribute can be either a key—except in root tables—or a nonkey. A root table attribute cannot be a foreign key because the primary key of a root table can only identify an entity type. Normally, foreign keys are found in *relationship* tables because these tables contain data that results from the intersection of entity types.

A *recursive* foreign key is a *nonkey* attribute in a table that permits that table to be accessed by the foreign key. The nonkey attribute in the student-instructor-alumni table of person-number-advisor contains the identifying value of the instructor who is advising a specific student. To obtain any attributes about that person-number-advisor other than the identifying value requires that the same table be logically accessed by the identifying value. Recursive foreign keys should occur only in root tables that contain multiple roles for the identified entity type.

IDENTIFYING FOREIGN KEYS

Root Tables

Examine each nonkey attribute against the key attributes of the host root table *and* each table in all *other* entity sets. Any equal comparison identifies a foreign key (a match on the host table identifies a recursive foreign key).

Nonroot Tables

Examine each attribute (key or nonkey) against the key attributes of each table in all other entity sets. Any equal comparison identifies a foreign key.

AUGMENTING GRAPHIC MODEL

Bubble

Foreign keys are treated as primary keys in bubble charts since they represent a 1 : 1 relationship. The foreign key is considered the parent (owner) and therefore the arrowhead is placed on the bubble to be the foreign key attribute. I recommend placing an ''F'' in the foreign key bubble rather than an *.

Canonical

Draw a line from the foreign key attribute rectangle to the table name attribute rectangle with a single arrowhead pointing to the table name attribute on the *left* side of the model.

DBTG

Place the foreign attribute name in the ''third'' portion of the DBTG rectangle.

IDENTIFYING SUBSETS OF FOREIGN KEYS

Adding all the connecting lines that all foreign keys would require in a bubble or canonical model can cause the model to look like the diagram of the New York (or London or Moscow) subway system. The original reason for transforming the Codd or ADPAC relational notation to a graphic model was that the model would be easier to visualize and understand. A model that looks like a subway map is not easy to understand. The analyst has two choices:

1. Add lines only for those foreign keys that the analyst believes necessary (Mr. Murphy guarantees that the analyst will be wrong).
2. Add an appendix that lists all the foreign keys.

My recommendation is that analysts add the lines for their guesses *and* provide an appendix for all foreign keys with an identifier for all foreign keys that have been drawn on the model.

Normally, a single table does not contain many foreign keys; therefore it is typically easy to list all the foreign keys in the ''third'' portion of the DBTG rectangle.

AUTOMATED TOOLS

Only the ADPAC DESIGN software package identifies foreign keys automatically. Figure 13.1 is a listing of all foreign keys in the Logic University logical database and Figure 12.8 is the complete DBTG diagram with foreign keys identified by an F prefix.

```
     Left half of the report

  FOREIGN KEYS

     RPT    FOREIGN KEY                        IN RELATION
     LINE   DATA NAME                          SYMBOLIC IDENT    OF:
            1...5...10...15...20...25...30  ----------------    OF:
       1    H-NAME-CURRICULUM                  COURSE            OF:
       2    H-NAME-CURRICULUM                  COURSE            OF:
       3    C-NUMBER                           CLASSROM.RDAYOFWK  OF:
       4    C-NUMBER                           CLASSROM.RDAYOFWK  OF:
       5    C-NUMBER                           CLASSROM.RDAYOFWK  OF:
       6    C-NUMBER                           CLASSROM.RDAYOFWK  OF:
       7    I-NUMBER                           CLASSROM.RDAYOFWK  OF:
       8    I-NUMBER                           CLASSROM.RDAYOFWK  OF:
       9    S-NUMBER                           CLASSROM.RDAYOFWK  OF:
      10    S-NUMBER                           CLASSROM.RDAYOFWK  OF:
      11    S-NUMBER                           CLASSROM.RDAYOFWK  OF:
      12    S-NUMBER                           CLASSROM.RDAYOFWK  OF:


    Right half of the report

                      PM/SS, USE BY AGREEMENT ONLY 07/22/85 PAGE   1

  OF RELATION                       OF RELATION
  DATA NAME                         SYMBOLIC IDENT
  1...5...10...15...20...25...30  ----------------
  MAJOR-MINOR                       MAJIMIN
  MAJOR-MINOR.M_C-REQUIREMENTS      MAJIMIN.M_C-REQR
  COURSE                            COURSE
  COURSE.C-PREREQUSITE              COURSE.C-PREREQ
  COURSE.C_E-SPECIAL                COURSE.C_E-SPEC
  MAJOR-MINOR                       MAJIMIN
  INSTRUCTOR.I_C-HISTORY            ST-IN-AL.I_C-HIST
  INSTRUCTOR.I-DEGREE-PREVIOUS      ST-IN-AL.I-DEG-PV
  STUDENT.S_C-HISTORY               ST-IN-AL.S_C-HIST
  STUDENT.S_M<MAJOR>                ST-IN-AL.S_M-MAJR
  STUDENT.S_M<MINOR>                ST-IN-AL.S_M-MINR
  STUDENT.S_R-NUMBER-ATTENDING      ST-IN-AL.S_R-#-AT
  DYNAMIC DATA CHART
```

Figure 13.1   Foreign Keys for Logic University

14

Secondary Keys

DEFINITION

Computers like numbers. Human beings like names. This basic dichotomy is the principal—but not the only—reason for secondary keys. A secondary key is a user request to access a table by attributes other than the primary key within that table. A primary key returns a single occurrence, a secondary key n occurrences. A primary key is $1:1$; a secondary key is $1:M$.

DERIVING SECONDARY KEYS

User Views

Most DP shops that have DBMSs have also provided some form of user inquiry to that DBMS. Typically, DP has programmed these "ad hoc" inquiries and provided formatted screens for the user (4GLs should permit the user to perform these and other ad hoc inquiries by themselves). These user repetitive ad hoc inquiries should be shown as secondary keys.

User Interviews

Most computer trade publications have articles that state both the "real" and the "hidden" backlog of user requests. Real means that the request has been submitted to DP, where hidden means that the user—for whatever reason—has decided not to submit the request because the user knows that DP cannot answer the request in a timely fashion. The hidden requests often contain request for secondary keys. The only way for an analyst to uncover the unknown secondary keys is to *talk* to the user. (I know that this is a *radical* idea!) Secondary keys are determined from user views and user interviews.

DETERMINING VALUE AND PRIORITY OF SECONDARY KEYS

Not all secondary key requests are created equal. There is *always* a user priority—i.e., some request is more important than any other. Once upon a time, most DBMSs had some restriction on secondary keys. That restriction has largely disappeared. However, physical design of a specific DBMS that is responsive to the user may hinge on the proper prioritization of the user secondary requests.

The best scheme that the author knows is described in Chapter 7.5.3 of Gane/Sarson *Structured Systems Analysis*. The method is simplicity. Ask the user: If I could provide you (user) the answer to your question for $1 tomorrow, what would you pay to get the same answer immediately?

This question is particularly effective in an organization that uses a charge back system because the user knows that any DP processing is costly. To make the question really effective requires two additional parameters:

1. How many times per hour (minute, day, week, etc.) are you going to ask the question?
2. What is your organizational rank?

The first question permits proper evaluation of the particular query's value to an organization. A $2 query asked 10,000 times per day ($20,000) is "twice" as important as a $2,000 query asked 5 times per day ($10,000).

The second question allows the analyst to assess the "political" value of the query. If the CEO states that he/she would like to ask a particular query but does not know how often or how much it's worth, my recommendation is that the database designer provide that facility or start looking for a new job.

Many ineffective physical designs are caused by the inability of the database designer to obtain this type of vital information from the analyst or the user. (I am sure that by now the reader is tiring of this phrase but I will repeat it again, *The analyst must know the data, the data relationship, and how the user expects to use the data.*

AUGMENTING GRAPHIC MODEL

Bubble

Secondary keys use an ** in the bubble to signify a secondary key. A line with a double arrowhead (>>) connects the secondary key bubble with the secondary attribute bubbles.

Canonical

Draw a *dotted* line on the *right* side of the model from the secondary key attribute rectangle to the table name rectangle that the secondary key points to. Again, a $>>$ is used to indicate the $1:M$ relationship.

DBTG

Place the secondary key attribute names in the "fourth" portion of the DBTG rectangle.

IDENTIFYING SUBSETS OF SECONDARY KEYS

As with foreign keys, adding all the secondary keys may create a bubble or canonical model of the "subway" system. In the case of secondary keys, however, all the secondary keys are necessary because they were derived from user views or user interviews. The only way to reduce the complexity of a bubble or canonical model is to place the secondary keys into an appendix. Again, most single tables do not contain many secondary keys; therefore, it is typically easy to list all the secondary keys in the fourth "portion" of the DBTG rectangle

AUTOMATED TOOLS

Data Designer and ADPAC permit secondary keys to be entered manually and thereafter displayed on the printouts.

SUMMARY

Figure 12.5 is a bubble chart for the instructor table from the 3NF set, Figure 12.6 is a canonical model, and Figure 12.8 is the full DBTG model (secondary keys have a prefix).

I believe that the DBTG diagram is the best alternative because of its simpler syntax. It is easy to clutter a bubble or canonical model to make it undecipherable to anybody, including its author.

15

Logical Records

DEFINITION

Cullinet was the first database vendor to offer a full logical record facility for its DBMS (IDMS). Cullinet has defined a logical record to be:

A logical record allows a program to access data fields from multiple database records as if they were data fields in a single record.[1]

Cullinet has defined the logical record facility (LRF) to be:

The IDMS Logical Record Facility (LRF) provides the ability to define a view of the IDMS database that is entirely independent of the database structure as defined in the schema. LRF takes advantage of relational database concepts by presenting user applications with logical data constructs that do not reflect or depend on schema-defined structures and relationships. With LRF, user programs do not issue database-navigation instructions; they issue only functional request for the desired data constructs, which provide flat-file views of the database. Programmers and end users therefore are not required to be familiar with IDMS network structures or database-navigation logic. Additionally, since the logical view of the database is independent of the schema definition, the physical structure of the database can be changed without always requiring either modification or recompilation of application programs.[2]

---

[1]Cullinet Logical Record Facility Classroom Aids.
[2]Cullinet IDMS Logical Record Facility.

My definition is that a logical record is a user view where the user can be the end user *or* the *programmer* writing an application program. The end-user view is typically a single transaction processed on-line; the programmer view is the data required to be processed in a single application (usually batch) program.

DERIVING LOGICAL RECORDS

User Documentation

The best source for user views is the *user*! Again, I recommend extensive discussion with the user because it is the user and only the user who knows. An unprepared analyst, however, will frustrate the user and lead to an unsuccessful investigation and the loss of many user views. My recommendation is that the analyst follow Ken Orr's basic principle of reviewing existing output documents. These can be documents such as: purchase order, invoice, credit statement, customer inquiry, etc.; "Private" documents such as "real" inventory, "real" credit status (these documents are usually maintained manually by the user because the user does not trust the "automated" reports); management request for data necessary for decision making (usually handwritten notes to "Joe" or "Jill" requesting all the sales by salesperson X in territory Y for the first quarter Z that were undiscounted and profitable, etc, etc.).

Gane/Sarson

The business logic represented by the lowest-level process box in a Gane/Sarson data-flow diagram should be expressible in approximately one page of structured English (or pseudocode, or a "small" decision table, or . . .). The structured English requires data and that data represents that process box's logical record. Stradis[3] has a SDLC (System Development Life Cycle) activity requiring the development of "design units." A design unit is defined as:

> A collection of processes (with their associated data stores) which make up a schedulable work unit (which can potentially all be active at a given time without console operator intervention) to be designed as a whole.[4]

Consequently, the data required by that design unit represents the logical record. Normally, a design unit represents:

What one clerk can reasonably perform (manual system)
What one structured application program can reasonably process (batch)
What one transaction can reasonably accomplish (on-line)

---

[3]Stradis is a methodology developed by Gane/Sarson and currently supported by McAuto (St. Louis).
[4]From my class notes of the McAuto ASAD course.

It turns out in the real world that what one clerk can do manually is roughly equal to what one on-line transaction can process through the computer.

Yourdon

As with Gane/Sarson, the business logic represented by the lowest-level dataflow diagram should be expressible in one page of structured English (Yourdon refers to this page as a "mini-spec"). I do not believe that Yourdon has a concept comparable to design units, but certainly it would be easy to adapt to Yourdon.

Jackson

Jackson begins by diagramming both the input and output data structures. The next step is to attempt to merge the data structure into the corresponding program structure. This usually leads to a "structure clash"[5] which Jackson normally solves by "program inversion." The next step is to list the operations required, which includes the data required. This listed data is then the logical record for this Jackson diagram. Again, I do not believe that Jackson has the concept of a design unit, but it could be easily applied to Jackson.

Warnier/Orr

Orr starts at the "output" and works backward, eventually incorporating the input at the right edge of the diagram. As with Jackson, the data diagram is merged with a program structure. The final diagram again contains the data required and therefore the logical record. Design units can easily be applied to Orr also.

Bubble

The final bubble chart is a synthesis of user views; therefore, each individual bubble chart is the user view and therefore the logical record.

Existing Programs

Most companies have had data processing in some form for over 15 years. I contend that in that period of time all entity types and most of the entity type attributes are present in the data portions of the existing programs. The problem is making any sense of the mishmash of attribute names that pervade the typical DP shop. The author has conducted numerous studies at Fortune 500 companies which have shown that there are 20 bad attribute names (alias, homonym, synonym)[6] for each good attribute name. This poses an almost impossible identification task if the process is manual. Consequently, most companies do not attempt to utilize one of their most precious resources—existing data. If attribute

---

[5]An excellent basic explanation of Jackson, Warnier, and Warnier/Orr is provided in K. Hansen, *Data Structured Program Design*, Ken Orr & Associates, Inc., Topeka, Kansas, 1983.

names are rationalized[6] or "cleaned," the procedure for developing program logical records is simple: Cross-reference all Data Division input file names from Cobol programs to the Procedure Division. Those that have a reference plus the Procedure Division literals form the program logical record.

The entire input file cannot be used because virtually all "old" Cobol programs bring in the entire input record regardless of the actual number of attributes used. Output files and the Working Storage Section are not used since they should contain input data or data derivable from the input data.

User Screens

An end-user view is a logical record. The typical current end-user view is the data necessary to process an on-line transaction. Most new applications are on-line and use screens for end-user communication with the database. These screens are "painted" and processed by telecommunication software packages such as CICS (IBM) or ADS/O (Cullinet). Each screen normally represents a user view, although it is possible that a user view is represented by a series of programmatically linked screens. The development of screens is either early in the SDLC if prototyping is used or late if a standard development cycle is used.

AUTOMATED TOOLS

Gane/Sarson or Yourdon

DFDP (ADPAC) constructs logical records from the dataflow definitions provided by the analyst for each diagram. The logical record can be a single process box or a design unit.

Jackson

PDF (Jackson) and PACT (3D Systems) can construct logical records from data descriptions provided by the analyst in the development of each diagram.

Warnier/Orr

Structure(s)® (Orr) can construct logical records from the coded Warnier/Orr diagrams.

Bubble

Data Designer (Database Design, Inc.) can construct logical records from the coded bubble charts.

---

[6]See Chapter 4 or the Glossary for definition.

Existing Programs

Virtually all Cobol compilers provide various cross-reference reports as standard options. These reports can be used to construct the program logical record assuming that the attribute names are clean. Two automated software packages are available to clean the attribute names:

1. PM/SS (ADPAC)
2. Data Dictionary Composer (Composer Technology Corp.)

SUMMARY

Logical records are important because they assist in:

> User verification
> Developing security and privacy algorithms
> Physical database design (see Chapter 23)
> Eliminating programmer navigation (see Chapter 24)

Logical records should form the cornerstone of the logical database design!

16

LOGICAL DATABASE VERIFICATION

DEFINITION

The logical database produced by the techniques described in this book should represent the minimal cover—the smallest amount of data necessary to satisfy a particular user application. The data has been clustered (see Chapter 7) to its entity type, normalized (see Chapter 8), and converted to a graphic model (see Chapter 12).

The next step is to verify that the final logical database really does represent the minimal cover. One method is to produce actual sample tables of the logical database and give them to users for verification. Users are requested to verify that they can answer any question from the data provided in the tables. The problem with this approach is that normalized tables disperse the data over many tables and it is difficult for a user to envision how they would or the computer would handle the tables to answer a specific question. My preferred method is to have the user write down some ''normal'' questions and as many ''oddball'' questions as they can conceive of. The questions are given to the analyst who uses relational algebra to perform the verification.

RELATIONAL ALGEBRA

Relational algebra is a language that provides a set of operators for manipulating tables (relations). The normal operator set is: (1) project, (2) select, (3) join and unjoin, (4) Cartesian product (union); and, (5) ''usability'' operators.

Project

The project operator allows specific columns to be extracted in any sequence from a specific *single* table. An accepted graphic is | |. A sample syntax of the project operator is:

```
temporary-table-name¹ = | | table-name (column-name, column-name,...)
```

For instance, to create a temporary table of all instructors and their curriculum-school from the instructor table:

```
Instructor.curriculum-school = | | Instructor (instructor-name,
curriculum-school)
```

The resultant temporary table contains all instructor names with their curriculum school in "physical" storage sequence. Most human beings like their lists alphabetized and there is a "sort" operand for this purpose. For instance, sorting the instructors alphabetically within curriculum school could have the following syntax:

```
Instructor.curriculum-school = | | Instructor (instructor-name,
curriculum-school); SORT BY curriculum-school, instructor-name
```

Select

The select operator can use all the arithmetic operators $\{<, <=, =, =>, <>\}$ and can use all the Boolean operators (and, or, exclusive or, not) for multiple qualifications. The select operator allows qualification of the inquiry. An accepted graphic is Q. It can be used with most other relational operators. For instance, to list all instructors alphabetically that are in the Law curriculum school:

```
Instructor.law = | | Instructor (instructor-name)
                Q curriculum-school = "law"; SORT BY
                instructor-name
```

Join and Unjoin

The join operator permits two or more tables (relations) that have a common column (attribute) to be joined together in a new temporary table. Only rows (record tables) that have

---

¹All relational operators create temporary tables, which can then be the targets of other relations operators. The temporary tables exist during the life of the "inquiry."

identical attribute (column) values (domains) are placed in the new table. An accepted graphic is *. The basic syntax is

```
temporary-table-name = first-table-name * second-table-name
```

It is possible to join multiple tables by multiple *:

```
temporary-table-name = table1 * table2 * table3*...
```

The only requirement for a multiple table join is a common column (attribute).

The equations above would combine all unique attributes in all requested tables to form a "super" temporary table for all rows that had a matching attribute value in the specified column. For instance, Student.course-history-temporary-table = Student*Student.course-history would combine all the attributes in both tables, eliminating one occurrence of student-number since it occurs in both tables (and is the "join" attribute). This means that the new table contains student-home-address, em-ployer-name, employer-address, etc., in addition to course-number, course-grade, course-credit-hours, and instructor-number. If the inquirer only wanted the data in the student.course-history table, the equation could be

```
Student.course-history-temporary-table = Student () *
Student.course-history
```

where () = null—the table is used only for the join operation. If the inquirer also wanted the student-name from the Student table:

```
Student.course-history-temporary-table = Student (student-name) *
Student.course-history.
```

If the inquirer would again like the student name alphabetized within the curriculum school:

```
Student.course-history-temporary-table = Student (student-name) *
Student.course-history; SORT BY curriculum-school, instructor-name
```

Note: Curriculum-school can be used as a sort parameter even though it is not included in the new temporary table.

The select operator can also be used with a join operator. Again, if the inquirer only wanted law students:

```
Student.course-history-temporary-table = Student (student-name) Q
curriculum-school = "law" * Student.course-history; SORT BY
student-name
```

A join without qualification is often called a *natural join;* a join with qualification is often called an *equi-join.*

The unjoin operator creates a new temporary table from two or more tables that have a common column (attribute) but only for rows that do *not* have a matching value in the other tables. The new temporary table contains *only* rows (records, tables) that do not have a match. For instance, if the Logic University Registrar wanted an alphabetized list of entering students, the inquiry could be

```
Entering-students = Student (student-name) * Student.course-history ()
```

where $\overline{*}$ is an accepted graphic for unjoin (the overbar is math notation for negation).

Student.course-history is used only to eliminate students with course-history and therefore presumably not entering this semester; () after Student.course-history is the null graphic.

Cartesian Product (Union)

The Cartesian product operator combines two or more tables that have a common column (attribute). The Cartesian product differs from a join because there does *not* have to be a matching value in the tables; it differs from an unjoin because there does *not* have to be an *unmatch* value in the tables. An accepted graphic is u.

Duplicate Rows (Records, Tuples)

A basic premise of relational algebra is that all rows that have exactly the same attribute values are not repeated (this is analogous to "hex" dumps that do not print a line if that line is the same as the previous print line). For instance, if the Registrar wanted a list of unique courses taken by each student (i.e., he/she was not interested in knowing that a specific student had audited, failed, and finally passed the same course), the query could be

```
Student.courses = Student (student-name) Student.course-history
(course-number, course-title); SORT BY student-name
```

If the Student.course-history table contains

STUDENT NUMBER	COURSE NUMBER	SEMESTER	COURSE[2] TITLE	COURSE GRADE	COURSE HOURS
0001	22	FAL 8	ENGL I	PASS	3
0001	33	FAL 8	LITR I	PASS	4
0169	13	FAL 8	MATH I	AUDIT	NULL
0169	13	SPR 9	MATH I	FAIL	0
0169	13	SUM 9	MATH I	PASS !	3
1001	22	FAL 8	ENGL I	PASS	3

[2]Included for illustration; FNF table would not contain course-title.

then the new temporary table of Student.courses would contain, before removing duplicate rows (and sorting):

STUDENT NUMBER	COURSE NUMBER	COURSE TITLE
JONES	22	ENGL I
JONES	33	LITR I
VESELY	13	MATH I
VESELY	13	MATH I
VESELY	13	MATH I
SMITH	22	ENGL I

An analysis of the table above indicates that *each* entry for Vesely is identical; therefore, only one entry will remain in the final table. Note that if any other column (semester, course-grade, couse-hours) had been included in the query, then all *three* Vesely rows would have been included in the final version of Student.courses.

Multiple Relational Operations

Each new temporary table can be used in further operations to satisfy a specific inquiry. In the discussion of 3NF in Chapter 8 the table of

```
Course-tally.semester (course-number, semester-number)
tally-of-students, number-of-major-students,
number-of-minor-students, number-of-free-attendees)
```

was completely eliminated because it was stated that "major," "minor," and "free" could be derived from

1. Student.course-history which contains all courses taken
2. Student.major.minor which contains each student's majors and minors
3. Major.minor.course-requirements which contains the courses required for each major and minor

If that assertion were correct, there should be some combination of relational operands that would return the tally of "major," "minor," and "free" for each course taken per semester. A possible solution (there is more than one solution):

1. To retrieve all courses taken for a specific semester:

```
Courses-taken-in-a-specific.semester = | | Student.course-history
(student-number, course-number) Q semester = XXXX
```

a. XXXX = specific semester.

b. Semester can be used as qualifier because it is a column in the Student.course-history-table even though semester is not included in the new table.

c. Student-number must be included:

  (1) For future operations.

  (2) To prevent the relational operation from eliminating duplicate rows (if 40 students took course-number 13 and that was the only column in the new table, there would only be *one* entry).

d. New table = student-number, course-number.

2. To retrieve all majors for all students

```
Student.major = | | student.major-minor Q
major-minor-type="major"
```

a. New table = student-number, major-minor-name, major-minor-type

b. Notes 1b and 1c apply to major-minor-type and student-number.

3. To ''insert'' the specific majors that each student in the Courses-taken-in-a-specific.semester table:

```
Potential-major.courses-taken-in-a-specific.semester =
Courses-taken-in-a-specific.semester * Student.major
```

a. This join operator is joining the two new temporary tables created in steps 1 and 2.

b. new table = student-number, course-number, major-minor-name, major-minor-type.

4. To retrieve actual courses taken for a specific major:

```
Actual-major.courses-taken-in-a-specific.semester = Potential-
major.courses-taken-in-a-specific.semester * Major-minor.course-
requirements ()
```

a. This is a multiple-column join; the two tables are joined ''over'' major-minor-name *and* major-minor-type *and* course-number. The new table contains *only* those courses that are actually required for a specific major. It is possible that a specific course can be required for both majors of a specific student. Operation 5 eliminates the duplication.

b. New table = same as 3b table except that only courses required for majors remain.

5. To eliminate "duplicates" and tally the actual number of courses taken for a major prerequisite in a specific semester:

```
Unduplicated-major.courses-taken-in-a-specific.semester =
| | Actual-major.courses-taken-in-a-specific.semester (student-
number,course-number); COUNT
```

    a. If a specific course is a prerequisite for both majors of a specific student, then the first version of the new table would contain a duplicate entry:

```
    0169   (student-number)    0013   (course-number)
    0169                       0013
```

which would be eliminated from the final table because both rows are identical. The final table then contains the actual courses taken to fulfill the prerequisites.

    b. COUNT is an additional operand that returns the number of entries (rows) in the new table.

    c. new table = student-number, course-number.

6. To eliminate "major" courses from all courses taken in a specific semester:

```
Nonmajor.courses-taken-in-a-specific.semester = Courses-taken-

in-a-specific.semester * Unduplicated-major.courses-taken-in-a-
specific-semester; COUNT
```

    a. new table = same as 1d table except that only nonmajor courses remain.

7. Redo steps 2 to 5 for minors by substituting "minor" where applicable.

8. The final unjoin operation provides the tally of "free" students:

```
Free-courses-taken-in-a-specific.semester = Courses-taken-in-a-

specific semester * Unduplicated-minor.courses-taken-in-a-
specific-semester; COUNT
```

    a. new table = same as 1d table except that only "free" courses remain.

I believe that it would be onerous to ask a user to try to perform the relational operations above; I also believe that it is onerous to ask analysts to perform this procedure very often. There must be a simpler way and there is!

REVISITING THE GRAPHIC MODEL

The graphic models described in Chapter 12 provide the necessary information to "navigate" the logical database to determine if a query can be answered. The basic technique is to determine what attributes are required to answer the query and what tables those attributes are in. If there is a common ''column'' (usually a primary, secondary, or foreign key) or a common column can be created, there is some set of relational algebra that *absolutely positively* can provide the answer.

''USABILITY'' OPERATORS

The relational operators described previously in this chapter form the basic set. Many query languages that use relational algebra (such as IBM's SOL) have added ''usability'' operators to make the query language more user ''lazy.'' Some of these operators are:

SORT:	Sort the new table by the specified column(s); a *descending* option is usually included.
COUNT:	The number of rows (entries) in the new table.
SUM:	Total the numeric values in a specific column of the new table.
AVERAGE:	SUM divided by COUNT.
MIN:	Return the minimum value in a specific column in the new table.
MAX:	Return the maximum value in a specific column in the new table.

Some query languages (such as Computer Corporation of America Model 204 QLI) provide for ''intermediate'' calculation, looping, if statements, etc. Model 204 QLI can almost be considered a stand-alone programming language.

SEMANTIC DISINTEGRITY

No discussion of relational algebra would be complete without a discussion of semantic disintegrity. *Semantic disintegrity* occurs when a legal set of relational algebra produces a new table that has ''garbage'' values (analogous to comparing apples to oranges). This can happen only if the database contains homonyms (same attribute name for two or more *different* attributes). For instance, if ''type'' was the full attribute name for major-minor-*type* and special-equipment-*type,* two tables containing ''type'' as the column name could be joined. The resulting new table would contain nonsense data. The moral is to eliminate homonyms.

RELATIONAL CALCULUS

Relational calculus is the term used to describe ''expert'' query languages that can interpret English statements and produce the relational algebra operators necessary to answer the query. A relational calculus language would take the query:

```
Give me a tally of all major, minor and free course for semester XXXX
```

and produce a set of relational algebra operations similiar to those described in this chapter to answer that query.

AUTOMATED TOOLS

I do not know any software tools that can automatically navigate the logical database. All the software tools described so far provide various cross-reference reports that can assist in the navigation.

17

Statistical Information

DEFINITION

The logical database developed so far is often called a *static database*. It shows entity types, the tables developed by normalization, and secondary and foreign key pathways—i.e., static information. The static logical database is valuable input to physical database designers, but they need "dynamic" information before an effective physical database design can be produced. This dynamic information is the statistical data. The resultant logical database is usually called a *dynamic database*.

TABLE INFORMATION

The basic "sizing" information is the quantity of occurrences in each table of the logical database.

Volume and Growth

Simply stated, volume and growth represents how many of each table exist with a projected growth rate over an established time frame. This statistic allows the physical database designer to allocate sufficient physical space to the database to maximize storage efficiency and minimize the need to reorganize the physical database because it exceeded the physical space.

Volatility

Volatility is the percentage of each table that changes over an established time frame. The "change" includes inserts, updates, and deletes. This statistic assists in the physical placement of the database on the storage devices to maximize multiple input/output operations and thereby minimize response time.

Asymmetrical Distribution   There is a special form of volatility that requires careful physical storage for optimum results. This form is often called asymmetrical distribution, which means that a small portion of a table receives a large portion of the changes (analogous to the 80/20 rules, except in this case 20% of the table has 80% of the changes). A real world example is an airline reservation system where today's flights receive the bulk of the accesses, tomorrow's flights receive the next most accesses, the day after tomorrow's flights receive the next most accesses, and the flights one year from today receive hardly any accesses. This statistic is vital for correct physical database design.

Planned Inquiries

The static logical database contains the user-requested secondary keys. The physical database designer needs to know the volume and growth of these inquiries.

Ad Hoc Inquiries

If the user is provided a query language for access to the physical database, a "guesstimate" as to the volume and growth is necessary. I can guarantee a huge increase in ad hoc inquiries if the query language is user lazy.

TRANSACTION PATH

A transaction path is the transversal of the logical database required to satisfy the data requirements of a particular transaction. The best way to define the data requirements of a transaction is the logical record (see Chapter 15). The transaction path information is vital if the physical database designer is to have any chance of providing a responsive physical database to the user. This information permits the physical database designer to intelligently decide when and where to "optimize" the physical database by doing such things as:

> Placing calculable data into the physical database
> Replicating data
> Adding pointers and/or chains
> Adding indices
> Combining tables for better access
> Etc.

Without this information the physical database designer is guessing; and Mr. Murphy guarantees that they are more often wrong than right.

Priority

Priority is the user need for this transaction. Many texts recommend that the user (or analysts!) rate transactions as high, medium, or low priority. This helps, but how does the physical database designer know which "high" transaction is the most important? (They don't.) I prefer forcing the user (this is often a painful exercise for both the user and the analyst) to rate all transactions in numeric sequence with *no* duplicates (i.e., the most important is 1, the second is 2, etc.). This commits the user and provides the physical database designer with the necessary priority statistics.

Note: I actually prefer—if the user is willing—to permit the user to rate the transactions on a scale (such as 1:1000). This provides both absolute *and* relative transaction priority. Figure 17.1 is a sample table for deriving the data.

USER TRANSACTION PRIORITY

Rel. Pri.	Transaction Name	O/B	Transaction Path										Response Time
			1	2	3	4	5	6	7	8	9	10	

Notes:
Rel. Pri. = Relative Priority.   No number can be *duplicated*.
O/B = Online or batch
Transaction Path = Table-number of all tables in logical
   database that must be accessed to satisfy request.

Figure 17.1 Transaction Priority Table

User Response Time Requirements

How fast does the user want it, or how long is the batch-processing window? Some people recommend or try to use response time as a priority measurement. This procedure has the same difficulty as high, medium, and low discussed above and should not be used. In fact, it is probably worse because users tend to place minimal response time on *all* transactions (one of my client companies has users that always request 3-second response time on all transactions). The combination of priority and response time provides the physical database designer with the hard facts required to design the best user-responsive physical database. It also provides the baseline for measuring predicted performance versus requested performance.

Volume and Growth

Volume and growth are again essential. My only caution is that the quantity and growth of inquiries is often badly underestimated.

AUGMENTING GRAPHIC MODEL

I prefer to augment printed copies of the logical database with the relevant statistics. I would place the table information on the complete logical database; I would place each transaction information on a *separate* portion of the logical database that shows the required tables.

AUTOMATED TOOLS

Most of the automated tools discussed permit statistical information to be incorporated.

18

The Logical Database

DEFINITION

The logical database—as advocated by this book—is a DBTG (Bachman) diagram that graphically portrays tables (flat files) that have been normalized through "final" normal form (FNF). Each table "rectangle" contains:

1. The table name
2. The primary key that identifies a single occurrence of the table
3. Any foreign keys (a logical pathway to other entity type sets and/or a recursive "pointer" to the same table)
4. Any secondary keys (user request to access that table by an attribute within that table)

Each DBTG diagram shows a "set" of tables that were created during the normalization process. Each set has a "root" table (the table that contains all 1:1 attributes about the entity type described by the table) and all the member tables belonging to that owner.

The solid lines with a single arrowhead represent the 1:M relationship between the owner and its members. The dotted lines represent the 1:M or M:1 relationships created by foreign keys.

A logical database without statistical information is "static"; a logical database with statistical information is "dynamic" (see Chapter 17). The dynamic logical database is the best input document for the physical database designer to create a user-responsive physical database.

STABLE

The logical database is a stable view of the data and the data relationship that it portrays. Within an application logical database it is improbable that new entity types would be added. Even if new entity types are added, it is generally simple to incorporate them into the logical database and show the relationship between the existing entity type sets by the foreign keys existing in the new entity type set.

A method of building an enterprise (corporate, organizational) logical data model is to combine (synthesize) separate logical databases into a single logical database. I advocate this approach for enterprise modeling because it is simple and it *works!*

The major permutation in most data models is the attribute (data element) volatility: (1) new attributes, (2) deleted attributes, (3) changed attributes (usually—but not limited to—physical storage size). Attribute volatility usually has minimal effect on a normalized logical data model.

New Attributes

The first step of processing a new attribute is to determine which entity type it describes. If it is a new 1:1 attribute, add it to the *Codd* relational database entity type root table. Unless the new attribute is a new user secondary key or a new foreign key, do nothing to the DBTG model.

If the attribute is 1:*M,* determine if any of the member tables contain a set of primary keys on which the new attribute would be fully functionally dependent (see 2NF in Chapter 13). If so, add it to that table in the Codd relational database. Again, unless the new attribute is a new user secondary key, or a new foreign key, do nothing to the DBTG model.

If the attribute cannot be placed into an existing member table, create a new table in *both* the Codd relational and DBTG model. Check for secondary and foreign key associations.

Deleted Attributes

Simply remove the deleted attribute from both the Codd relational and the DBTG model. If the deleted attribute is a secondary key, remove from the DBTG diagram and inform the physical database designer—if the logical database has been implemented—that the secondary key is no longer required by the user. (It was the user who requested that the attribute be deleted—wasn't it?) If the deleted attribute is a foreign key, remove it from the table "rectangle" and remove the dotted line representing the foreign key relationship. Again, inform the physical database designer of the deletion.

It is theoretically not possible to delete an attribute that is a primary key attribute because that means that the normalization process was wrong. The real world—as stated before—is usually not kind to the analyst and this situation does occur. It does mean that the normalized database is wrong! Fortunately, only the entity type set containing the deleted primary key usually needs to be renormalized.

Changed Attributes

Changes to attributes do *not* affect either the Codd or the DBTG model. Obviously, the physical database schema requires modification and all the procedural language programs that referenced the changed attribute require modification and/or recompilation.

ADVANTAGES

The stable logical database provides significant advantages: Analysts can be provided with a data "map" before they start a new project. This map provides a complete understanding of the entity types, their attributes, and their relationships with other entity types of existing models. It is often possible for the analyst to make minor modifications to the Codd relational and DBTG models to reflect the *entire* data required by the new user application. Then the analyst can spend time on the difficult portion of the task—what to do with the data. Users can be provided with a data "map" that actually allows the users to determine how they would probe the logical database to answer a particular ad hoc inquiry. This can be invaluable in 4GL environment and for developing user views. Each senior manager can be given visual assurance that a valuable resource—data—is being managed correctly.

PORTABLE

The logical database is independent of both specific hardware and specific physical DBMS. As such it can be used to develop physical databases for any computer for any DBMS (Chapter 21 provides conversion rules for some of the more popular DBMSs). This is important because:

1. It provides precise input to the physical database designer, thereby increasing the productivity of a scarce data processing resource.
2. Organizations without a DBMS can determine the kind of physical DBMS that would best fit their requirements before committing substantial funds (usually in excess of $1 million when all costs, such as education, conversion, salaries of database personnel, etc., are considered).
3. Organizations with "old" DBMSs and a logical database can again choose the new DBMS that fits their new requirements and can *also* plan their conversion from old to new using the logical database as the primary mechanism.

DUAL DBMS STRATEGY

A new trend with vendors that have both "old" DBMSs and new DBMSs (usually relational or "quasi-relational") is a dual DBMS approach. The old DBMS should be used for production and the new DBMS should be used for user inquiries. IBM is advocating this approach with IMS/VS for production and DB2 for user inquiries.

This strategy has the advantage of preserving the ''old and true'' DBMS while providing the user with the opportunity to use 4GL-type languages to query the new DBMS. The real question is how to perform the magical feat of having two concurrent DBMSs that have different access methods access to the same data. I believe the only practical way is to use the logical database as *the* input to both [or tri or quad (!)] concurrent physical DBMSs.

USER VIEWS

The graphic logical database provides a visual approach to developing user views. The ''picture is worth a thousand words'' simplifies the deductive process of isolating user views.

AUTOMATED TOOLS

The various automated tools that produce logical databases in this book usually provide the modification of and the redrawing of the graphical logical database.

SUMMARY

The graphic logical database provides a stable view of the data and the data relationships that increases the productivity of analysts and physical database designers by providing precise metadata (data about data).

19

The Role of the Data Dictionary in Logical Database Design

DEFINITION

A catalog of all data types giving their names and structures (Martin). A catalog of all data elements in a database, giving their definition, format, source, and usage; frequently computer based (Teorey and Fry). A data store that describes the nature of each piece of data used in a system; often including process descriptions, glossary entries, and other items (Gane/Sarson). In other words: metadata or data about data.

TYPES

Manual

The simplest data dictionary, but the least effective in the real world, is the manual data dictionary. This dictionary is often kept (but not maintained) on 8 × 5 index cards. It is ineffective because:

Manual ''anything'' in most DP shops is not maintained.

It is easy to lose vital metadata.

All benefits, such as cross-reference reports, must be performed manually.

Etc.

Automated

The ineffectiveness of manual data dictionaries and the failure of early attempts to use various computer software "editors" led to the development of automated software packages known as data dictionaries.

Standalone   A stand-alone data dictionary is a separate software package that maintains its own meta-database. The most popular stand-alone data dictionary is DataManager (Figure 19.1 is a list of data dictionaries).

Integrated   Most DBMS vendors decided that a data dictionary was a worthwhile option. Accordingly, these DBMS vendors developed a data dictionary that uses the host DBMS to maintain its meta-databases. There are three types.

A GAGGLE of DATA DICTIONARIES

DICTIONARY NAME	VENDOR	HOST	NAME	C	P	B	O	E	SPECIAL FEATURES
DATA CATALOGUE 2	TSI	F1	67	X	X	X		X	Test Data Generation
DATACOM/DD	ADR	F2	15	X	X	X		X	Unlimited entity type relationships
DATA DICTIONARY	SOFTWARE A.G.	ADABAS	32	X			X		
DATA DICTIONARY	CINCOM	TOTAL	8						
DATA MANAGER	MSP	F3	32	X	X	X	X	X	User exit facility
DB/DC	IBM	IMS	31	X	X	X		X	
IDD	Cullinet	IDMS	32	X	X	X	X	X	Very active
S2000 IDD	SAS	S2K	250	X			X		
UCC/10	University Computing	IMS	8	X	X	X	X		User exit facility

NOTES:

HOST = The DBMS that provides the access mechanisms for the data dictionary; DATA CATALOGUE 2 and DATAMANAGER do NOT require a DBMS for access (they are standalone data dictionaries).

NAME = The maximum size in characters for data names

C = Cobol interface

P = PL/1 interface

B = BAL (assembly language) interface

O = other language interfaces

E = Extensibility feature; permits an organization to define its own unique subjects, attributes of those subjects, and the relationships between those subjects.

F1 DATA CATALOGUE 2 is a standalone data dictionary that interfaces to IMS, DL/1, TOTAL, ADABAS, IDMS, DMS 1100, IDS II, S2K, MARK IV, and probably lots of others.

F2 DATACOM/DB and IMS

F3 DATAMANAGER is a standalone data dictionary that interfaces to ADABAS, IDMS, IMS, DL/1, MARK IV, S2K, TOTAL and probably lots of others.

Figure 19.1   A Gaggle of Data Dictionaries

1. *Passive:* A passive data dictionary contains a snapshot of data at some specific time frame but exercises no control over the host DBMS. Probably the best known passive data dictionary is IBM's DB/DC.

2. *Subsumed:* A subsumed data dictionary is automatically created by the host DBMS and can be either passive or active.

3. *Active:* An active data dictionary uses the host DBMS to maintain its meta-database *but* also controls the data operations of its host DBMS. For instance, Cobol programs must be precompiled through Cullinet's data dictionary (IDD) to provide the appropriate entries in the Cobol Data Division. Programs not precompiled through IDD do not execute against IDMS.

Most DBMS vendors are "activating" their data dictionaries as they "relationalize" their DBMS. A relational DBMS requires an active data dictionary to resolve the access "paths" at the execution of a database request (planned or ad hoc).

Uses

Manual or automated data dictionaries can provide most of the uses listed below. The difference is that manual requires data professionals to waste their valuable time performing clerical tasks better performed by an automated data dictionary.

Communication   Data dictionaries can provide unlimited reports, such as:

1. Complete descriptions of all entries (all the metadata)

2. Summary reports that provide statistics such as the number of entity types, the average number of attributes per entity type, the number of foreign and secondary keys, etc.

3. Composite reports that combine the metadata about multiple entries

4. Cross-reference reports that provide "directory" metadata, i.e., where an attribute is referenced (program, file, database, etc.) or in reality, everything you wanted to know about your data but were afraid to (or did not know how to) ask

Development   Data dictionaries can increase the productivity in the development cycle. (This is contrary to the general opinion that any data dictionary is similar to the "Black Hole of Calcutta" or the blackhole of astronomy in that lots of "things" go in but nothing ever comes out.) It can provide the unlimited reports mentioned previously and also:

Consistency checking: verifying that data naming standards are being adhered to; that undesirable homonyms, aliases, and synonyms are not creeping into the database, etc.

Entity type analysis: assisting the analyst in determining the entity types required for the user application

Normalization: assisting the analyst in performing normalization

Data division generation: automatically generating the *correct* data element names in Cobol Data Divisions

Other   The following data dictionary uses are not strictly for development of the logical database but display the versatility of a well-constructed data dictionary:

On-line editing: Editing rules for attributes can be placed in the data dictionary and verified at entry time by the data dictionary. This eliminates the necessity of placing editing logic in application programs and provides a *single* place to read, change, or delete editing rules.

Relational inquiries: Relational DBMSs require an active data dictionary to resolve database inquiries at execution time.

Impact analysis: Where zipcode is used in all programs so that it can be changed to Zip + Four.

Data name rationalization: A ''superset'' of impact analysis in which homonyms, aliases, and synonyms are identified and changed to the ''right'' names.

Not where used analysis: The ''reverse'' of impact analysis in which data that is *not* being used *anywhere* is uncovered. The question is why bother to input, maintain, and worry about data that nobody is using.

Population

Population is the buzzword for entry of metadata into the data dictionary. This is usually the responsibility of analysts working on new projects and usually requires large amounts of manual clerical entry. This combined with the fact that the data dictionary is usually under the jealous control of a database person who considers it as a private domain accessible only to ''noble'' DP people causes the ''blackhole'' syndrome. The analyst spends *user* project time in populating the dictionary without—in many cases—the ability to obtain any of the benefits listed previously in this chapter.

There are two automatic methods to populate a data dictionary:

1. With garbage
2. With correct metadata

All the existing data dictionaries have a utility that allows the extraction of metadata from existing programs and/or files and/or databases. This is effectively populating the data dictionary with 20 (!) bad names for every good name.[1] Not only is the data dictionary

---

[1]The author has conducted several studies at Fortune 500 companies of data names in old programs and discovered that there are approximately 20 ''bad'' names for each good name. I would appreciate any thoughts on why the number of bad names is 20.

going to be enormous but it is also going to be unusable and a drain on DP resources. The answer is either automatic collection or software-assisted "purification."

Automatic Collection

Many of the various software tools described in this book permit metadata to be entered once, verified, and prepared for normalization (single data entry is what DP preaches to users). Many of these tools can also transfer metadata to "mainframe" data dictionaries, thereby permitting population with correct metadata.

Software-Assisted Purification

Some of the software tools permit extraction and purification of metadata from existing programs/files/databases. Purification means that homonyms, aliases, and synonyms are identified and processed according to an organization standard. These tools also generally allow transfer to mainframe data dictionaries.

The basic theme is that it is about time for DP to use the computer to assist DP (the analogy is the cobbler who does not have sufficient time to produce shoes for his/her children). The automated tools section in this chapter contains greater detail.

DATA ELEMENT (ATTRIBUTE) NAMING STANDARDS

One of the largest DP quagmires is data element naming standards. There are absolutely no generally accepted standards and not even IBM could make its OF language an acceptable standard. This section explores the quagmire with recommendations by the author (only fools rush in where angels fear to tread).

OF Language (Global Naming)

The IBM OF language is a technique for creating unique readable object names. The object name is formed with a single class word followed by a prime word followed by one or more modifiers word with each word separated by a predefined connector. The syntax is

```
CLASSWORD/CONNECTOR/PRIME-WORD/CONNECTOR/FIRST-MODIFIER-WORD/
CONNECTOR/SECOND-MODIFIER-WORD/CONNECTOR/.../LAST-MODIFIER-WORD
```

The classword is a single alphabetic character with a specific meaning. The most commonly used letters and meanings are:

A	amount (currency)	C	code
D	date	F	flag
G	group	I	indicator
K	constant	M	name (identifier)
N	number (identifier)	P	percent
Q	quantity (count)	T	text
U	unidentified (!)	X	control

The connector is a single special symbol. The most commonly used symbols and meanings are:

	of			of
*	which is/are	.	/	which is/are
|	or : or		$	or
&	and		#	and
/	by, per, within		@	by, per, within
-	compound-word		_	initiator

A cursory review of the table above indicates that there is significant disagreement over the special symbols and their meaning. Most of these differences arise from available print "trains" (fonts) and/or the dominant programming language within an organization. The leftmost column is the set specified in Appendix A of Guide Publication GPP-41, "DB/DC Data Dictionary Usage Manual" (Guide is an IBM user group—see Appendix D for address).

The prime-word and the modifier-words are usually taken from a list of predefined key words. The modifier-words are inserted in most general to most specific sequence. The key words are usually nouns and are usually limited to four, five, or six characters. At Logic University, the unabbreviated key word list could contain:

student	instructor	alumni
course	major	minor
equipment	classroom	semester
history	dayofweek	degree (academic)

There is of course no generally accepted standard for forming abbreviations. A relatively easy technique is to force all names to the same length, eliminating all vowels unless the vowel is the first letter of the word. If the name is still too long, eliminate consonants, beginning with the last consonant working forward to the beginning of the word. If the name is too short, add vowels from the beginning of the name or zeros (0) up to the fixed length. Reserve the last character (byte) of the name for a tie-breaker digit. The key word list for Logic University with the last character reserved for the tie-breaker digit:

std0	stdn0	stdnt0
ins0	inst0	instr0
alm0	almn0	alumn0
crs0	cors0	cours0
mjr0	majr0	major0
mnr0	minr0	minor0
eqp0	eqpm0	equmn0
cls0	clss0	class0
sms0	smst0	smstr0
hst0	hstr0	histr0	(y is treated as a vowel)
dfw0	dfwk0	dafwk0
dgr0	degr0	degre0

The rules may be easy, but is the name created understandable? Following is the course table from final normal form (Figure 10.1) with the attribute names created using the classword table, the "Guide" connectors, and a four-character key word list:

N	crs0	T crs0*tt10	M	crs0 crr0-sch0*name0
Q	crs0*hrs0&crd0&mnm0		Q	crs0*hrs0&crd0&mxm0
Q	crs0*cls0&mnm0		Q	crs0*cls0&mxm0
Q	crs0*hrs0&drt0			

These OF names to me are gibberish! They may be useful to data administration personnel, but what use are they to users, analysts, programmers, etc.? If these are the only names provided, the other users of the data dictionary have a right to believe that they have stumbled into the "Black Hole of Calcutta" or possibly the Twilight Zone. Granted that longer key words would help (using six letters without tie-breaker digit):

N	course	T course*title	M	course crrclm-school*name
Q	course*hours&credit&minimm		Q	course*hours&credit&maximm
Q	course*classz&minimm		Q	course*classz&maximm
Q	course*hours&duratn			

Certainly better, but to me still confusing (*Note:* I apologize if I have incorrectly constructed any of the names and/or used the wrong connectors. I do not believe the OF language is a solution.)

Prime Word and Class Word

A variation of the OF language suggested by Duncan Connall in the *Data Base Newsletter* (see Appendix D for address) is to place the prime word first followed by class word modifiers from general to specific. Using the identified entity types as prime words and the OF class words (not the single alphabetic character) and the "Guide" connector symbols yields the following for the course table:

```
course-number                        course-title
course*name school&curriculum        course-hours*credit&minimum
course-hours*credit&maximum          course-classize*minimum
course-classize*maximum              course-hours*duration
```

Definitely more understandable! Using the period(.) as the "of" symbol to confirm that a set of words is a single name helps:

```
course*name.school&curriculum
```

instead of

```
course*name school&curriculum
```

Modified English Genetive Structure

The syntax of this structure is

```
ENTITY-TYPE/ADJECTIVE-MODIFYING-TYPE/
ADJECTIVE-MODIFYING-ATTRIBUTE/ATTRIBUTE-NAME/ATTRIBUTE-TYPE.
```

Example for Logic University:

ENTITY TYPE	student
ADJECTIVE MODIFYING ENTITY TYPE	undergraduate
ADJECTIVE MODIFYING ATTRIBUTE	current
ATTRIBUTE NAME	home address
ATTRIBUTE TYPE[2]	T (text)

The full attribute name of the above is

```
student-undergraduate-current-home-address-T
```

A suggested list of attribute-type suffixes for this syntax is:

A	amount (currency)	C	code
D	date	I	identifier (numeric or alpha)
P	percent	Q	quantity (count)

This list is shorter than the OF classword list, but the idea is the same. The course table is in this syntax:

```
course..number-I                    course..title.
course.curriculum-schoolname-I
course.credit&minimum-hours-Q       course.credit&maximum-hours-Q
course.minimum-classize-Q           course.maximum-classize-Q
course.duration-hours-Q
```

```
= no entry;   course..number-I means that there is no adjective
              modifying course AND no adjective modifying number.
& = and       credit&minimum means that both adjectives are
              applied to hours.
```

And Into the Valley of Death Rode . . .

My personal syntax is:

1. For an attribute of a single entity type:

[2]Attribute type is similar to OF classword.

```
ENTITY-TYPE/ATTRIBUTE-NAME/ATTRIBUTE-MODIFIER-1/ATTRIBUTE-
MODIFIER-2.../ATTRIBUTE-MODIFIER-LAST
```

where a hyphen (-) is used to separate the components.

2. For an attribute which is an intersection (junction of two or more entity types)

```
ENTITY-TYPE-1/ENTITY-TYPE-2/.../ENTITY-TYPE-LAST/ATTRIBUTE-NAME/
```

where:
> A period (.) separates entity types.
> A colon (:) separates the subtypes of a supertype entity type.
> Braces ({}) defines a specific *role* that the attribute is playing
> in the definition.
> A slash (/) identifies an ''or'' attribute modifier.
> A hyphen (-) separates the attribute name from the entity type and
> attribute modifiers from the attribute name.
> And compound names such as day of week are space compressed
> to dayofweek.

Entity type is a ''thing'' requiring storage of independent data (see Chapter 6). The attribute name should be a generic noun: the attribute modifiers should be specified from general to specific.

Chapter 10 describes the process of generalization which identifies supertype entity type and the subtypes (entity occurrences) associated with the supertype. The original entity type analysis at Logic University identified

```
STUDENT          ALUMNI          INSTRUCTOR
```

as separate entity types (see Chapters 6 and 7).

Chapter 10 correctly identified student, alumni, and instructor as subtypes of a more generic supertype of person-involved-with-courses. The recommendation in Chapter 10 was to show each subtype where possible separated by colons (:). Therefore, anything in the supertype of students and instructors and alumni should have a ''prefix'' of

```
student:instructor:alumni
```

Occasionally, an attribute modifier is not an ''adjective'' such as

```
current          taken          tally
```

but a description of the role that the attribute is playing at the instant of time of the table definition. The student:instructor:alumni table could contain two instances of

```
student:instructor:alumni-number
```

The first occurrence is the identifier number (primary key) of a specific student:instructor:alumni; the second occurrence is the identifier number (foreign key) of a specific instructor who is playing the *role* of advisor to that specific student. The addition of the role braces {} clarifies the situation.

```
student: instructor: alumni-number              primary key
student: instructor: alumni-number{advisor} role (foreign key)
```

Another occurrence is the course-prerequisite table. How would you interpret the following?

```
course-prerequisite(course-number, course-number)
```

Why is course-number repeated? Why are both keys? etc.? I believe the confusion can be eliminated by adding the role

```
course-prerequisite(course-number, course-number; (prerequisite}
```

Because multiple subtypes and/or roles can occur, it is sometimes necessary to include a multiple (or) attribute modifier. Student and alumni roles take a course; instructor teaches a course. The attribute modifier is taken/taught. The now familiar course table looks like this:

```
course-number                    course-title
course. schoolname-curriculum    course-hours-credit-minimum
course-hours-credit-maximum      course-classize-minimum
course-classize-maximum          course-hours-duration
```

This is very similar to the prime word and class word syntax. The difference becomes more apparent when trying to name subtypes: what one prime word describes student:instructor:alumni, or what class word describes a role, or what combination of prime word and class words describes an intersection attribute such as that portrayed in the student:instructor.course-history table?

```
student: instructor: alumni-number
student: instructor: alumni. course-number-taken/taught
student: instructor: alumni. course-hours-credit-taken
student: instructor: alumni. course-hours-credit-earned
student: instructor: alumni. course-grade-earned
```

I believe that my data naming standard is understandable because:

No abbreviations are used.

The sequential syntax approximates normal English syntax.

The special symbols (-.:/{}) describe *classes* rather than adjectival phrases (of, which is/are, or, and, etc.).

The major complaints are:

> The name is too long (most data dictionaries have a restriction of 32 characters or *less*; the Cobol restriction is 30 characters).
>
> The special symbols are not implementable in programming languages such as Cobol.
>
> There are no classwords.

I do not believe in abbreviations because there is no foolproof method of deriving standard abbreviations and/or which words to abbreviate. As a good DP person, I do grudgingly accept mnemonics. I ''mnemonisize'' the ''prefix''—the entity types or the subtypes. This is a short list of words and should be printed on all data dictionary reports.[3] At Logic University:

C	Course
H	School-name
M	Major:minor
R	Classroom
S	Student:instructor:alumni
T	Semester

I prefer one-character mnemonics, but have no objection to more characters. My recommendation is that the mnemonic always be the same physical size. The mnemonisizing should reduce the name to acceptable lengths for most data dictionaries and programming languages. If the name is still too long, you must abbreviate (good luck!).

The special symbol problem is a problem. Cobol restricts names to

A through Z   0 through 9   - (hyphen)

There is a solution since all data names are constructed from alpha characters—substitute numbers for the special symbols:

0 for .   1 for :   2 for /
6 for {   9 for }

The Cobol name for

```
student:instructor:alumni.course-number-taken/taught
```

is

```
s0c-number-taken2taught
```

---

[3]A better user-lazy alternative is to have an expansion routine that converts the mnemonic to its full name.

instead of

```
s.c-number-taken/taught
```

Mnemonics and number substitution solve the length and special symbol complaints.

What about the lack of class words? Is anybody besides data administration personnel interested in class words? I do not believe so. In any case, I would add the OF classword mnemonic as the final suffix and place it in the data dictionary as an approved data administration *alias*. If the class word is desirable, make it the final suffix of the primary name.

The next personal question is: Have I survived the valley . . . ?

AUTOMATED TOOLS

There are no tools that the author knows of—at this book's writing—that automatically construct standard data names. The various data dictionaries can enforce naming standards (usually via user exits). A few tools can expand ''short'' data names into the ''real'' data names.

20

Physical Database

DEFINITION

A database in the form in which it is stored on the storage media, including a pointer or other means of interconnecting it (Martin). A collection of interrelated data stored as one or more types of stored record (Teorey and Fry). The logical database converted to the physical model usually represented by a schema (Vesely). In other words: a map of the data as it is stored on the storage media.

PHYSICAL TYPES

The DBTG committee was probably the first group to classify DBMSs by their physical storage characteristics. There are generally four classifications: (1) tree (hierarchical), (2) plex (network), (3) inverted (list), and (4) relational.

Tree (hierarchical)

A tree structure is composed of data groups (usually called segments) in which there is an implicit hierarchical relationship between the parent segment and its children segments. Figure 20.1 is a graphic representation of a tree structure.

The characteristics of tree DBMSs are:

A Graphical Representation of a Tree DBMS (Hierarchical)

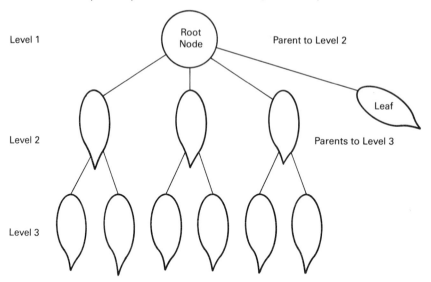

Figure 20.1 Graphic Representation of a Tree DBMS

1. The tree is composed of data groups. The data groups are called segments in IMS (IBM) and the highest level is the ''root'' segment. (Another indicator that DP people are a bit wacky since they place the root of the tree at the *TOP!*) Each segment (other than the root) is a child of the higher-level segment (lower-level number) and a parent of any lower-level segments (higher-level number) that it ''sires'' (owns). A widow segment (parent without any children segments) is a ''leaf''(?!).

2. The relationship between the parent segment and the children segments that it owns is implicit and descends from parent to child. A child segment is normally accessible *only* through its parent segment. (The IMS command is Get Next Within Parent.)

3. Each relationship between parent and child is $1:M$, i.e., there is one parent that can have many children (including *none*).

4. Each child can *only* have *one* parent. (IMS has attempted to alleviate this ''biological'' problem by permitting a physical child to have *one* physical parent *and one* ''logical'' parent. The use of the word ''logical'' is deceiving since the ''logical'' parent is a *physical* segment with physical interconnections.)

The major disadvantages in implementing a physical tree DBMS include:

1. Multiple ''parentage'' $(M:M)$ requires ''link'' segments, which can cause integrity problems and does cause complexity.

2. Insertion of new segments requires the application programmer to have the program "pointed" to the precise hierarchical block for correct execution (programmer navigation—see Chapter 24 for more details).

3. Deletion of a parent causes any "living" children and grandchildren and great-grandchildren and . . . to be "killed." Deleting the children may be what was intended, but most of the time the deletion of a parent with existing children is a mistake with the users suddenly discovering that important data is "lost."

4. Child segments are normally accessed through their parents. This means that a child on level 15 (maximum level for IMS) must initially be accessed through the root segment, then the level 2 segment, then the level 3 segment, then. . . .

Plex (network)

A plex structure is composed of data groups in which a member (child) can have more than one owner (parent). The association between an owner and its members is a "set." Figure 20.2 is a graphic representation of a plex structure.

A plex model becomes *com*plex if there are *any M:M* relationships, which is graphically shown by a double arrowhead line:

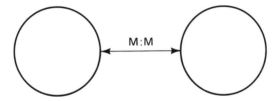

Most plex structures cannot directly model *M:M* relationships and use an intersection (junction, connector) to achieve the desired result:

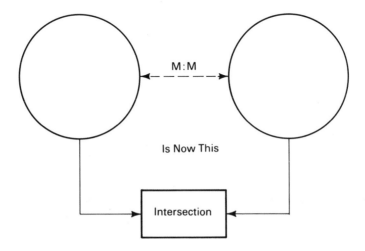

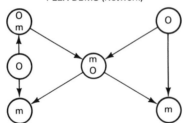

A Graphical Representation of a
PLEX DBMS (Network)

*SIM*PLEX Model because All Mapping is 1:M

DBTG (CODASYL) DBMS
O = Owner
m = Member

Figure 20.2   Graphic Representation of a
Plex DBMS

The characteristics of plex DBMSs are:

1. The plex is composed of data groups usually called "nodes." Related nodes are placed into "sets," with each set having *one* owner and one or more members.
2. The relationship between owner and members is explicit since members may have many owners and participate in many sets.
3. A node can be both an owner and a member. The original DBTG-proposed standard prevented a node from being an owner and a member in the *same* set. This restriction has been lifted.

The major disadvantages in implementing a physical plex DBMS include:

1. *M:M* relationships require intersection nodes, which can cause integrity problems and does cause complexity.
2. Application programmers must *always* be aware of the physical structure before they perform any DBMS operation. The buzzword for this knowledge is "currency" and means "programmer beware" lest you may do irreparable damage to your users' data! Programmer navigation (Chapter 24) is more severe in plex than in tree.
3. Insertion requires all DBMS keys to have nonnull values.
4. Deletion of owner can cause the "death" of all existing members.

Inverted (list)

An inverted structure is composed of base records (maybe—see next) and prespecified indices. A user—or an analyst representing the user—identifies the data elements within the original data group that are to be "inverted" (converted into indices). The remaining data elements are the base record; if no data elements remain (i.e., all data elements were inverted), the resultant structure is ''fully'' inverted. Figure 20.3 is a graphic representation of an inverted structure.

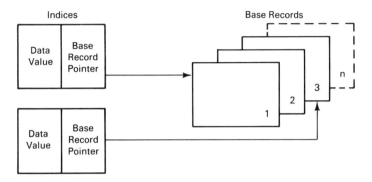

Figure 20.3   Graphic Representation of an Inverted DBMS

The characteristics of inverted DBMSs are:

1. The inverted is composed of multiple indices that contain the current data values for selected data elements and a ''pointer'' to all base records that contain a specific data value.
2. The indices are normally maintained in separate external tables (not as an internal part of the base record), thereby permitting fast retrieval.

The major disadvantages in implementing a physical inverted DBMS include:

1. Data element maintenance can be significant because all indices must be updated or at least verified.
2. Performance considerations may require complex structures to implement $M:M$ relationships.

The major advantages in implementing a physical inverted DBMS include:

1. Physical design is simpler than tree or plex.
2. External indices provide for fast retrieval.
3. New user-required ad hoc inquiries can be satisfied by creating new indices. Most inverted DBMSs have a utility that can add (or delete) indices easily.

Relational

A relational ''structure'' is composed of normalized tables (flat files). Figure 20.4 is a graphic representation of a relational ''structure.'' Note that there are no connecting

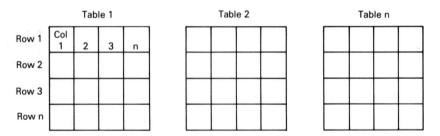

Figure 20.4 Graphic Representation of a Relational DBMS

"lines." "Joining" of tables is performed dynamically at execution using relational algebra.

The characteristics of relational DBMS are:

1. Prespecified indices are *not* required. An active data dictionary resolves user inquiries at execution time.
2. Temporary tables are created, which in turn can be used in further relational operations.
3. Attributes are stored *once;* attribute names are unique.

The major disadvantage in implementing a relational DBMS is that the dynamic execution of a request may cause unacceptable response times because of the many accesses required to mechanical memories.

This disadvantage is "solvable" by:

1. Prespecifying paths for known queries
2. Using compaction/expansion algorithms to allow the DBMS to retrieve more data per access

and, of course:

3. Using nonmechanical memories when they become commercially feasible for your organization.

The major advantages in implementing physical relational DBMS include:

| *User verification:* | Most users use tables; what better way to present a user with data to verify but in a table? |
| *Flexibility:* | Users can "cut and paste" tables to answer their questions; they can perform these operations without programmer assistance if a user-lazy language is available. |

Precision:	Pointers are eliminated; results are always accurate provided that unique attribute names are used to prevent "semantic disintegrity."
Implementation:	The normalized tables developed in the logical database can usually be directly implemented in the physical DBMS; the need for physical DBMS designers is reduced (not eliminated).
Data Independence:	Relational structures provide the opportunity to achieve data independence. (The application program does *not* have to change because the physical structure of the DBMS changes and/or the physical DBMS does not have to change because the application program was revised; this will significantly reduce future maintenance costs.)

A future advantage of the relational structure is the ability to utilize associative memories when they become commercially feasible. An associative memory is a storage device that is addressed by the data value or content of the data elements stored rather than by the physical address of a "packet" of data. Associative memories significantly extend the capabilities of users to ask (and receive answers) for complex ad hoc inquiries.

PHYSICAL STORAGE METHODS

The actual physical DBMSs are implemented by a variety of physical access methods. The most common are: (1) chain file linked, (2) hierarchical blocking, (3) page blocking, (4) inverted (list), and (5) relational.

Chain File Linked

A chain-file linked DBMS uses a link or pointer file to implement the association between entity types. These DBMSs originated with BOM (bill of material—manufacturing) explosions. Each pointer file contains how many parts comprise a product and two chain file links. One chain is the "explosion" chain, which permits a product to be decomposed into its component parts; the other chain is the "cross-reference" chain, which specifies all the products in which a part is used. Figure 20.5 is a graphic representation of a chain-file-linked physical storage method.

Hierarchical Blocking

The original and simplest form of hierarchical blocking (storage) was that each segment in the hierarchical sequence was stored in a *contiguous physical* sequence. The *actual* physical position determines the hierarchical sequence and was the *implicit* path. Most tree

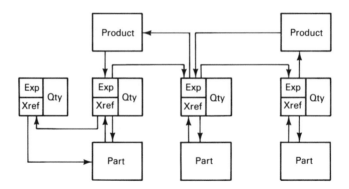

Figure 20.5   Graphic Representation of a Chain-File-Linked Storage

DBMSs have modified the original hierarchical blocking sequence to provide more flexibility—however, the original concept is still ever-present. Figure 20.6 is a graphic representation of a hierarchical-blocking physical storage method.

Page Blocking

A common concept permeating all DBMSs is to return the maximum data to the DBMS *buffer* so that the DBMS can minimize *disk* accesses in retrieving *subsequent related* DBMS accesses. The DBTG recommendation (implemented in IDMS and IDS/II) is to retrieve a "page" of data. This page of data can contain a mixture of owner/member records whose composition is basically under the control of the physical database designer. IDMS and IDS/II retrieve the full page containing the owner "node" when a "calc" command is issued. This permits either DBMS to perform in-memory searches for members that were placed on the same page rather than the time-consuming accessing of

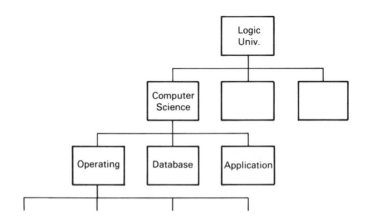

Figure 20.6   Graphic Representation of Hierarchical-Blocking Method

Data Page

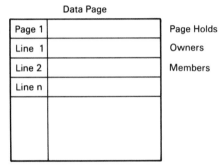

Page 1		Page Holds
Line 1		Owners
Line 2		Members
Line n		

Database Key (DBKEY) = Page Number + Line Number

Figure 20.7   Graphic Representation of Page-Blocking Method

disc memories. Figure 20.7 is a graphic representation of a page-blocking storage method.

Inverted (list)

There are probably $n + 1$ physical methods of storing inverted DBMSs, where $n =$ the number of actual physical DBMSs. The basic premise is to store the "inverted" indices separately and have those indices point to the appropriate base record. Figure 20.8 is the elementary ADABAS physical storage approach.

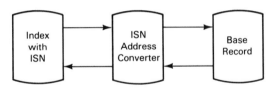

Index with ISN → ISN Address Converter → Base Record

ISN = Indexed Sequence Number

Figure 20.8   Graphic Representation of Inverted Method

Relational

A relational DBMS uses an active data dictionary to resolve which tables to use at execution time. Prespecified pointers are *not* necessary. Figure 20.9 is a graphic representation of a relation storage method. Note that there are no differences between Figures 20.9 and 20.4.

Table 1

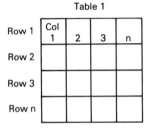

Row 1	Col 1	2	3	n
Row 2				
Row 3				
Row n				

Table 2

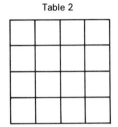

Table n

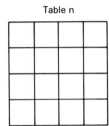

Figure 20.9   Graphic Representation of Relational Method

POINTERS

A pointer is the absolute, or relative, or symbolic address of a data group (segment, node, etc.) that has an association with the original data group. Pointers are the "pathways" that allow tree, plex, and inverted DBMSs to perform their operations (relational DBMSs do *not* require pointers). Figure 20.10 is a simple graphic presentation of pointers.

Embedded With Data

The early DBMSs embedded their pointers with the actual data. This means that the DBMS actually has to read the *data* record to retrieve the pathway to the "next" associated data group. This requires a minimum of *one* disk access to find any data group and usually more.

External

"Newer" DBMSs have attempted to increase performance by placing the pointers in separate "records" external to the actual data. This permits the DBMS to use in-memory searches for the indices *and* to locate the address of the requested data group. This is the basic technique for most inverted DBMSs, although S2K (SAS), which is a "tree" database, uses external pointers.

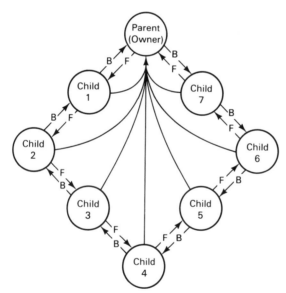

F = Forward Pointer
B = Backward Pointer
All other are parent (owner) pointers.

Figure 20.10 Graphic Representation of Pointers

Types

The tree and plex DBMSs share a common "set" of pointers that are somewhat under the control of the physical database designer.

Forward   The forward pointer allows a parent-child (owner-member) to be "walked" in a forward direction starting with the parent (owner) and continuing with the "first" child (member) through . . . until the parent (owner) is again retrieved (end of chain or walk).

Backward   The backward pointer allows a parent-child (owner-member) to be "walked" in a backward direction starting with the parent (owner) and continuing with the "last" child (member) through the "last-1" child (member) through the "last-2" child (member) through . . . until the parent (owner) is again retrieved (end of chain or walk).

Parent   The parent (owner) pointer allows the parent (owner) to be *directly* accessed from *anywhere* in the "chain." This permits a "user" to shortcut a "walk through" a chain whenever the appropriate child (member) has been retrieved.

Twin (IMS—forward or backward)   The physical twin pointer in IMS points either forward or backward to the specific segment occurrence of a specified segment type of a specified parent.

COMPONENTS

The "standard" DBMS consists of these "mandatory" components:

DDL   Data Definition Language: a "language" that defines the data to the DBMS. This is usually a schema (a map of the overall logical structure of the database plus subschemas (a map of a specific view of the total schema)).

DML   Data Manipulation Language: a "language" that permits programmers to access the database using conventional *"third"-generation "batch" languages (Cobol, PL/1, Fortran, etc.).*

and the following "optional" components:

DSDL   Data Storage Definition Language: a language that permits the actual storage of data groups on the storage media.

DD   Data Dictionary: provides metadata and up to full active control of the DBMS.

DBIOC   *DataBase I/O Controller):* accepts logical data record requests from "users" and navigates the database to satisfy the request.

QUERY/REPORT WRITER: a "language" that permits "users" to access the database using a "nonprocedural" language to specify the question and its required values.

CLASSIFICATION OF SELECTED DBMSs

The DBMSs selected for review were those DBMSs with which the author has some familiarity. I apologize for any DBMSs omitted since I do not intend to slight any DBMS offering. The classification uses the criterion identified in this chapter. Figure 20.11 is a summary table.

ADABAS

Vendor:	Software AG of North America
Physical Type:	Inverted
Physical Storage:	Partially inverted using multilevel indices
Pointers:	External to base record
DDL Defines:	Associator: "schema," including all inverted indices
	Base records: all data elements that were not inverted
	Work: temporary
	Cobol, Fortran, PL/1, and BAL
DMS:	Direct using a single index (descriptor)
Access methods:	Direct using a combination of indices
	Direct using the ISN (internal sequence number)
	Sequentially using any data element as a primary key
	Physical serial sequence
	None available at the time of publication
DSDL:	Data Dictionary (integrated—slightly active)
DD:	None available at the time of publication
DBIOC:	ADASCRIPT + (query)
Query:	ADACOM (report writer)
	NATURAL (an "expert" query language)

Features:

1. Data compression available on initial database loading; this can save significant disc space.
2. Excellent security. Up to 15 levels of security can be specified on each field defined. Ciphering is also available. Record relationships can be defined to produce a plex (network) type database. These relationships may be established at initial load or afterward.

3. Adabas's implementation of partially inverted lists and its internal sequence number (ISN) permits quick searches on indices.

4. Interfaces to Data Base Machine.

5. Multithreaded and multiuser.

6. Variable-length segments.

7. Checkpoints, restart, logging (before/after) with auto restart.

8. Micro/mini link.

9. Distributed data processing using ADABAS/VTAM.

Database 2 (DB2)

Vendor:	IBM
Physical type:	Relational
Physical storage:	Collection of tables accessible through a "subsumed" data dictionary (SQL–*S*tructured *Q*uery *L*anguage)
Pointers:	None required: may be prespecified to reduce response time
DDL:	SQL
DMS:	Cobol, Fortran, PL/1, BAL
Access methods:	Relational algebra
DSDL:	None available at the time of publication
DD:	SQL and via IMS DB/DC dictionary
DBIOC:	SQL
Query:	SQL
	QMF (Query Management Facility)

Features:

1. Fully relational database

2. Powerful query languages

3. Able to "download" data from IMS/VS databases

4. Standard IBM security and an authorization mechanism

5. Variable-length segments

6. Checkpoint, restart, and transaction backout logging

7. Multithreaded and multiuser

8. Can coexist with IMS/VS

DATACOM/DB

Vendor:	Applied Data Research (ADR)
Physical type:	Inverted
Physical storage:	Partially inverted using multilevel and compound indices
Pointers:	External to base record

DDL: Defines:
                                  Database: "schema"
                                  File: "subschema"
                                  Area: "physical schema"
                                  Key: data element defined as an index (inverted)
                                  Element: "base record"
DMS: Cobol, Fortran, PL/1, BAL, RPG
Access method: Sequentially, using any data element as a primary key
DSDL: None available at time of publication
DD: DATACOM/DD (integrated—passive)
DBIOC: Limited "logical record facility"
Query: DATAQUERY (query)
                              DATAREPORTER (report writer)

Features:

1. The ability to concatenate and exclude indices provides significant flexibility in accessing data. The feature is further enhanced by the ability to establish synonomous indices in several areas or files.
2. ADR/IDEAL is a 4GL development tool.
3. Security includes update passwords, terminal validation, and encryption.
4. Variable-length segments.
5. Checkpoints, restart, logging with auto restart.
6. Multithreaded and multiuser.
7. Micro/mini link.

DBMS[1]

Vendor: Handle Technologies
Physical type: Hybrid
Physical storage: Page with multilevel primary and secondary indices
Pointers: External to documents and records
DDL: None required for documents; schema for records
DMS: C
Access method: Directly using a primary index read
                              Directly using a single secondary index
                              Sequentially
                              Relational algebra
DSDL: None available at time of publication
DD: Subsumed—active

[1]The author and Lee Bollinger were codesigners.

DBIOC:	None available at time of publication
Query:	WRITER (word processor)
	CALC (spreadsheet)

Features:

1. Extensive access methods to data
2. Supports office automation software tools
3. Minimal memory requirements (<128K)
4. Checkpoint and restart

DMS-90

Vendor:	Sperry Univac
Physical type:	Plex (network)
Physical storage:	Page blocking
Pointers:	Imbedded; forward, backward, owner
DDL:	Schema (conforms to CODASYL DBTG recommendations)
DMS:	Cobol
Access methods:	Direct using actual physical database key
	Direct (calculate or "calc") using a hashing algorithm (requires synonym chaining)
	Member (child, detail) via owner (parent, master)
DSDL:	DMCL
DD:	Data Dictionary
DBIOC:	None available at time of publication
Query:	UNIQUE (query)

Features:

1. CODASYL database.
2. Subschemas provide the ability to achieve data independence for both the database and application programs.
3. DMCL provides the physical database designer with the ability to optimize performance by controlling storage of nodes on physical storage pages.
4. Checkpoint, restart, and logging (before/after).
5. Multithreaded and multiuser.

IMAGE (3000)

Vendor:	Hewlett-Packard
Physical type:	Limited network
Physical storage:	Chain file linked

Pointers:	Imbedded; forward, backward, and owner
DDL:	Schema
DMS:	Cobol, Fortran, Basic, RPG, assembler
Access methods:	Master (parent, owner) directly via a hashing algorithm (requires "synonym" chaining) detail (child, member) via master
DSDL:	None available at time of publication
DD:	DICTIONARY/3000 (passive)
DBIOC:	None available at time of publication
Query:	QUERY/3000

Features:

1. Easy to implement and use
2. Extensive security to field level
3. Multithreaded and multiuser
4. Can be distributed

IMS/VS

Vendor:	IBM
Physical type:	Tree (hierarchical); limited network
Physical storage:	Hierarchical blocking
Pointers:	Imbedded; forward, backward, twin, owner
DDL:	Schema (approximates CODASYL DBTG recommendations)
DMS:	Cobol, PL/1, BAL
Access methods:	Direct using a hashing algorithm (requires synonym chaining) Child (member, detail) via parent (owner, master) Direct using indices
DSDL:	None available at time of publication
DD:	DB/DC—passive
DBIOC:	None available at time of publication
Query:	GIS/VS and IQF [query and report writers are available from third-party vendors such as Informatic (Mark IV and V) and Application Software (ASI/Inquiry)]

Features:

1. Most popular DBMS on IBM mainframes
2. Extensive options, including Fastpath and data-entry databases
3. Can coexist and/or "download" data to Database 2 (DB2)
4. Security includes passwords and terminal access
5. Variable-length segments

6. Checkpoint, restart, and transaction backout logging
7. Multithreaded and multiuser
8. Micro/mini link

INGRESS

Vendor:	Relational Technology
Physical type:	Relational
Physical storage:	Relational
Pointers:	None required
DDL:	None required
DMS:	Cobol, C, Fortran, Pascal, Basic
Access methods:	Relational algebra
DSDL:	None available at time of publication
DD:	Subsumed—active
DBIOC:	QUEL and EQUEL
Query:	QUERY (query)
	REPORTS (report writer)
	Application-By-Forms (ABF—combines QUERY and RE-PORTS)
	GRAPHICS (business graphics)
	QBF (query update)

Features:

1. Extensive security available via Define Permit Command
2. Two-phase commit protocol to maintain database integrity
3. Extensive utilities
4. Checkpoint, restart, and transaction backout logging
5. Software cache for shareable systems

INQUIRE

Vendor:	Infodata Systems
Physical type:	Inverted
Physical storage:	Partially inverted using multilevel indices
Pointers:	External to base record
DDL:	Schema
DMS:	Cobol, Fortran, PL/1, BAL
Access methods:	Directly via multikey indices
	Proximity searching using Boolean operands
	Relational algebra
DSDL:	None available at time of publication

DD: Subsumed—active
DBIOC: None available at time of publication
Query: INQUIRE (query)
                   IRMS (text processing)

Features:

1. Flexible indexing with support of multiple database at execution time; conjunctive and unidirectional searches are efficient
2. Password protection and data independence to field
3. Variable-length segments
4. Warm restart and automatic logging with backout
5. Multithreaded and multiuser
6. Micro/mini link
7. Interfaces to external files, text processing, and SAS products

Integrated Database Management System (IDMS)

Vendor: Cullinet Database Systems
Physical type: Plex (network)
Physical storage: Page blocking
Pointers: Imbedded; forward, backward, owner
DDL: Schema (conforms to CODASYL DBTG recommendations)
DMS: Cobol, Fortran, PL/1, BAL
Access methods: Direct using actual physical database key
                   Direct (calculate or calc) using a hashing algorithm
                   (requires synonym chaining)
                   Member (child, detail) via owner (parent, master)
DSDL: DMCL
DD: Integrated Data Dictionary (IDD—active)
DBIOC: Logical Record Facility (LRF)
Query: CULPRIT (report writer)
                   OnLine Query (OLQ—query)
                   OnLine English (OLE—"expert" query)
                   INTERACT (text and word processing)
                   EDP-Auditor (query for auditors)

Features:

1. CODASYL database
2. Subschemas provide the ability to achieve data independence for both the database and application programs. LRF provides additional data independence.

3. DMCL provides the physical database designer with the ability to optimize performance by controlling storage of nodes on physical storage pages.
4. Development facilities, including ADS/O and ADS/BATCH.
5. Multithreaded and multiuser.
6. Checkpoint, restart, and logging.
7. Micro/mini link.

IDMS/R

Vendor:	Cullinet Database Systems
Physical type:	Inverted/relational
Physical storage:	Relational
Pointers:	External multilevel indices
DDL:	Schema
DMS:	Cobol, Fortran, PL/1, BAL
Access methods:	Direct using multilevel indices
	Relational algebra
DSDL:	DMCL
DD:	IDD—active
DBIOC:	LRF
Query:	CULPRIT (report writer)
	OLQ (query)
	OLE (''expert'' query)

Features:

1. See IDMS
2. Additional development facility (Automatic System Facility) permits non-database personnel to define database components on-line and generally bypass the normal technical steps.
3. Abend detect and warm restart.

Integrated Datastore II (IDS/II)

Vendor:	Honeywell Information Systems
Physical type:	Plex (network)
Physical storage:	Page blocking
Pointers:	Imbedded; forward, backward, owner
DDL:	Schema (conforms to CODASYL DBTG recommendations)
DMS:	Cobol

Access methods:	Direct using actual physical database key
	Direct (calculate or "calc") using a hashing algorithm (requires synonym chaining)
	Member (child, detail) via owner (parent, master)
	Direct using indices
DSDL:	DMCL
DD:	None available at time of publication
	Data Catalogue 2—TSI—is available for IDS/II
DBIOC:	None available at time of publication
Query:	Query and Reporting Processor (QRP—query and report writer)

Features:

1. Subschemas provide the ability to achieve data independence for both the database and application programs.
2. DMCL provides the physical database designer with the ability to optimize performance by controlling storage of nodes on physical storage pages.
3. All pointers specified and created.
4. Variable-length segments.
5. Checkpoint, restart, and logging (before/after).
6. Multithreaded and multiuser.
7. Micro/mini link.

Model 204 (M204)

Vendor:	Computer Corporation of America
Physical type:	Inverted
Physical storage:	Partially inverted with multilevel indices
Pointers:	External to base record
DDL:	DEFINE (data elements are stored as data element/name/data value pairs)
DMS:	Cobol
Access methods:	Direct using a hashing algorithm
	Direct using secondary indices
	Physical sequence
	Sorted sequence
DSDL:	None available at time of publication
DD:	Dictionary/204—active
DBIOC:	M204 User language
Query:	M204 User language (query and report writer)
	ACCESS/204 (query by example)

Features:

1. Extensive utilities for space optimization, channel utilization, and search optimization.
2. Extensive access and crossreferencing methods; data independence.
3. Capable of supporting very large databases (in excess of 500 gigabytes) and hundreds of concurrent on-line users.
4. Security includes seven levels of password protection to field.
5. Variable-length segments.
6. Multithreaded and multiuser.
7. Micro/mini link (PC/204).
8. M204 user language provides most of the power of conventional third-generation languages.
9. Interfaces to text editing and electronic mail.
10. Distributed directory version under development.

ORACLE

Vendor:	Oracle
Physical type:	Relational
Physical storage:	Relational
Pointers:	External indices to tables (all indices are B-trees)
DDL:	SQL
DMS:	C, Cobol, Fortran, Pascal, PL/I
Access methods:	Direct using primary (unique) index
	Direct using secondary (nonunique) index
	Relational algebra (via SQL)
DSDL:	Storage Manager
DD:	SQL—active
DBIOC:	SQL
Query:	SQL (query)
	Report Writer (report writer)
	Application Generator (application generator)

Features:

1. Extensive query language.
2. Security includes password protection to database, table, record, and to fields by value. Views can also be protected.
3. Variable-length segments.
4. Checkpoint, restart, and logging (after).
5. Multithreaded and multiuser.

6. Micro/mini link.
7. On-line development facility (Interactive Application Facility).
8. On-line help facility.
9. Reentrant.

RAMIS II

Vendor:	Mathematica Products Group
	Martin Marietta Data Systems
Physical type:	Hybrid
Physical storage:	Hierarchical blocking
Pointers:	External to hierarchical block
DDL:	RAMIS II
DMS:	Cobol, Fortran, PL/1, BAL, RAMIS II
Access methods:	Direct using multilevel indices
	Physical sequence
	Sorted sequence
	Relational algebra
DSDL:	None available at time of publication
DD:	Subsumed—active
DBIOC:	RAMIS II
Query:	RAMIS II (query and report writer)
	SAS interface (statistical analysis)
	Graph Generator (business graphics)
	Financial Planning (financial statements)
	High Resolution Graphics (business graphics)
	APL interface (algorithmic query)

Features:

1. Nonprocedural "English" language can be used for record maintenance.
2. RAMIS II provides extensive report generation facilities.
3. Logical data structures that provide data independence.
4. Password protection to file, record, and field.
5. Variable-length segments.
6. Checkpoint, restart, and user-specified logging.
7. Multithreaded and multiuser.
8. Micro/mini link.

Structured Query Language/Data System (SQL/DS)

Vendor:	IBM
Physical type:	Relational

Physical storage: Relational
Pointers: None required, but SQL/DS creates external indices to increase performance
DDL: SQL
DMS: Cobol, PL/1, BAL
Access methods: Relational algebra (via SQL)
DSDL: VSAM Entry Sequenced Data Sets (ESDS); also called DBEXTENTS
DD: SQL—active
DBIOC: SQL
Query: SQL (query and report writer)

Features:

1. Extensive query language
2. Security includes access control to table, record, and field
3. Variable-length segments
4. Checkpoints, restart, and journal
5. Multithreaded and multiuser
6. Micro/mini link

System 2000/80 (S2K)

Vendor: SAS
Physical type: Tree (hierarchical)
Physical storage: Hierarchical blocking
Pointers: External to hierarchical block
DDL: S2K (free-form English-based syntax)
DMS: Cobol, Fortran, PL/1, BAL
Access methods: Direct using multilevel inverted indices Physical sequential
DSDL: None available at time of publication
DD: Integrated Data Dictionary (IDD—active)
DBIOC: None available at time of publication
Query: QUBE-X ("expert" query)
    TAPS/80 (application generator)
    Report Writer (report writer)
    QUERY (query)

Features:

1. All user interfaces use "English."
2. Extensive query languages.

3. Nonprocedural languages can be used for record maintenance.
4. Password protection to field.
5. Variable-length segments supported logically.
6. Checkpoint, restart, and auto transaction recovery.
7. Multithreaded and multiuser.
8. Micro/mini link.

TOTAL

Vendor:	Cincom Systems
Physical type:	Limited network
Physical storage:	Chain file linked
Pointers:	Imbedded; forward, backward, and owner
DDL:	Schema
DMS:	Cobol, Fortran, PL/1, BAL, RPG, Basic
Access methods:	Primary (parent, owner) directly via a hashing algorithm (requires "synonym" chaining)
	Related (child, member) via primary (parent, owner)
	Physical sequential
DSDL:	None available at time of publication
DD:	Data Dictionary (passive)
DBIOC:	None available at time of publication
Query:	T-ASK (query)
	SOCRATES (report writer)

Features:

1. Large customer base using virtually all major computers.
2. The limited network chain file linked structure is simple to implement and use. This structure also provides data independence.
3. Security is implemented by hardware/software locks utilizing a password protected library.
4. Variable-length segments supported logically.
5. On-line task recovery; logging (before/after).
6. Multithreaded and multiuser.
7. Micro/mini link.
8. Upwardly compatible to TIS.

Total Information System (TIS)

Vendor:	Cincom Systems
Physical type:	Limited network

Physical storage:	Chain file linked
Pointers:	External; forward, backward, and owner
DDL:	Schema
DMS:	Cobol, Fortran, PL/1, BAL, MANTIS
Access methods:	Primary (parent, owner) directly via a hashing algorithm (requires "synonym" chaining)
	Related (child, member) via primary (parent, owner)
	Physical sequential
DSDL:	None available at time of publication
DD:	Directory Management (active)
DBIOC:	None available at time of publication
Query:	QUERY (query)
	Report Writer (report writer)

Features:

1. See TOTAL.

2. Directory-driven database supported by a user-lazy language.

3. Supports unstructured data which may provide interface to external database machines and associative memories.

Physical Type (PhyType)

T	Tree (hierarchical)
P	Plex (network)
I	Inverted (list)
R	Relational
H	Hybrid (not classifiable according to the "standard" types)

Physical Storage (PhyStor)

C	Chain file linked
H	Hierarchical blocking
P	Page blocking
I	Inverted (list)
R	Relational

Pointer (Pnt)

E	External (not imbedded with data)
I	Imbedded (with data)

DDL

C	CODASYL DBTG schema
S	Schema
O	Other

SUMMARY OF DBMS CHARACTERISTICS

DBMS	Phy Type					Phy Stor					Pnt		DDL			DMS					D S	DD		I O	QUERY		
	T	P	I	R	H	C	H	P	I	R	E	I	C	S	O	C	F	P	B	O	S	P	A	O	Q	R	O
ADABAS			X						X		X		X			X	X	X	X			X			X	X	X
DB2				X					X		X	X	X			X	X	X	X			X	X		X	X	
DATACOM/DB			X						X		X		X			X	X	X	X	X		X			X	X	
DBMS					X			X			X			X						X		X				X	
DMS-90		X				X					X	X	X								X				X		
IMAGE/3000		X				X						X	X			X	X	X	X	X		X			X		
INQUIRE			X						X		X		X			X	X	X	X			X			X		X
IDMS		X						X			X	X	X			X	X	X	X		X	X			X	X	X
IDMS/R			X	X					X	X	X	X	X			X	X	X	X		X	X			X	X	X
IDS/II		X						X			X	X	X								X				X	X	
IMS/VS	X	X				X					X	X	X					X	X			X					
INGRES			X							X			X	X						X				X	X	X	X
MODEL 204			X					X			X		X	X									X		X	X	
ORACLE				X						X	X	X	X						X	X	X			X	X	X	X
RAMIS II					X	X					X		X			X	X	X	X	X				X	X	X	X
SQL/DS				X						X	X	X	X			X		X	X		X		X		X	X	
S2K	X					X					X		X			X	X	X	X			X			X	X	X
TOTAL		X				X						X	X			X	X	X	X	X		X			X	X	
TIS	X					X					X		X			X	X	X	X			X			X	X	X

Figure 20.11   Summary DBMS Table

DMS

C		Cobol
F		Fortran
P		PL/1
B		BAL or other assemblers
O		Other (C, Basic, Pascal, RPG, etc.)

DS   X = that DBMS has a data storage definition language (DSDL)

Data Dictionary (DD)
P	Passive
A	Active

IO   X = that DBMS has database I/O controller (DBIOC)

QUERY
Q	Query
R	Report writer
O	Other

21

First-Cut Executable Physical Model

DEFINITION

A first-cut executable physical model is created by applying the general conversion rules presented in this chapter to the logical database developed by the steps described in Chapter 11. First cut means that it will probably have to be "skewed" (see Chapter 23) to achieve user response requirements; executable means that the physical model is implementable and would "run" after being "compiled" by the appropriate DBMS component.

GENERAL RULES FOR CONVERTING LOGICAL DATABASE TO PHYSICAL STORAGE TYPES

The following general rules are appropriate for the specific physical storage type; they may need to be modified to satisfy a specific DBMS. These rules are suitable for IMAGE, TOTAL, and TIS.

Chain File Linked

1. All root tables become primary (master) "files." At Logic University:

```
student: instructor: alumni
major: minor
course
classroom
semester
```

2. All tables created by normalization become related (detail) "files" that "belong" to the root table primary (master).

3. Create an additional related (detail) "file" for all foreign keys that is "owned" by both the table containing the foreign key and the table to which the foreign key points.

Hierarchical Blocking

These rules are specifically for IMS/VS. Figures 21.1 to 21.3 show the first draft of IMS/VS through to the executable IMS/VS physical model.

1. All root tables become root segments. At Logic University:

```
student: instructor: alumni
major: minor
course
classroom
semester
```

2. All tables created during the first pass of 1NF (first normal form) as level 2 children (the first pass of 1NF removes the first repeating group).

3. All tables during the second pass of 1NF as level 3 children (the second pass of 1NF removes the first repeating group *within* the original repeating group).

4. Etc.

5. Place any table generated by 2NF or 3NF in the hierarchical leg of its major primary key data element.

6. Secondary keys become secondary indices.

7. A table containing a foreign key becomes the logical parent of the lowest segment that would contain the foreign key as a key.

The rules above create an *un*executable IMS/VS physical model because illegal relationships have been established. The possible illegal relationships with a suggested "cure" are:

Logical child cannot have associated secondary index.
Create physical child to logical child which forms a LINK segment to the logical parent.

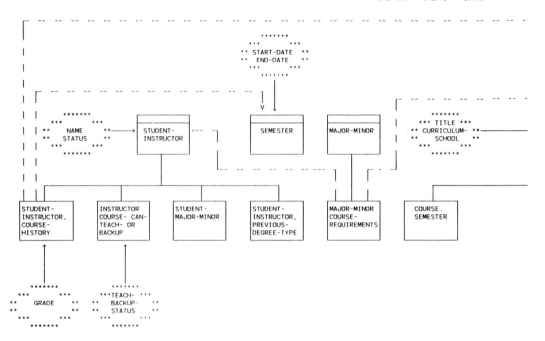

library name: IMSVS2A

Figure 21.1 First Draft: IMS/VS Physical

188

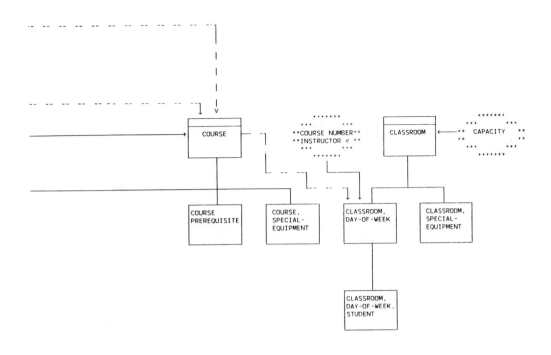

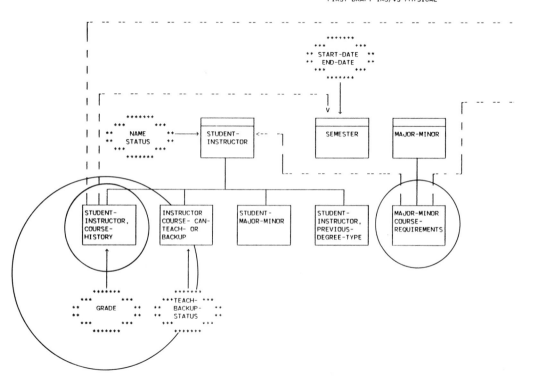

LOGIC UNIVERSITY
FIRST DRAFT IMS/VS PHYSICAL

library name: IMSVS2A

Figure 21.2 First Draft: IMS/VS Physical with IMS/VS Illegal Relations Noted

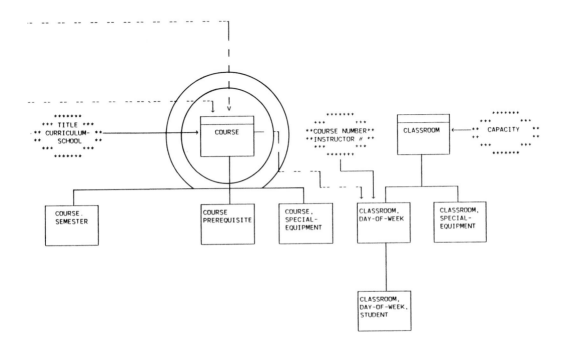

COURSE

TITLE
CURRICULUM-
SCHOOL

COURSE NUMBER
INSTRUCTOR #

CLASSROOM

CAPACITY

COURSE.
SEMESTER

COURSE
PREREQUISITE

COURSE,
SPECIAL-
EQUIPMENT

CLASSROOM,
DAY-OF-WEEK

CLASSROOM,
SPECIAL-
EQUIPMENT

CLASSROOM,
DAY-OF-WEEK,
STUDENT

library name: IMSVS2B

PREPARED BY DFDP
ADPAC

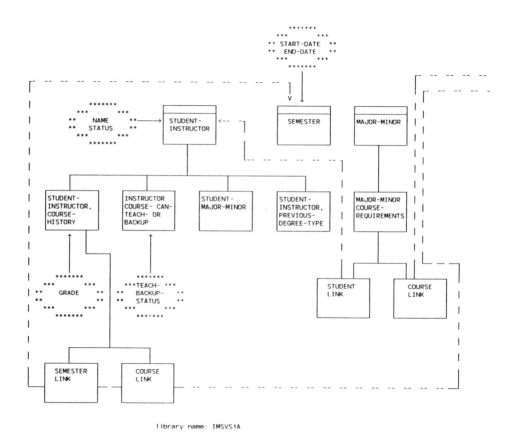

library name: IMSVS1A

Figure 21.3 IMS/VS Executable Physical

192

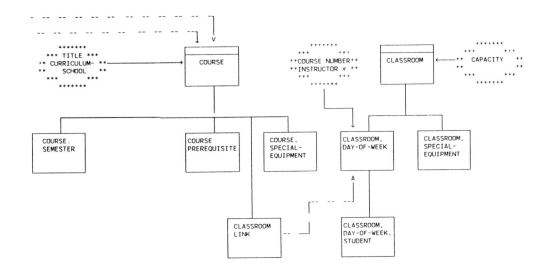

Logical child cannot have multiple logical parents.

Create physical child to logical child for each logical parent which forms LINK segment to logical parent.

Logical parent cannot be a logical child.

Create physical child to logical parent/child segment which forms LINK segment to its logical parent.

Logical child must be physically lower in hierarchical leg than logical parent.

Add necessary LINK segments.

Each hierarchical leg cannot only have one logical child.

Add necessary LINK segments.

Plex (network)

These rules are suitable for DMS-90, IDMS, and IDS/II. It is trivial to convert a DBTG logical database to a page-blocked plex DBMS since the DBTG diagram was developed to model plex databases.

1. All root tables are "calc" owners.
2. All other tables are "via" the root owner.
3. Foreign keys are implemented "non-via."
4. Secondary keys become indices.

Figure 21.4 is the executable page-blocked plex physical model.

Inverted (list)

These rules are specifically for ADABAS:

1. All primary keys become descriptor fields.
2. All secondary keys become descriptor fields.
3. All foreign keys become descriptor fields.
4. All nondescriptor fields become the (data) base record.

Relational

This rule should be suitable for all relational DBMSs.

1. *Do nothing* (the logical database should be directly implementable in the relational physical DBMS)!

AUTOMATED TOOLS

Many of the vendors in this book are developing logical to physical software; to the best of my knowledge none were available at the time of publication.

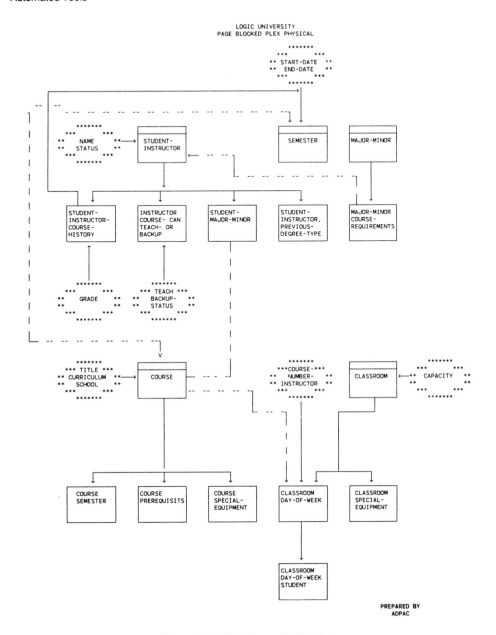

Figure 21.4 Plex Executable Physical

22

Response Timing
of Logical Records
and Transactions

DEFINITION

The first-cut executable physical model developed by the rules in Chapter 21 works but is probably unresponsive to the users' needs. How do we know this? One method would be to implement the physical model and wait for user reaction (usually angry). A better method is to estimate the performance of the physical model and "skew" it where necessary *and* where possible. This requires statistics that are often *not* collected in current system development life cycles (SDLC). The inputs to the process are:

DYNAMIC LOGICAL DATABASE

The dynamic logical database defined in Chapter 17 collected the following statistics:

Table volume and growth
Table volatility, including asymmetrical distribution
Volume of planned inquiries
Estimated volume of ad hoc inquiries
Transaction path identification and priority (see Figure 17.1)
User response-time requirements, including volume and growth

LOGICAL RECORDS

The logical record defines the data elements (attributes) required to process the user transactions. This preliminarily defines the transaction paths.

LOGICAL TRANSACTION PATHS

The logical transaction paths specify the tables that must be retrieved and the logical retrieval sequence. This information, coupled with the transaction path volumes, is probably the most *significant* statistic to the physical database designer. Unfortunately, it is usually a statistic that is not *collected* by the SDLC.

SYSTEM VALUES

The following system values should be obtainable from your system programming organization:

Average time for the application program to generate a DBMS ''call''
Average time for the operating system to process the DBMS call
Average time for the DBMS to process the call
Average storage access time (add in a synonym chaining factor if required)

The volumes for *each* transaction path plus the system values can be transferred to a form similar to Figure 22.1 which can then be factored to produce the ''minimum'' response time (on line) or processing time (batch) on an *unloaded* system.

PAGE BLOCKING

An additional timing problem is presented by the DBMSs that used page blocking *and* have a data storage definition language (DSDL). That problem is that the physical database designer must specify which owner/members tables should be stored on the same page. The ''improper'' placement means that ''walks'' must actually be done with physical read statements. There is a *few-orders-of-magnitude* timing difference between memory searches and physical disk reads. Figure 22.2 is a representative form for page planning.

RESULTS

The timing responses should be compared to the user requirements as defined on a form similar to Figure 22.1. The physical designer needs to attempt to skew the high-priority transactions that exceed the user timing requirements.

TRANSACTION TIMING DETAIL

TRANSACTION NAME _____ RUN NAME _____ NO _____ FREQ. _____

RECORD	DBMS CALL	NO PER TRANS	DISC ACCESSES				CPU TIME				COMMENT
			INDEX	INVEN	DATA	TOT	DBMS	TP MON	APP PROG	TOT	

Avg Disc Access × [ ] = Disc Time + [ ] = TOT TRAN TIME

COURTESY OF LEARMONTH-BURBETT

Figure 22.1 Transaction Timing Detail Plan

PAGE PLANNING CHART

PAGE TYPE _____ NO RECORDS _____ NO. PAGES _____ RANGE _____ (ALLOW 10% expansion)

RECORD	DATA SIZE	DBMS BYTES	POINTERS						RECORD TOTAL	NO. PER. OWNER	TOTAL SIZE PER OWNER	COMMENTS
			†P/P	P/B	P/H	†S/P	S/B	R S/H				

TOTAL

OWNER/PAGE

DATA SIZE/PAGE

PAGE HEADER 32

PAGE BYTES

† MANDATORY

R RECOMMENDED FOR SECONDARY DETAILS

COURTESY OF LEARMONTH-BURCHETT

Figure 22.2 Page Planning Chart

199

Note: Dear user: Please do *not* expect your physical database designer to create a physical database that will achieve *all* of your requirements. In almost all but the most trivial applications, it is a *physical* impossibility to satisfy *all* requests.

AUTOMATED TOOLS

Many of the vendors listed in this book have announced that a "what if" timing product will be available in the future. None, to the best of my knowledge, was available at the time this book was written.

23

Skewing Physical Model to Achieve User Response Requirements

DEFINITION

The transaction timing form (Figure 22.1), when compared to a user requirement form (Figure 17.1) highlights those user transactions that exceed the user requirements. Physical database designers need to use all their skills to manipulate (skew) the physical database to achieve as many user requirements as possible. This chapter presents some basic ideas for skewing, but the real optimization rests with the skilled professionals in your organization.

BASIC SKEWING RULES

Chain File Linked

These basic rules work for IMAGE, TOTAL, and TIS.

1. Place calculable, derivable, or other forms of redundant data into the physical database.
2. Move data from related (detail) to primary (master).
3. Add "link records" to permit multiple accesses.

Hierarchical Blocking

These basic rules are specifically for IMS/VS:

1. Place calculable, derivable, or other forms of redundant data into the physical database.
2. Move data up the hierarchy.
3. Add logical parents/children.
4. Add indices.

Plex (Page Blocking)

These basic rules work for DMS/90, IDMS, and IDS/II:

1. Place calculable, derivable, or other forms of redundant data into the physical database.
2. Change the storage of "via" and "non-via" nodes [i.e. redo the page planning form (Figure 22.2)].
3. Add indices where possible.

Inverted (List)

These basic rules work for ADABAS, DATACOM/DB, INQUIRE, and M204:

1. Place calculable, derivable, or other forms of redundant data into the physical database.
2. Invert more data elements for faster inquiries.
3. "De-invert" (reduce the number of indices) for faster updates.

For ADABAS:

4. Establish periodic groups.

Relational

These basic rules should work for any relational DBMS.

1. Place calculable, derivable, or other forms of redundant data into the physical database.
2. Use compaction/expansion algorithms if available.
3. Use prespecified "paths" for known accesses if available.

"WHAT IF" MODELING

The procedures above should be repeated over and over and over until the best mix is achieved. It is the responsibility of DP to deliver the best possible product to the user (who after all has—in one way or another—paid for the product).

AUTOMATED TOOLS

At this book's writing, IBM and Cullinet provided utilities for "what if" modeling. Other vendors are developing similar tools.

24

Eliminating Programmer Navigation

DEFINITION

Programmer navigation is the knowledge that an application programmer designer requires of the *physical* structure of the database to program a user system. It is my personal belief that much of what has gone "wrong" with DMBSs is that application programmers do not—and normally should not—need to know the physical structure (the other contributing reason is the lack of a logical database). The moral is that every organization should eliminate programmer navigation.

RATIONALE

Chapter 23 presented some basic optimization rules. Physical database designers are creative; they often develop ingenious solutions to specific problems. Unfortunately, the ingenious solution is usually not communicated to the application programmer and the application programmer develops a "disastrous" solution. It is very possible to achieve significant performance gains by making simple changes to the access calls within application programs. Logical records permit physical database designers to implement their best path.

    The Logical Record Facility (LRF) of IDMS provides an additional performance advantage. LRF remains in "contact" with IDMS until the logical records has been retrieved, thereby saving numerous calls between the application program and IDMS.

Data Independence

If properly incorporated into application programs, logical records provide data independence. The program accesses only the data that it actually needs. Changes to the physical structure of the database that do not affect the application program logical record do not affect the program! (An amazing concept!)

Data Security

Logical records provide an additional security provision—certain commands, such as update, delete, etc., can be made inaccessible to specific "programs." This means that future program modifications cannot destroy the original security.

Currency

The biggest programmer navigation problem is currency. *Currency* is a buzzword that means where the DBMS physical pointer is. Inappropriate knowledge of currency by application programmers *destroy* user databases. Logical records place currency where it belongs—with the physical database designer.

IMPLEMENTATION

Logical Record Facility

The only DBMSs that have a complete logical record facility (LRF), to the best of my knowledge, is Cullinet's IDMS and IDMS/R. To implement LRF under IDMS or IDMS/R requires the application programmer to:

> Specify the logical record
> Specify the messages that LRF should return upon completion of any LRF activity

COPYLIBs (COBOL)

LRF can be implemented by specifying a Data division COPYLIB for the logical record. The LRF "paths" and "path commands" can be coded by the database staff and placed into *Procedure* Division COPYLIBs for inclusion into specification programs.

CAVEAT

IBM has estimated that there are at least 1 billion calls accessing IMS databases. Those calls were normally coded by application programmers. Under LRF these calls would be coded by the database staff. This requires:

1. A new position: database LRF programmer

2. Staffing of that position

I believe—without empirical proof—that the overall programmer staffing will decrease by transferring the programmer navigation duties to the database staff.

SUMMARY

Programmer navigation is the major cause of database "corruption" and contributes to poor response times. LRF eliminates programmer navigation by transferring the responsibility to the people who should have it—the database staff.

25

Summary

The design cycle recommended in this book is:

1. Collect the user information by:
   a. Functional decomposition dataflow diagrams
      (1) Gane/Sarson
      (2) SADT
      (3) Yourdon
   b. Data decomposition diagrams
      (1) Jackson
      (2) Warnier/Orr
   c. Analyzing existing programs
2. Verify the collected user information by
   a. Eliminating homonyms
   b. Identifying and minimizing aliases
   c. Derive the minimal cover by normalization
      (1) 1NF
      (2) 2NF
      (3) 3NF
      (4) FNF (optimization and generalization)

3. Convert the static relational notation logical database to a graphic logical database model of your choice.

4. Augment the static logical database model with the necessary statistical information to convert it into a dynamic logical database model.

5. Convert the dynamic logical database model to a first-cut executable physical database model.

6. Estimate the minimum response times for the required logical transactions.

7. Optimize the response time to best satisfy user requirements.

8. Deliver a timely, correct, flexible, recoverable, user-friendly physical database to your happy, satisfied, glowing, and rapturous user.

Why use this design cycle? Because many companies have proved that it works! I have two last comments:

THANK YOU FOR READING THIS BOOK

and

GO FOR IT

Appendix A

Class Scheduling Application of Logic University

Logic University wishes to automate its rather hectic semiannual class scheduling exercise. Currently, the Registrar is responsible for ensuring that all changes to courses, curricula, and instructors have been made by the respective school deans, that Facilities have made all room changes, and that the Registrar has entered all new students and updates. Upon ensuring their completion, the Registrar says GO! The automated system will have to handle the various inputs but the Registrar's control function will remain.

The basic procedure is to determine what required courses each student must take for both his or her major(s) and minor(s)—dual majors and/or minors are allowed. The required courses are noted in the student schedule and a running tally by course is maintained. Concurrently, a three-semester average of students taking free courses (course not required for student major or minor) is determined and added to the tally. The number of classes required this semester is determined by dividing the final tally by the maximum size for each class. Classrooms are then assigned by size required, special equipment required, and course duration. After classrooms are assigned, instructors are assigned based on the courses they can teach. Instructors are given a preliminary schedule of their classes.

Meanwhile, the final classroom assignments are matched with each student's required courses and a student class listing indicating all required courses being offered this semester by instructor, by time, and by classroom is prepared for each student. A complete semester course listing is also provided. Each student fills in the required course listing by indicating his or her class preference numerically (1, 2, 3, . . .) and listing any free classes desired. Students also list up to three substitute courses if any course is unavailable.

The student class request is checked for necessary course, minimum and maximum credit hours, and prerequisites for free courses. Any bad requests are returned to the student with an explanation. All valid requests are saved for the big day of the course assignment. On the big day each course by classroom and by time is open for bid. All students requesting a course as their first priority are assigned up to the maximum class size. If more students than the maximum allowable want a particular course, the following priority scheme is used (preference given to left column).

Credit student	Auditing student
Major	Minor
Minor	Free
Most course credit hours	
Graduate	Undergraduate
Full-time	Part-time
Student failed course previously	
Student audited course	
Most accumulated credit hours	
Highest grade point average	
Postmark date of request	
Coin flip	

Any student denied a course will have their request changed in the following priority: instructor; coursedays; courseperiod (morning or afternoon). If no course is available, substitute course as requested by student. If no substitute course is available, request is sent to student faculty advisor for a resolution. After first priorities are resolved, then second, third, . . . are resolved as above. If any course has less than the minimum, it is then canceled and student courses resolved as above. Unresolved requests are sent to student faculty advisor. Otherwise, final schedule is returned to student and instructor.

Various other departments have heard of the automation plans and requested the following (with the President's approval).

1. Maintenance of all student records, including major(s), minor(s), expected graduation date, enrollment date, previous degrees with date, credits earned, credits being taken this semester, grades, grade point average.

2. Maintenance of all instructor records, including courses can teach and back up. LU also wants to introduce a summary rating for each instructor by course.

3. Generation of possible courses for three semesters in advance based upon instructor availability for courses they can teach.

4. Maintenance of alumni data to generate mailing list for fund raising and funds contributed.

The Registrar has also agreed to assign unique student and instructor numbers. The first two digits are the curriculum-school-number and the last six digits are the student or instructor number within the curriculum school.

Appendix B

Additional Reading Material Provided by Vendors

Many organizations and people have submitted material for this book. Some of the material is technically excellent and I believe would be valuable additional reading. Rather than force the reader to write for all the material, I have incorporated it in this book. All the material has a sales slant since it was written in support of a product. The articles are:

- JSD Technical Summary
  Michael Jackson Systems Limited
  Description of a SDLC from a data decomposition point of view.
- PSL/PSA: An Information Modeling Tool
  Dr. Hasan H. Sayani
  Advanced Systems Technology Corp.
  Description of the Problem Statement Language (PSL) and Problem Statement Analyzer (PSA) for specifying information systems.
- Entity Multityping
  Dr. Ken Winter
  Database Design, Inc.
  Description of subtypes, supertypes, and roles.
- Data Name Rationalization and Building the Data Dictionary
  Adpac Corporation
  A "how-to" article on populating a data dictionary with good data element names from existing systems.

- A Data Element Naming Convention
  Jim Odell
  Database Design, Inc.
  Another approach to naming standards.
- DATADESIGNER User Guide Introduction
  Database Design, Inc.
  A brief introduction to logical database design.
- A Database Design and Evaluation Workbench
  D. Reiner, M. Brodie, G. Brown, M. Chilenskas, M. Friedell, D. Kramlich, J. Lehman, and A. Rosenthal
  Computer Corporation of America
  Description of a future tool that will assist database analysts in designing databases.

JSD Technical Summary

Michael Jackson Systems Limited

JSD: AIMS AND SCOPE

- JSD is Jackson System Development, a method of developing computer-based systems.
- JSD applies to systems whose subject matter has a strong time dimension, that is to systems that are about an evolving reality (or an evolving simulated reality).
- JSD starts from a rough statement of need and covers the technical part of the rest of the life-cycle including the development of a detailed and formal specification, the implementation of this specification, and the subsequent maintenance (enhancements and adjustments to meet changed requirements, perhaps better termed system evolution).
- JSD aims to make software development more methodical, that is, to decompose the systems development task into a number of well-defined steps, each with formally defined outputs, that fit together into a harmonious whole.
- JSD fits very well with iterative approaches to development such as the prototyping or deliberate phasing of projects.

WHAT CHARACTERIZES A METHOD OF SOFTWARE DEVELOPMENT?

A method is an ordering and organization of the decisions that (explicitly or implicitly) make up the development. Examples of decisions are:

1. Specification decisions like
   a. Claims cannot be made on a policy for which the premiums have not been paid.
   b. The daily claims report looks like this.
   c. A telephone user is given a dial-tone if the other party to a call hangs up first.
2. Implementation decisions like
   a. The claims file should be an indexed sequential file.
   b. Claims updating will be done in batch.
   c. Premium updating will be done on-line using XYZ intelligent terminals.
   d. The telephone system will consist of a scheduler, one component capable of being scheduled per telephone and a number of common subroutines.

Of particular importance in the justification of JSD is an analysis of decision independence: Are decisions A and B independent or does one depend on the results of the other?

SPECIFICATION AND IMPLEMENTATION

The most important distinctions in JSD are between specification decisions and implementation decisions and within specification between modelling decisions and functional decisions. (This second distinction is explored in the following section.)

Everything to do with the target hardware/software environment is classified as implementation. Thus choice of machine is implementation; file design is implementation; database design is implementation; decomposition into batch runs is implementation. Most decisions commonly referred to as "design" decisions or "architectural" decisions are really to do with implementation. All these are rigorously excluded from the early specification steps of JSD.

Specification decisions concern what the system is about, what it has to output, how the outputs are to be calculated, and how fast the outputs have to be produced.

A JSD specification consists of a number (potentially a very large number) of sequential processes that communicate by writing and reading data streams and by inspection of state vectors. These forms of communication are described in Appendix 1. The state vector is a collective term for the local variables of a process, including the text pointer.

JSD specifications have the following characteristics:

1. They are, except for some timing constraints, formally expressed and directly executable.
2. For a complete system execution each process in the specification executes exactly once; there is no idea of repeated execution in JSD specifications; the lifetime of the processes may be very long (tens of years for a DP system); each process executes slowly because its inputs arrive gradually over its whole lifetime.
3. The only data in the system is the data local to the various specification processes;

thus although data can be accessed through state vector inspection of other processes, it can only be changed by the unique process to which it belongs.

In the following section we describe how a JSD specification is built up, and in the section after that we describe how such specifications are implemented.

MODEL AND FUNCTION

The major separation in the development of a JSD specification is between the model and the function. The model is an abstraction of the subject matter of the system expressed as a set of almost completely disconnected sequential processes. The elementary components of the processes are relevant actions (events); the processes describe their possible orderings. An entity in JSD is the name of one of these processes.

During the development of the model questions must be asked about the range of the abstraction (should more, or less, or different actions have been selected?) and about its accuracy (do the processes describe exactly the permissible sequences of actions?).

For a pure information system the actions in the model are exact reflections of events in the reality about which information is required. When one of these external events occurs, an input is created to the model. When the model process reads this input, and partially executes, it is coordinating itself with the reality that it is modelling.

For a simulation, the actions are events in the simulated reality. Inputs for each action are generated not by connection with the external world, as for an information system, but by additional processes that express the assumptions of the simulation.

In many control and data processing systems the model has a mixture of external, real-world actions and internally generated (simulated) action. In a telephone switching system, for example, there is a model process for each telephone. These processes are an abstraction that describes telephone service. Actions include external events like ''lift'' and ''replace'' handset and events like ''request to start a call'' that (with no switchboard operator) are generated by the system. The ordering of these different events is significant. A ''lift'' after a ''request'' means that the user is answering a call; a ''lift'' before a ''request'' means that the user is starting his own call and the request should be refused. The model processes describe telephone service by ascribing meaning to the permissible orderings of actions.

In JSD the model is developed first, before attention is focussed directly on

1. The outputs of the system and how they are calculated
2. Before the exact conditions are determined for the generation (simulation) of the actions that do not originate externally
3. Before the exact means of collecting data for external actions is worked out

These three areas are addressed, approximately in parallel, by the three subsequent steps of the method.

In JSD systems are not conceived as mathematical functions that map system inputs to outputs. Instead the model plays an intermediate role. Outputs are the result of functions whose domain is the model (and some functionally oriented inputs like enquiries). The role of the (rest of the) inputs is to coordinate the model with the actions in the external reality.

IMPLEMENTATION IN JSD

There are three major issues in the JSD implementation phase:

1. The scheduling of the many processes in the specification on (probably) a much smaller number of processors (often the scheduling is fixed by the design of a special purpose scheduler)
2. The transformation of the specification processes so that they fit with the general purpose or specially created schedulers and other implementation framework software
3. Designing the storage structures (tables, files, databases, etc.) and accessing capability on the state vectors (local data) of the specification processes

The most important transformations are program inversion, state vector separation, program dismemberment and state vector dismemberment. They are briefly described in Appendix 2.

A traditional implementation of a simple data processing system has

Some master files, perhaps on a database

Programs (on-line or batch) that update the master files

Reporting programs

Enquiry answering programs

Error checking programs

JCL and operator instructions

The records on the master files are the state vectors (local data) of the model processes. The updating programs partially execute the model processes, usually by calling the inverted model process (see Appendix 2) as an update subroutine. The reporting, enquiry, and error processing programs correspond to the non-model processes in the specification. JSC and operator instructions are usually implementations of a special purpose scheduler.

In JSD scheduling is largely fixed at build time (as opposed to run time) for efficiency reasons. A batch scheduling, for example, gives each instance of a process type enough processor time once per batch period to catch up on its backlog of input. In real-time embedded systems the binding of the scheduling is no less important; it allows many specification processes to be combined into a single schedulable unit.

JSD DEVELOPMENT STEPS

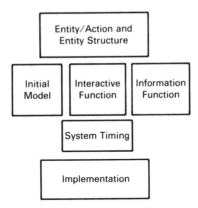

The arrangement of the diagram indicates that the second, third, and fourth step can be carried out largely independently of each other.

1. *Entity/action and entity structure step:* Actions are defined, and their possible time orderings expressed in a set of structure diagrams.

2. *Initial model step:* The actions are divided into those that are genuine actions in the world external to the system and those that have to be generated (simulated). A connection is established between the reality and the model processes. Error handling processes are added to make this connection more reliable.

3. *Interactive function step:* Processes are added to the specification to generate those model actions that are not external to the system. In general these processes extract information from the model as well as generating actions: hence the term interactive functions.

4. *Information function step:* Processes are added to the specification to extract information from the model, and to process it to produce the system outputs. In this and the previous step the model processes may be elaborated in limited ways, principally by the addition of new local variables (thus enlarging the state vector and, after implementation, the master records of the entity).

5. *System timing step:* Necessary timing constraints on the execution speeds of the various processes are added to the specification.

6. *Implementation step:* The scheduling of the many specification processes is settled, by using a general purpose scheduler, by creating a special purpose scheduling scheme, or by a mixture of the two. The specification processes are transformed (see Appendix 2) to fit with this scheme. The state vectors are organized into a suitable file or database design.

SHAPE OF A JSD SPECIFICATION

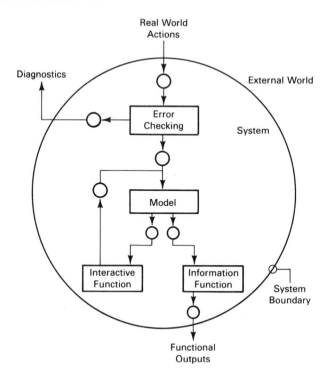

The diagram is highly schematic. Only one process type is shown for each of the first four major steps of the method; only data stream connections are shown; there is no multiplicity between any of the process types.

ADVANTAGES OF THE JSD APPROACH

The most important distinctive features of JSD are:

1. The separation of model and function in the development of the specification
2. The central role in JSD implementation of transformations on the specification

Defining and agreeing on a formal model forces the developer towards a deeper understanding of the problem area, eases difficulties of communication between user and developer and provides the basis for specifying and understanding the functional requirement. The function is defined in terms of the entities and actions of the model: that is, in terms of an abstraction with which a user is comfortable.

A model can support a coherent family of functions. In JSD this family of functions is (indirectly) specified first, and then the particular functional requirement is chosen. Subsequent maintenance within this family is relatively easy.

JSD uses the process as a modelling medium. In JSD specifications, data is not considered in isolation from the processes that change it. It is no more appropriate to define a database separately from updating routines than to declare the variables of a program completely separately from the procedures that use them.

Transformation yields a very attractive answer to the question posed during a system acceptance test, "How can we be sure that the implemented system meets the specification". Provided that the transformations used are known to preserve the specification, we only have to check that they have been carried out correctly.

A unity is established among a wide class of systems, particularly between data processing and real-time embedded systems. JSD *is* more methodical:

1. The specification is built up in increments, each of which is completely and formally defined.
2. There is no time-consuming and confusing restatement of system characteristics, for example, between requirements documents and design documents, or between program specifications and program.
3. The specification is transformed, not input to a design process that effectively starts from scratch.

APPENDIX 1: JSD SPECIFICATION MEDIUM

SYSTEM SPECIFICATION DIAGRAMS

A JSD specification consists of a set of communicating sequential processes. A System Specification Diagram (SSD) describes the way these processes communicate.

There are two basic types of communication: by data stream and by state vector. On an SSD, rectangles represent processes, circles represent data streams and diamonds represent state vector connections.

Data Stream Connection

The diagram shows the process P writing the data stream F which is read by the process Q. F is an infinitely buffered first-in-first-out queue. P writes records that are eventually all read by Q in the order they were written.

Data stream connection has the following characteristics:

1. The initiative for the communication lies with P; P decided when and what to write; Q cannot use the data stream F to influence P.

2. Because of the infinite buffering, P can never be blocked trying to write.

3. If Q tries to execute a "read F" operation and no record is available, the Q is blocked. It can only continue to execute when a record of F becomes available.

4. If, for some reason, Q does not execute "read F" operations for some time, no information is lost. A backlog of records will simply have built up in the buffer.

There are two variants of simple data stream connection involving, respectively, multiple inputs to a process, and communication with multiple instances of a process type.

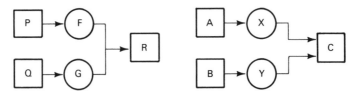

In the left diagram F and G are "rough merged" inputs to R. That means that F and G are read by R as if they were one stream by a single "read F/G" operation. The algorithm for merging F and G is as yet unspecified and must, at some level of granularity, involve some possible unfairness—hence the "rough" in "rough merge." Usually F and G are consumed more or less in the order they are written and then the merging depends on the relative speed of execution, or relative scheduling, or P and Q. The rough merge is indicated by the joining of the lines into R into a single arrowhead.

By contrast, the lines from X and Y into C have separate arrowheads. This implies that X and Y are read by C as separate data streams using distinct "read X" and "read Y" operations. The relative speed of consumption of X and Y is determined by the relative frequency of these operations in the execution of C.

The first of the diagrams below shows the process P writing an F data stream to each of many Q instances. When P writes a record it writes it to a particular named F. Double bars indicate relative multiplicity. In this diagram there could still be many P processes. Each P would write to many Qs; and Q would be written to by only one P. The second diagram shows many R processes each writing a G stream. The G streams are rough merged and read by a single S process. The final diagram shows a many-to-many communication between A type processes and B type processes. Each A process writes to many Bs. Each B process reads records from many As.

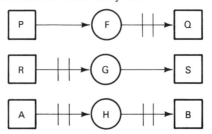

State Vector Connection

The diagram shows the process Q with a connection that enables it to examine the state vector of the process P. The state vector of a process is a collective term for all the local variables of the process including the text-pointer, the variable whose value indicates how far the process has reached in its text. When Q executes a "get SV of P" operation the state of P is made available to Q. No operation is executed in P for this communication to take place. State vector inspection is invisible to the inspected process.

State vector inspection has the following characteristics:

1. The initiative for the communication lies with Q. Q decides when to extract information.
2. If for some reason Q does not execute any "get SV" operations for a period, it simply misses what has been happening in P. No backlog of information builds up.
3. Q can never be blocked on a "get SV" operation.
4. State vector inspection is loose in the sense that the values returned depend on how much of P has executed, and therefore also on P's speed of execution. State vector inspection may only be used in a specification where we are prepared to accept the indeterminacy resulting from lack of knowledge of this speed.

The same multiplicity notation is used for state vector connection as for data stream connection.

Q inspects many Ps. Many Ys each inspect many Xs.

STRUCTURE DIAGRAMS AND STRUCTURE TEXT

Structure Diagrams and Structure Text both define the internal structure of processes using sequence, selection and iteration, the normal structured programming constructs. In JSD (and in Jackson Structured Programming, the related programming method) processes are defined first by expressing their structure diagramatically, elaborating the structure with the elementary executable operations of the process, converting the resulting diagram to a textual form, adding the conditions and, if necessary, handling any backtracking.

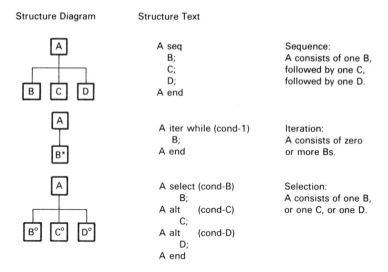

Structure Diagram   Structure Text

A seq   Sequence:
  B;   A consists of one B,
  C;   followed by one C,
  D;   followed by one D.
A end

A iter while (cond-1)   Iteration:
  B;   A consists of zero
A end   or more Bs.

A select (cond-B)   Selection:
  B;   A consists of one B,
A alt   (cond-C)   or one C, or one D.
  C;
A alt   (cond-D)
  D;
A end

There is also a textual form of the posit/quit/admit backtracking construct.

APPENDIX 2: COMMON TRANSFORMATIONS IN JSD IMPLEMENTATION

PROGRAM INVERSION

Program inversion transforms a process into a variable-state procedure by the addition of a suspend-and-resume mechanism. When the procedure is invoked the process resumes where it left off, partially executes and then suspends itself again. Suspend points are associated with the read/write operations of one or more data streams. The records of these data streams are passed across the procedure interface, downwards on resumption for a read operation in the inverted program, and upwards on suspension for a write.

In essence the suspend-and-resume mechanism is very simple, though some details must be handled with care. A variable, conventionally called QS, is assigned a different value at each suspend/resume point; the assignment is followed by a return statement and a label. A branch is inserted at the beginning of the procedure that transfers control to the appropriate label, according to the value of QS.

QS must be initialized so that on the very first invocation the procedure begins at the beginning of the process text; if the inversion involves two or more data streams the interface must include information so that the invoking level knows the reason for the suspension; in many languages, the structured coding constructs cannot be used for the selections and iterations in the process specification because they prevent a branch to a resume point in their middle.

STATE VECTOR SEPARATION

JSD specifications almost always contain many instances of different process types. For example there may be one process in the specification per insurance policy or per telephone. The instances of one type have the same text, but as they execute concurrently they do so at their own pace and with their own particular local variables.

The state vector of a process is a collective term for its local variables, including its text pointer. (The variable QS is a text pointer whose values are limited to a restricted set.) State vector separation implements many instances of a single process type by a single copy of their text and multiple copies of their state vectors. The local variables, including QS, of the inverted process are made part of the procedure interface. The invoking level is made responsible for the storage and retrieval of the state vectors. To execute process instance X partially, the invoking level retrieves the state vector of X, calls the generalized inverted procedure with the state vector as a parameter, and stores the updated state vector of X when the procedure returns.

The results of state vector separation are familiar in many computer systems, for example in the software that handles the multiple terminals of a teleprocessing system.

PROGRAM DISMEMBERMENT

Program dismemberment is a term covering those transformations that take a process text and implement it in several parts, perhaps in different languages. A report producing process may have a high level iteration. The iterated component produces, for example, one report. Input accumulates for the process at a rate corresponding to one report per week. The whole process may be dismembered into two parts: the iterated component becomes a weekly batch program that produces one report; the upper iteration becomes the operator instructions that run the program.

Another example of dismemberment comes from an on-line or real-time environment. A process is inverted with respect to its single input stream. For a given type of input record, or for a given value of QS, only a subset of its text can be executed on a single invocation. Separate (possibly overlapping) modules can be created, either for each input record type, or for each value of QS. In practice values of QS are usually grouped and separate modules are created for subsets of QS values.

STATE VECTOR DISMEMBERMENT

Any program dismemberment may give rise to a corresponding state vector dismemberment. Some local variables may not be used by a particular module. It may be more economical to store these parts of the state vector separately.

State vector dismemberment may be desirable quite separately from program dismemberment. A function process may deal with a high volume of enquiries each of which requires inspection of only a part of the state vector of another process. For example in a banking application there may be many enquiries on customers' balances. The balance part of the account state vector may be stored separately from the rest, for efficiency reasons.

The useful size of the state vector of the telephone process in a call processing application varies from very small when the telephone is not in use; large when a call is being set up; much smaller when the call is in progress; large again when the call is ended; and then back to very small. Space can be optimized by dividing the state vector into parts that are needed at these different times of the telephone's life. There may be a similar variable useful size of the state vector during the life time of an insurance policy.

PSL/PSA: An Information Modeling Tool

Hasan H. Sayani,
Advanced Systems Technology Corp. (ASTEC),
Greenbelt, Maryland

INTRODUCTION

The Problem Statement Language (PSL)/ Problem Statement Analyzer (PSA) is a tool for specifying information systems (IS). PSL is a language for specifying the IS, and PSA is a software package that supports the use of PSL. PSL/PSA has been under development since 1968 and is now in its fifth major revision. It is used in government and commerce and at universities.

The development of IS can be thought of as a problem-solving process. PSL/PSA is particularly suited to the support of the major phases of the problem-solving process:

The formalization of tentative visualizations

The expression of these formalizations

Reflection on these specifications

Analysis of the specifications

Modification of the specifications

Delivery of these specifications to the next phase

The basis of PSL is the popular entity relation model. The entities and relations used in PSL are those relevant for describing an IS. A formal syntax is placed around this model to allow for linguistic specification of an IS. A graphic expression is also feasible if a graphic terminal is available.

The PSA software utilizes a network-oriented database management system to store the specifications and to provide the support needed to review these specifications, analyze them, modify them, and to present them for further development along the life cycle.

PSL

While the text focuses attention on the data aspects of an IS, PSL allows not only data but also functional and control aspects of an IS to be specified. Moreover, PSL may be used to specify not merely the "logical" facets, but also the "physical" aspects of an IS.

Aspects of PSL

The scope of the language may best be categorized by the aspects of an IS that may be described. PSL can describe the flow of an IS, its architecture, dynamics, quantification, and other characteristics.

Levels of Formality in PSL

PSL permits three levels of formality. Expressions made in the highly formal fashion are well understood by PSA and permit the highest degree of analysis via the PSA software. Statements made in the very informal mode are merely carried in the database and associated with the IS components. These are in the form of narrative descriptions. There is also an intermediate form which allows the specifier to assign special properties to the components. PSA is not able to interpret the appropriateness of these values, but is able to retrieve the components by those characteristics, and to present the information in various forms, such as tables.

Adaptability to Methodologies

Most IS development approaches recognize the need for a systematic method of specifying or designing it. Hence, rather than haphazardly flail at various facets of the system, advocates specify a particular approach to the development process. The method of Gane and Sarson is one such approach. PSL/PSA may be adapted to any methodology. It does not insist on any particular starting point, nor does it require a prescribed set of steps to be followed. PSL/PSA lets the IS developers start at their focus (e.g., at the central process) and proceed either layer by layer, or all the way down to the primitive process without regard to relevant data, as desired. Typically, PSL/PSA is used with some methodology.

PSL's Role in the Problem-Solving Process

Whereas methodologies such as the approach suggested by Gane and Sarson specify techniques for "visualizing" the IS being developed, PSL is used for formally expressing these visualizations, to remove ambiguity that remains even in these well-defined diagrams and accompanying data dictionaries.

PSA

PSA is a software package that accepts PSL statements. These statements may be made at different times, by various team members (perhaps even geographically dispersed). PSA synthesizes these statements and maintains them in a database; of course, statements that contradict prior statements are not accepted. However, incomplete specifications are not brought to the user's attention unless explicitly requested. Requests for snapshots of portions of the database may be made at any time via PSA reports. With the capabilities described above, PSA is a good tool for supporting the problem-solving process referred to earlier.

PSA as a Support for the Remaining Facets of Problem Solving

PSL takes care of the formalization of visualizations prescribed by an IS development methodology. It also allows for the expression of these formalizations linguistically. It is PSA that supports the remaining phases of the problem-solving process.

Reflecting on the Specifications To-Date   For any system that needs more than a page of specifications, it becomes necessary periodically to review the specifications to-date. This is helpful to pick up and move on from where the specifier left off the previous day, or to examine retrospectively to see if the specifications are appropriate. PSA has a set of reports which allow the user to evaluate these specifications without critical comments; i.e., they present an ''as-is'' snapshot of the system. These reports can be obtained as indented-lists (e.g., the CONTENTS report), as diagrams (e.g., the PICTURE report), or as text (e.g., the DICTIONARY report). Examples of some of these reports are included at the end of this appendix.

Analyzing the Specifications   When a significant milestone is reached (as specified by the methodology), PSA may be used to analyze the completeness of that facet of the specifications. There are standard reports that check for loose ends (e.g., the DATA-ACTIVITY-INTERACTION report), and also customizable checks that can be made via the QUERY SYSTEM, which is part of PSA. Examples of some of these reports are also shown here.

Modifying the Specifications   Typically, both reflection and analysis may lead one to change the specifications in the PSA database. PSA provides comprehensive and convenient mechanisms for changing any facet of the specifications made—whether they be at the formal or informal level, and in any characteristic: flow, structure, control, or properties. PSA modifier commands ensure that a change made in one portion is properly reflected everywhere else that it is relevant. Moreover, the modifier commands also guard against the introduction of inconsistencies as a result of their use. Finally, they leave behind both a paper and an electronic audit trail to mark the changes.

Delivery of the Specifications to the Next Phase   Typically, an IS development process progresses from sketches, to formal specifications, to design specifications, to coding specifications, etc. Hence it is important to take the specifications at any phase and hand them over to the next phase with minimum distortion. Current techniques call for the production of standard documents that must be produced at the end of each phase. PSA comes with the Documentation Generator, which permits the intermingling of free-form text with PSA commands and formatting commands. Hence it is possible to produce a document which follows the organizational standards (e.g., DoD 7935), without requiring a manual transcription of the specifications already in the PSA database.

If, the next phase happens to use an automated tool, PSA databases can be presented to these tools without the necessity of producing any paper (unless, of course, the organizational standards require it). An example of such an automated tool is the Logical Database Designer produced by ASTEC. This tool accepts a PSA database and a directive about the portion of the data specifications that are to be used for design, and produces a logical database design wherein data is appropriately normalized. An example of this product is also shown in the attached.

Once the database has been designed and program specifications have to be generated, PSA can aid in this process, too. For example, a Cobol Data Division may be generated from a PSA design database (via the DATA-DIVISION report).

Characteristics of PSA Relevant for Managers

PSA is written in a machine-portable fashion and is available on most major main-frames, midis, and minis. Although it can be run on super-micros, it is unreasonable to expect an adequate performance for large databases on a small machine. However, current technology makes it quite appropriate to run PSA on a desktop machine (e.g., it is being used successfully on the 32-bit Hewlett-Packard 9000/series 500 machines).

PSA databases are transportable across implementations of PSA. Hence, if a contractor wished to develop an IS on his local minicomputer but was required to transport the specifications to his customer's main-frame, it would literally be a question of making sure that the tape produced by him would be readable on the main frame.

Finally, PSL/PSA is adequately supported with courses, consulting and other help from ASTEC. The tool has a history of usage by various organizations and user groups.

EXAMPLES OF PSL/PSA AND LDBD

PSL Statements Showing the Flow To and From STUDENT:

```
DEFINE INTERFACE STUDENT;

    RECEIVES STUDENT-CLASS-CAT, STUDENT-CLASS-SCHEDULE,

        STUDENT-REPORT-CARD;

    GENERATES STUDENT-CLASS-REQUEST, INSTRUCTOR-GRADE;
```

PICTURE report

This report depicts the information flow to and from the STUDENT.

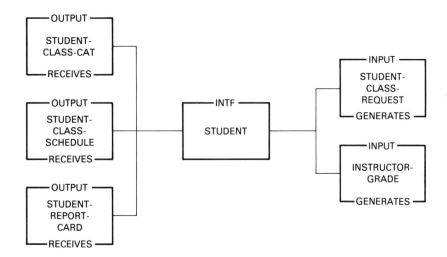

DATA-ACTIVITY-INTERACTION report

This report shows the analyses of information flow at the top level. In this data activity interaction matrix, the rows are data names, the columns are activity names.

```
8  FACILITIES
7  DEAN-OF-SCHOOL
6  INSTRUCTOR
5  REGISTRAR
4  STUDENT
3  STUDENT-FACULTY-ADVISOR
2  SCHEDULE-CLASSES
1  ALUMNI-ASSOC
```

1	ALUMNI-CHANGES	D	R		
2	ALUMNI-MAILING-LIST	R	D		
3	UNRESOLVED-CLASSES		D	R	
4	STUDENT-CLASS-CAT		D		R
5	THREE-SEM-COUR-LIST		D			R
6	STUDENT-CLASS-SCHEDULE		D	R	
7	STUDENT-REPORT-CARD		D	R	
8	PREL-CLASS-SCHD		D			R
9	INST-CLASS-SCHD		D			R
10	INST-RATING		D			R
11	INSTRUCTOR-SUMMARY-RATING		D				R
12	CLASSROOM-CHANGES		R					D
13	STUDENT-CHANGES		R		D
14	STUDENT-CLASS-REQUEST		R	D	
15	INSTRUCTOR-GRADE		R	D	
16	STUDENT-GRADE		R		D
17	INSTRUCTOR-SUMMARY		R		
18	INSTRUCTOR-CHANGES		R			D
19	CURRICULUM-CHANGES		R			D
20	COURSE-CHANGES		R			D

The data activity interaction matrix analysis is

```
Activities
----------

FACILITIES                    (INTERFACE) (Column   8)
    Does Not Receive Any Data
```

(*Note:* The error diagnostic indicates that FACILITIES provides data but does not receive any data.)

QUERY-SYSTEM

This usage shows

> All ENTITIES that "course-number" IDENTIFIES
> All ENTITIES or GROUPS that are not IDENTIFIED

Enter query:

```
LIST course-number IDENTIFIES ?;

        Set Name: ** not defined **
        Query:    course-number IDENTIFIES ?
        The Number of Objects is:    2
        The Objects are:

        Object Name                      Object Type
        -----------                      -----------


        COURSE-ATTENDANCE-HISTORY        ENTITY
        COURSE-DATA                      ENTITY
```

Enter query:

```
LIST (ENTITY OR GROUP) AND NOT ? IDENTIFIED BY !;

        Set Name: ** not defined **
        Query:    (ENTITY OR GROUP) AND NOT ? IDENTIFIED BY !
        The Number of Objects is:    9
        The Objects are:

          Object Name                    Object Type
          -----------                    -----------


          alumni-degree-previous         GROUP
          classroom-dayofweek            GROUP
          classroom.equipment-special    GROUP
          classroom.instructor-name      GROUP
          instructor-degree-previous     GROUP
          instructor.course-history      GROUP
          major/minor.course-rqmts       GROUP
          student-degree-previous        GROUP
          student.course-history         GROUP
```

CONTENTS report

This report shows the structure of STUDENT-DATA before normalization.

```
        (ENTITY)      1 STUDENT-DATA
        (ELEMENT)     2   student-number
        (ELEMENT)     2   student-name
        (ELEMENT)     2   student-status
        (ELEMENT)     2   student-home-address
        (ELEMENT)     2   student-home-phone
```

(ELEMENT)	2	student-dt-graduation-expected
(ELEMENT)	2	student-date-enrollment
(ELEMENT)	2	student.instructor-num-advisor
(ELEMENT)	2	student.curriculum-school-name
(GROUP)	2	student.course-history (many)
(ELEMENT)	3	student.course.semester-taken
(ELEMENT)	3	student.course-number-taken
(ELEMENT)	3	student.course-title
(ELEMENT)	3	student.course-hr-credit-taken
(ELEMENT)	3	student.course-hr-credit-earned
(ELEMENT)	3	student.course-grade-earned
(ELEMENT)	2	student.major (upto-two)
(ELEMENT)	2	student.minor (upto-two)
(GROUP)	2	student-degree-previous (many)
(ELEMENT)	3	student-degree-type-previous
(ELEMENT)	3	student-dt-graduation-previous

Examples of Use of the Logical Database Design Software[1]

ALUMNI-DATA as received by the Design Analyst

(ENTITY)	1	ALUMNI-DATA
(ELEMENT)	2	alumni-number
(ELEMENT)	2	alumni-name
(ELEMENT)	2	alumni-home-address
(ELEMENT)	2	alumni-home-phone
(ELEMENT)	2	alumni-employer-name
(ELEMENT)	2	alumni-employer-address
(ELEMENT)	2	alumni-contribution-year-this
(ELEMENT)	2	alumni-contribution-summary
(GROUP)	2	alumni-degree-previous (many)
(ELEMENT)	3	alumni-degree-type-previous
(ELEMENT)	3	alumni-data-gradn-previous

ALUMNI-DATA as modified by the Design Analyst

(ENTITY)	1	ALUMNI-DATA
(ELEMENT)	2	alumni-number
(ELEMENT)	2	alumni-name
(ELEMENT)	2	alumni-home-address
(ELEMENT)	2	alumni-home-phone
(ELEMENT)	2	alumni-employer-name
(ELEMENT)	2	alumni-employer-address
(ELEMENT)	2	alumni-contribution-year-this
(ELEMENT)	2	alumni-contribution-summary
(GROUP)	2	alumni-degree-previous (many)
(GROUP)	3	alumni-degree-previous-key

[1]In the following examples, identifiers are underlined.

```
(ELEMENT)        4         alumni-data-gradn-previous
(ELEMENT)        4         alumni-number
(ELEMENT)        3         alumni-degree-type-previous
```

ALUMNI-DATA as designed by the Logical Database Design Software   As the report on the next page shows, it has been broken up into two entities with a Relation between them:

```
(ENTITY)        1 ALUMNI-DATA
(ELEMENT)       2   alumni-number
(ELEMENT)       2   alumni-name
(ELEMENT)       2   alumni-home-address
(ELEMENT)       2   alumni-home-phone
(ELEMENT)       2   alumni-employer-name
(ELEMENT)       2   alumni-employer-address
(ELEMENT)       2   alumni-contribution-year-this
(ELEMENT)       2   alumni-contribution-summary
```

Reports produced by the Logical Database Design software for what used to be ALUMNI-DATA

Report 1: Created entity linkage report

```
          From Created Entity: alumni-degree-previous@5


Thru                              Linkage To Created Entity
----------------------------      ------- -------------------------
RD1@5                             many: 1  ALUMNI-DATA
```

Report 2: Created entity summary

```
**
**   Created Entity: alumni-degree-previous@5
**

Key or Concatenated Key
-----------------------

(alumni-number + alumni-data-gradn-previous)

Members
------------

alumni-number
alumni-degree-type-previous
alumni-data-gradn-previous
```

```
Thru                                To   Created Entity              Link
--------------------------        -----  --------------------------  ----
RD1@5                                    ALUMNI-DATA                  many
```

Report 33: Created entity diagram

```
┌── alumni-degree-previous @ 5 ───────────── ENTITY ──┐
│                                                      │
│   alumni-number, alumni-data-gradn-previous          │
│                                                      │
│   alumni-degree-type-previous                        │
│                                                      │
└──────────────────────────────────────────────────────┘
```

Entity Multityping

Ken Winter Database Design, Inc.

Get ready for multityping—you're going to be hearing a lot about it in the months to come. It provides a major advance in the richness and completeness of the information that an information system can handle.

Standard data modeling languages have the following troublesome limitation: Each entity—each individual thing about which an information system is supposed to contain data—is supposed to be an instance of exactly one entity type (data group, in DATA DESIGNER parlance). All we can use to describe that entity are the attributes and associations of that one entity type. We call such a data language a *monotyping language*.

But the things we have to describe are not that simple. Take an entity type such as good old EMPLOYEE. Suppose that every EMPLOYEE works for a DEPARTMENT, has a PHONE #, is assigned to one or more PROJECTs, and so on. In other words, EMPLOYEE has legitimate attributes and associations and is a perfectly respectable entity type.

But there are attributes and associations that only some EMPLOYEEs can have. Only FEMALE EMPLOYEEs, let's suppose, can take MATERNITY LEAVEs; only MALE EMPLOYEEs can have a DRAFT STATUS; HOURLY EMPLOYEEs have a WAGE, belong to a UNION, and have a certain PENSION PLAN; SALARIED EMPLOYEEs have a SALARY, never belong to unions, and have a different PENSION PLAN, requiring different attributes to describe it. So we have at least four more valid entity types: MALE EMPLOYEE, FEMALE EMPLOYEE, HOURLY EMPLOYEE, SALARIED EMPLOYEE.

Now take the individual entity named Sally Smith. If we can put her in only one of these categories, then whichever one we choose we lose some of the information we need to describe her. If we call her a FEMALE EMPLOYEE we lose the fact that she's also an EMPLOYEE, we don't know whether to pay her a wage or salary, etc. Other classifications of Sally would lead to similar dilemmas.

Moreover, this is not just a case of bad data modeling. There is no obvious way to reorganize a monotyping data model so that it will capture even these fairly simple differences among different groups of employees.

The best answer is a *multityping* data language, whose basic premise is that each individual entity can be an instance of one *or more* entity types—as many as are needed to describe that individual. The entity types themselves are like those in a monotyping system, that is, each has its own complement of attributes and associations (which we now refer to collectively as the *predicates* of the entity type). What's new is that an entity's description now consists of the predicates of *all of the entity types into which that individual has been classified.*

In our example, if Sally Smith is classified as an EMPLOYEE, a FEMALE EMPLOYEE, and a SALARIED EMPLOYEE, her description will include a DEPARTMENT assignment, possibly some MATERNITY LEAVEs, a SALARY, etc.; and it won't include a DRAFT STATUS or a UNION membership. We can know all this just by knowing how Sally is (and isn't) classified. And all of this information remains undisturbed if Sally turns out to be an instance of still more types (perhaps SUPERVISOR, STOCKHOLDER, or CUSTOMER): the predicates of these types are simply added to her description.

A multityping data system can capture many kinds of information that lie beyond the grasp of monotyping systems. One is to keep track of which instances of various entity types are actually the same individual, enabling it to answer queries such as "Is the EMPLOYEE named 'Sally Smith' the same person as the STOCKHOLDER named 'Sally Smith'?"

Another new kind of information in multityping models is what we call *classification constraints*. These are rules specified in the data model about what entity types can and can't have members in common. Classification constraints come in three kinds:

1. The most important is *subtype/supertype*. This says that one entity type (the subtype) is a subset of another (the supertype). In other words, the subtype is a particular "kind" or "special case" of the supertype. FEMALE EMPLOYEE in our example is a subtype of EMPLOYEE. Every entity that is an instance of the subtype is also an instance of the supertype, and therefore has all the supertype's predicates. If we know that Sally Smith is a FEMALE EMPLOYEE, we also know that she is an EMPLOYEE, and thus that she is assigned to one or more PROJECTs. This kind of inference is called "property inheritance" in artificial intelligence circles.

2. The *exclusivity* constraint says that two entity types cannot have any members in common: An entity that is an instance of one can't be an instance of the other. For example, if Sally Smith is a FEMALE EMPLOYEE, then she can't be a MALE

EMPLOYEE, and so won't have the predicates of MALE EMPLOYEEs. Somewhat more subtly, an exclusivity constraint between HOURLY EMPLOYEE and SALARIED EMPLOYEE would document a company policy that no EMPLOYEE can be both hourly and salaried, while the absence of that constraint would mean that the company permits an EMPLOYEE to have both statuses.

3. The *covering* constraint indicates that some set of subtypes "covers" its supertype: every instance of the supertype must be an instance of at least one of the subtypes. For example: Could there be an EMPLOYEE who is neither hourly nor salaried? Yes, unless the data model contains a covering constraint asserting that HOURLY EMPLOYEE and SALARIED EMPLOYEE "cover" EMPLOYEE, their common supertype.

The enumeration of an entity supertype, its subtypes, and their exclusivity/covering constraints we call a "subtyping" of the entity.

SUBTYPINGS AREN'T RELATIONSHIPS

As the above discussion makes clear, each entity subtype is a respectable entity type in its own right, having attributes and associations with other entity types. But we now have two kinds of connections that can exist between entity types:

1. Those that represent a way of relating *two distinct real world individuals,* as in "EMPLOYEE works for DEPARTMENT"

2. Those that say "ENTITY A is a subtype of ENTITY B," that is, *two different classifications of the same real world individuals.*

Unfortunately, in a monotyping data language, there is no way to distinguish between these two cases, so both end up (improperly) called "relationships." We now reserve the word "relationship" for associations of the former kind, above.

HOW TO REFLECT SUBTYPINGS IN DATA DESIGNER

Today's DATA DESIGNER is based on a monotyping language. (I am pleased to add that a new multityping version was released during 1984.) While, as such, you can't describe a full subtyping with all its classification constraints, you can at least describe the differences in attributes and links between a supertype and its subtypes. The steps to follow are:

1. If you find yourself about to model an attribute that is a "type code," e.g., MALE, FEMALE, or SALARIED/HOURLY—STOP! Ask yourself, "Are there important differences in attributes or relationships that depend on the type code value?" If so, follow the rest of the rules below.

2. Append the type-code values to the supertype key name to form ''subtype pseudo-keys.'' For example, if EMP# is the key for EMPLOYEE, you might make the MALE/FEMALE subtype keys EMP #-M'' and EMP#-F.'' Be sure to indicate in your data dictionary that all three of these keys have identical domains (i.e., the set of valid employee numbers).

3. When bubblecharting attributes or relationships of all members of the subtyping (e.g., of all EMPLOYEES, regardless of sex) show them as dependent on the supertype key (EMP#).

4. When bubblecharting attributes or relationships that pertain to only one subtype, show them as arrows off the appropriate subtype pseudo-key.

5. On at least one bubblechart, show a one-to-one association between the supertype key and each of its subtype pseudo-keys. (Some analysts like to label each one-to-one arrow with an IF statement that clarifies the basis of the subtyping).

The accompanying figure shows a bubblechart that accomplishes the above for our EMPLOYEE example of sex-based subtypes.

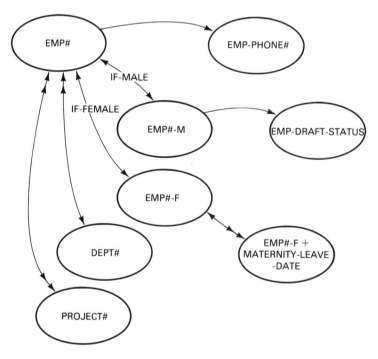

Be aware that under this scheme, EMP#, EMP#-F, and EMP#-M will be listed as candidate keys on Report 6 because of the one-to-one relationship used to identify the subtyping. As these are all really names for the same data item, you can ignore these Report 6 entries.

Here are a few other hints:

1. Some user views will pertain only to one subtype (for example, a view for the transaction "record maternity leave" pertains only to FEMALE EMPLOYEEs). Be sure to use the subtype key in such views.
2. Use the DATA DESIGNER reports (Report 2 is my favorite) to verify that your subtyping was worthwhile. That is, if a subtype has no important attributes or relationships that are peculiar to it, go back to using a type-code attribute off the supertype key. There's no sense cluttering a model with data groups that add little or no additional information.

THE POWER OF MULTITYPING

So why should you care? Because a multityped model:

1. Minimizes "null violations," that is, empty fields in your database (e.g., female employee records with blank draft statuses) because you can make each supertype and subtype a distinct data group.
2. Provides more exact transaction control (for example, you would know that the "Record Maternity Leave" only needs to process FEMALE-EMPLOYEE instances). Considerations of this sort may lead you to make separate physical files for the various subtypes to cut processing time for some transactions.
3. If proper administrative and program controls are built in to ensure that the same real world individual has the same key value in all its supertype and subtype instances, you can suddenly deliver more information to your users. Now you *can* tell if Sally Smith, the EMPLOYEE, is the same Sally Smith, the STOCKHOLDER.
4. Your data model can contain new kinds of information. If properly implemented it can, for example, automatically ensure that no FEMALE EMPLOYEE is ever assigned a draft status. Data entry people would not have to worry about enforcing these rules.
5. Your databases will be better positioned to make use of advances in DBMSs that support automatic "property inheritance" and other sophisticated, artificial-intelligence-like inferences.

These are just a few of the powers that multityping adds to information systems. We continue to discover further benefits that follow from this fairly simple innovation, and through future DDI tools, we will make them available to you.

Programming Machine/ Standard Solutions:[1] Application 4—Data Name Rationalization and Building the Data Dictionary

Adpac Corporation

Data-name rationalization is the procedure used to identify all of the same physical data elements in a system of code, regardless of their given names, and reassigning each a unique self identify name. There are many steps in the complete procedure. Some of these PM/SS fully automates, others require man/machine interaction. Once a 'clean' list of unique names has been prepared, they can be globally substituted throughout the system. As the final step, PM/SS automatically creates the particular input file required for virtually any data dictionary such as DATAMANAGER, DB/DC, IDMS, etc.

Most data dictionaries include procedures for converting existing COBOL record layouts into data dictionary input. Unfortunately, while there is a great deal of software available to perform this mechanical step, *it is undesirable to enter data elements into a dictionary in this manner*. The difficulty is that the existing COBOL programs contain the accumulated history of improper names (aliases) that, once entered into the dictionary, are difficult to remove. Thus, when these methods have been applied, the integrity of the data dictionary is compromised and, therefore, its usefulness diminished.

Application Nos. 3, 8, and 9 should also be read, since they contain additional analysis relevant to the subject of data dictionary development and other data administration functions.

Acknowledgments

Data-name rationalization, as this subject matter is now called, is an everyday assignment at The Catalyst Group of Peat Marwick. The general concepts outlined in this Application

[1]PM/SS has been developed by the Adpac Corporation, and is its solely owned proprietary product.

were expanded on, and made a very practical tool, by the following members of their organization.

Peat Marwick
The Catalyst Group
303 East Wacker Drive
Chicago, Ill. 60601
Tel: (312) 938-1000

Jon Cris Miller, Partner
Albert J. Travis, Senior Manager
Marc D. Gimbel, Analyst

Blue Cross and Blue Shield of Greater New York provided Adpac with a great deal of technical assistance in interfacing PM/SS to the DATAMANAGER dictionary. The following members of the BC/BS organization made significant contributions to the success of this phase of the application.

Blue Cross/Blue Shield of Greater New York
622 Third Ave.
New York, N.Y. 10017
Tel: (212) 490-4871

Harvey M. Smith, Jr., CDP, DBA Manager
Tony Gordon, Senior DA Analyst
William Colangelo, Analyst
Alexander Gollinge, DA Analyst

Functional Task List

1. Library member identification
2. Initial attribute list
3. Homonym identification
4. Synonym identification
5. Alias identification
6. Renaming
7. Preparing the WAS/IS list
8. Substitution of data-names
9. Substitution validation
10. Special problems
11. Entering the data elements into the dictionary
12. Entering other data into the dictionary
13. Entering process information into the dictionary

Glossary of Terms

Before beginning the procedural analysis it will be helpful to define some standard terms that will be used throughout this application.

Logical length: The length of the item that would result if all edit characters were removed from its PICTURE clause, except for the codes X, A, B, or 9. Thus an item's logical length is not affected by the picture codes V or P used to specify an implied decimal point, or any of the special edit characters such as: $, . * CR DB, etc. Note also that an item's logical length is also not affected by its COMP, SYNCH, OCCURS, or VALUE clauses.

Homonym: Two data elements with identical data-names but with *different logical lengths*.

Synonym: Two data elements with identical data-names and the *same logical lengths,* but with different picture clauses.

Alias: A single data element that has two or more data-names pertaining to the same physical element. Each data element will have the same logical length, regardless of the differences in their pictures.

Derived elements: An element that is operated upon in the Procedure Division and is the result of a data transfer or computation.

1. LIBRARY MEMBER IDENTIFICATION

The first task is to identify all of the members of the source library (programs) and Copylib members that pertain to the system being studied. Data elements may be located either in the Cobol programs or in separate Copylib (or Include) members. Furthermore, such members may be contained in one or more libraries resident throughout the entire operating system. In some cases, members may be all contained in one PDS, in other cases they are intermixed in a consolidated library masterfile such as PANVALET.

Before we can analyze all of the data elements that are contained in one system, we must first identify all of the members of the system. Refer to Application No. 2, Vector Processing, for a complete description of the various methods of performing this step.

2. INITIAL ATTRIBUTE LIST

Let us assume that we have now created a processing vector (MLIST), or have otherwise segregated all of the relevant members for processing in various PM/SS runs. The first run(s) are to create an Attribute List of data elements contained anywhere in the Data Division of all the members in the application system. This can be done by the following 2 runs:

Run 2a: @PM INPUT:

```
---> @PM. ATTRIBUTE MLIST-SYSXC
---> @PM              SOURCE-COPYLIB
---> @PM              CATAL-SYSXATLC
```

MLIST-SYSXC: SOURCE-COPYLIB   SYSXC is the member name of the MLIST that contains the vector of all Copylib members. This Attribute List is based upon the elements found only in the Copylib members. If Include members (in the primary source library) are used in place of, or in addition to the Copylib, a second run using an appropriate MLIST should be done.

The following attributes will be retained for each data element.

1. Member name
2. Program Ident
3. Level number
4. Data name
5. Library indicator (C)
6. Record sequence number
7. Positional location
8. Logical length
9. Physical length
10. Occurs
11. Picture
12. Data format code
13. Value
14. 01 level record name
15. Next higher group level
16. Next higher group data-name
17. Redefines name
18. Indexed by name
19. 88 level Data-names and values

Run 2b: @PM INPUT:

```
---> @PM. ATTRIBUTE MLIST-SYSXP
---> @PM              COPY-NO, INC-NO
---> @PM              CATAL-SYSXATLP
```

COPY-NO, INC-NO   This run is almost identical to Run 2a, except that it processes the Data Division of the programs in the MLIST-SYSXP, but excludes the 'explosion' of their Copylib (and Include) members. Note that preparing two separate lists in this manner is more efficient than a single run involving all programs and expanding their COPY statements. Obviously, if this were done, each COPY statement would be unnecessarily re-processed each time it was encountered. This would require an additional run to drop the duplicates.

3. HOMONYM IDENTIFICATION

Homonyms are two data elements with identical names but different logical lengths. PM/SS will automatically detect and mark homonyms in the Attribute list. Of all of the misnomers in a system of code, the homonym is the most offensive, and should be eliminated. Elements within the same name but different logical lengths are clearly different items, that can only add continued confusion to the maintenance programmers.

Run 3a: @PM INPUT:

```
---> @PM.LIST    ATLIST = (SYSXATLC, SYSXATLP)
---> @PM         CATAL = SYSXATL1
---> @PM         HOMONYM
```

LV No.	Data Name	Logical Length	From–To	Format Picture	N Y
03	CHRG-CODE	1	219	ALPNUM X	
03	CHRG-CODE	2	38–39	ALPNUM XX	H
07	CLASS-CODE	1	7	ALPNUM X	
03	RPT-CLIENT	12	17–28	ALPNUM X(12)	
03	RPT-CLIENT	14	29–42	ALPNUM X(14)	H
05	CC4-CLIENT-NAME	30	17–46	ALPNUM X(30)	
05	CC4-CLIENT-NAME	10	7–16	ALPNUM X(10)	H
07	CC4-CLIENT-NO	4	2–5	ALPNUM X(4)	
03	MS-COMMENT	36	357–392	ALPNUM X(36)	
03	TR4-COMMENT	30	17–46	ALPNUM X(30)	
03	RPT-COMMENT2	14	337–350	ALPNUM X(14)	
03	RPT-COMMENT2	30	47–76	ALPNUM X(30)	H

Homonym   The letter H will be placed in position 68 of the homonym data-name record (Record-1) of the Attribute List.

A second homonym run can also be made if the record or program prefixing has been used. Record prefixes such as TR- (for transaction), IN- (for input), etc., are commonly found in older systems of Cobol code. The use of the PREFIX-IGNORE option marks the attribute list just as in Run 3a above, but the comparison ignores the prefix of each data-name. The option SUFFIX-IGNORE may also be used with or without the PREFIX option.

Run 3b: @PM INPUT:

```
---> @PM.LIST    ATLIST = SYSXATL1
---> @PM         CATAL = SYSXATL2
---> @PM         PREFIX = IGNORE
```

4. SYNONYM IDENTIFICATION

Synonyms are two data elements with identical data-names and logical lengths, but with different pictures. PM/SS will automatically mark synonyms. Synonyms are usually obvious variations in the same data element's picture to allow for different input/output formats required by the computer's processing language. Most dictionary systems have a means of carrying a synonym indicator field.

Run 4a: @PM INPUT:

```
---> @PM.LIST    ATLIST = SYSXATL2
---> @PM         CATAL = SYSXATL3
---> @PM         SYNONYM
```

Synonym The letter S will be placed in position 68 of the synonym data-name record (Record-1) of the Attribute List.

If record prefixing has been used, the same run (as in Run 4a) using the PREFIX-IGNORE option will frequently find many more synonyms, by ignoring data-name prefixes (or suffixes if the SUFFIX-IGNORE option is used).

5. ALIAS IDENTIFICATION

To begin with, it should be recognized that alias identification is more of an art than a science. For that reason, this description should not be regarded as a universal set of rules to be applied in all cases. Rather it shows a series of typical runs that can be made that should yield a very high percentage of successful alias name identifications.

An alias is a single data element that has two or more data-names pertaining to the same physical element. Each data element will have the same logical length but need not have the same picture.

It is agreed by most analysts that the identification of aliases is the most difficult problem to resolve in a system of programs. If the system has been maintained over a number of years, with many people adding to and modifying the programs, the same physical field may be known under many different names. Under these circumstances, the same physical element, with different names, may occur in many different record layouts and in different positional locations, etc.

To further explain, let us take the case of a field that is called 'zip code'. When the programs were first developed, the name ZIP-CODE describing a five byte numeric field may have been a unique data-name. When other programmers added additional code, they may have used other abbreviations such as Z-CODE, etc. In many systems, a prefix was sometimes given to the same field to denote whether it is to be found on a transaction record or a master record, etc.

Certainly it is not appropriate to enter all of these different names for the same field into the data dictionary. What we are trying to achieve here is to find all of the implied uses of the same physical field 'zip code', and to find all variations in its name.

Alias identification here is based primarily upon the 'data transfer rule'. Under this rule, all pairs (or sets) of data-names involved in a data transfer instruction (MOVE) that are not homonyms or synonyms, are highly likely to be aliases. Furthermore, this pairing can be traced across program boundaries, so that all data transfer sets involving all common data elements may be collected into a single alias group. Consider the following case:

Program 1:

```
MOVE D-DESC TO D-FUNC
MOVE D-FUNC TO FUNC-CODE
```

Program 2:

```
MOVE FUNC-CODE TO CC2-DC-ID-PRE
```

Most analysts might agree that all of the data-names used above are probably aliases of each other. As will be seen this is a good first assumption, but it is not necessarily true of all such relations. The exceptions will be discussed later in this report (see Section 10), after the basic alias identification procedures have been presented.

Run 5a: @PM INPUT:

```
---> @PM.DNAMES   MLIST = SYSXP
---> @PM          DTRANS
---> @PM          CATAL = SYSXDNL1
```

DTRANS   The DTRANS options cause the standard @PM.DNAMES function to modify its normal processing rules in the following ways:

1. Only the Procedure Division of each program will be processed.
2. Only MOVE instructions with two or more data-names will be provided.
3. The XREF field in the DNLIST, positions 62–67, are set to the line number of the data transfer MOVE instruction. Thus, even instructions in the form:

```
MOVE A TO B
         C
         D
```

will all have the same XREF number. This number will be used in the @PM.DTRANSFER run shown next, to identify each data transfer set.

Run 5b: @PM.INPUT:

```
---> @PM.DTRANS   DNLIST = SYSXDNL1
---> @PM          ATLIST = SYSXATL3
---> @PM          CATAL = SYSXATL4
```

DNLIST = SYSXDNL1; ATLIST = (SYSXATLC,SYSXATLP)   Both the data-name and the attribute lists previously created are now brought together to prepare the complete data transfer list. A unique 5 digit number is placed in position 2–6 of each ATLIST record of each alias group. Naturally, elements shown in the printed report that have their attributes displayed were taken from the ATLIST, while those that do not were taken from the DNLIST.

It is important that all data transfer elements of a group be shown in the list as all of its corresponding attributes, in order to facilitate the data administrator's analysis of those elements that are truly aliases, homonyms, synonyms, etc. Unlike the output of the earlier runs, this report should be printed. The printed report will make it somewhat easier to analyze the output of later runs that will be viewed using SPF Browse, Edit, and the Worksheets.

User Code	Member Name	Program Ident	LV No	Data Name	Logical Length
00001	PC34	PC34		CC1-EMP-FULL-NAME	
00001	PC34	PC34		CC1-EMP-FULL-NAME	
00001	PC34	PC34	05	D-EMP-NAME	30
00001	PC34	PC34	05	D-EMP-NAME	30
00002	PC34	PC34		CC2-DATA-CEN-NAME	
00002	PC34	PC34	03	DC-NAME	30
00003	PC34	PC34		CC2-DC-ID-SUF	
00003	PC34	PC34	03	DC-SUF	2
00004	PC34	PC34	05	D-DESC	42
00004	PC34	PC34	05	D-FUNC	2
00004	PC34	PC34	03	FUNC-CODE	40
00004	PC34	PC34		CC2-DC-ID-PRE	
00004	PC34	PC34	03	DC-PRE	2

Data Element Worksheets

To assist data administration in the very comprehensive task of identifying unique data elements and assigning them new names, a Worksheet describing each existing data-name found anywhere in the system should be created. This Worksheet, one page per data-name, contains all of the attributes of each element. It also should contain space for users or analysts to enter additional narrative or other formatted fields, that may be entered into the data dictionary. Consider the following illustrative Data Command Model that will be used in Run 5c to actually create the Worksheet page for each data-name.

DATA ELEMENT WORKSHEET

Group: &2,6

Data name	: &DNAME
Located in Copylib	: &MEMBER
On line number	: &XREF
In record	: &RNAME
Contained in group	: &GNAME
Positional location	: &LOCAT
Logical length	: &LENGTH
Physical length	: &BYTES
Picture	: &PICTURE
Redefines	: &REDEF
Homonyn Synonym code	: &NYM
Indexed by	: &IBNAME
Occurs	: &OCCURS TIMES

NEW NAME IS: _____

DESCRIPTION: _____

_____

_____

_____

RANGE OF VALUES: _____

_____

_____

SUBMITTED BY: _____ APPROVED BY: _____

Run 5c: @PM INPUT:

```
@PM. DATA      DCMODEL = WRKMOD
@PM            ATLIST = SYSXATLC
@PM            ETS+ELEMENT, DICT = NO, FIXED
```

ETS = ELEMENT,DICT = NO,FIXED   To suppress the preparation of a dictionary relational structure that is the default assumption when processing an ATLIST. The following is one such example of a Worksheet page. Additional runs similar to Run 5c may be made for the data elements found in the Data Division of the program, etc.

```
                GROUP:  0009

1 DATA NAME              : FUNC-CODE
2 LOCATED IN COPYLIB     : PC34
```

```
 3 ON LINE MEMBER                 :  000484
 4 IN RECORD                      :  FUNCTION-RECORD
 5 CONTAINED IN GROUP             :  FUNCTION-GROUP
 6 POSITIONAL LOCATION            :  1
 7 LOGICAL LENGTH                 :  40
 8 PHYSICAL LENGTH                :  40
 9 PICTURE                        :  X(40)
10 REDEFINES                      :
11 HOMONYM SYNONYM CODE           :
12 INDEXED BY                     :
13 OCCURS                         :  25 TIMES
14
15 NEW NAME IS:  _____
16
17 DESCRIPTION:  _____
18 _____
19 _____
20 _____
21
22 RANGE OF VALUES:  _____
23 _____
24 _____
25
26 SUBMITTED BY:  _____ APPROVED BY:  _____
```

It should be emphasized that identifying all unique data element name groups, and giving the appropriate ones a unique new name, is the technical substance of the data-name rationalization project. This is, of course, the most difficult and time consuming part of the project. As will be seen, the mechanics of substitution are quite straightforward. The most difficult steps are establishing the data-name standards and control policies.

As a minimum, most of the policies and procedures described in Application No. 8 (Data Name Validation) must be in place before data-name assignment and substitution can be done. As a part of this overall procedure, data administration must develop their own control procedures to correlate the Worksheets prepared by Run 5c with the special homonym, synonym, and DTRANS reports, etc.

6. SOME SUGGESTIONS ABOUT RENAMING

More and more organizations are developing specific, and in some cases quite sophisticated, naming standards or conventions. The following are some DO's and DON'Ts that have been frequently observed as they apply to data dictionaries.

For dictionizing purposes, potential data-names should be defined without consideration of the requirements of the programming language's requirements for uniqueness. The Cobol language has several methods of allowing the same record layout to be addressed differently in the Procedure Division, e.g., qualified (OF) names, or the COPY REPLACING option.

Similary, most data dictionaries have record layout 'synthesis' techniques to allow a prefix or suffix to be added to each data element's name for purposes of compilation.

Except for such computation uniqueness, data-name construction rules are usually based upon:

1. A simple, honest, meaningful name, or standard syllable abbreviation
2. A (user) responsibility code or Entity Type
3. A data type Classification description

ENTITY TYPE (3 character):

PCH: purchasing
EMP: employee
SAL: sales
CUS: customer

Another component (syllable) of a complete data-name is its data 'class'. These are frequently entered as a suffix.

CLASS (3 character):

AMT: dollar amount
QTY: quantity
CNT: counter
TOT: total accumulation
SWI: switch

Refer to Application No. 8 for a complete description of various data-name validation runs that can be made by PM/SS.

7. PREPARING THE WAS/IS LIST

We will now assume that all, or a significant volume of the Worksheets have been completed, in preparation for the actual data-name substitution phase. To simplify this initial explanation of the complete data-name rationalization procedure, the special and more difficult cases will be deferred until later in this report. For the moment, let us assume that the procedures used so far have perfectly identified all aliases. However, this complete procedure should be studied before making actual production runs. It will also increase your understanding of these procedures to make a few experimental runs on a small subset of members. Actually seeing examples of the output of these runs based upon your program files will add considerable insight into the entire process. The Attribute List SYSXATL3 output from Run 5b is the source of input to form the WAS/IS list used for the data-name substitution process.

Run 7a: @PM INPUT:

```
---> @PM LIST  ATLIST = SYSXATL3
---> @PM          SORT = (LIBRARY, MEMBER, XREF)
---> @PM          CATAL = (SYSXWIL, WILIST)
```

SORT = (LIBRARY,MEMBER,XREF)   The Attribute List that now contains each element's alias group name (in position 2–6), is now sorted into a sequence that will facilitate the preparation of the WAS/IS substitution lists. Sorting by the fields shown here will cause all of the elements, by copylib, etc., to be grouped together. This is in the same order that renaming and substituting will be done.

CATAL = (SYSXWIL,WILIST)   At this time only the data-name information needs to be retained, and the more extensive attribute data dropped. Using the 2 parameter forms of the CATAL statement, the WILIST option value creates the WAS portion of the WAS/IS list, leaving a blank space for the desired IS name. Manul data entry is now used to place the new name from the Worksheet into the WAS/IS list. This step is usually done via normal interactive member editing procedures.

8. SUBSTITUTION OF DATA-NAMES

Substitution by Subsystem Groups

Depending upon the size of the complete system being rationalized, the actual process of substitution should be done as a series of runs, each dealing with a manageable set of records and their related programs. This description suggests some of the run groupings that seem practical in a typical situation: First, substitution runs must always be done in at least two runs: (1) the Copylib and/or Include library records; and (2) their corresponding programs. If it is desirable to process small groups (subsystems) of programs, rather than the entire system at one time, the programs must still be grouped by their Copylib records. To perform the grouping the following runs should be made.
    Run 8a: @PM INPUT:

```
---> @PM. COPY  ALL = SYSX, CATAL = SYSXCOP1
```

Separate process vectors may be selected from this list that will insure that all of the programs that use only certain Copylib records will be processed together.

Unique Name Validation

Before the actual substitution run(s) are made, the new names must first be validated to insure that they are not already in use. This is done by the following two search runs. These two runs insure that all of the IS names that are to be substituted into the current programs are not already in use. The rationale for performing this function in two separate runs is the same as applied to runs 2a and 2b earlier.
    Run 8b: @PM INPUT:

```
---> @PM. DNAME   MLIST = SYSXC, KWIC
---> @PM          DNLIST = SYSXWIL
---> @PM          SOURCE = COPYLIB
```

Run 8c: @PM INPUT:

```
---> @PM. DNAME   MLIST = SYSXP, KWIC
---> @PM          DNLIST = SYSXWIL
---> @PM          COPY = NO, INC-NO
```

DNLIST = SYSXWIL   In this case the WILIST is treated as a DNLIST. Thus, the IS names in positions 31–60 will form the second argument to be used by the @PM.DNAMES search function.

KWIC   To report on the entire record on which a 'hit' occurs.

All names appearing in this report must be examined and the duplicates ('hits') resolved, before the final @PM.REFORMAT substitution run can be made.

Copylib Substitution

The final substitution run uses the @PM.REFORMAT function of WHERE. In addition to performing the data-name substitutions, if the REFORM-NO option is not entered (to suppress the feature), each member will also be reformatted as part of the substitution process. Refer to the PM/SS Reference Manual for a complete description of the reformatting rules.

As with Runs 2a/2b and 3a/3b, this substitution function should be done in two separate runs. Run 8d applies to the copylib records and Run 8e applies to the programs. Before submitting the substitution Run 8d, the following additional steps should be done.

1. Review the @PM.REFORMAT section of the PM/SS Reference manual to see what custom options are preferred for your circumstances. Make any necessary modifications to the PMRUNSTD member in your PMLIB.

2. Perform a sample run on any member of the Cobol source library. Cataloging the results of that sample run is not necessary. The only purpose of this run is to obtain a sample of the reformatted program to make sure it is satisfactory to your standards.

3. Examine the allocation size of the OUTLIB PDS to insure that there will be sufficient space to receive all of the programs that are performed.

Run 8d: @PM INPUT:

```
---> @PM. REFORMAT  MLIST = COPYSET1
---> @PM            SOURCE = COPYLIB
---> @PM            WILIST = SYSXWIL
---> @PM            CATAL = *
```

WILIST = SYSXWIL; CATAL = * All of the Copylib records in the MLIST have their WAS names replaced by their IS names if the Copylib member name in position 61–70 of the WAS/IS list corresponds to the Copylib member being processed. If position 61–70 of any line of the WAS/IS list is blank, such names will be globally substituted wherever they occur. If position 1 of the IS name field (position 31) is blank, no substitution of the WAS name will be done.

Program Substitution

Run 8e: @PM INPUT:

```
---> @PM.REFORMAT MLIST=PGMSET1
---> @PM           WILIST=SYSXWIL,CATAL-*
```

CATAL = * The updated Copylib members will be cataloged in the DDNAME = OUTLIB library. The CATAL = * form of this option specifies that the name given to the reformatted member in OUTLIB is the same name it is cataloged in SYSLIB (or COPYLIB). If it is desirable to change its name, it may be done by entering each new member name in positions 21–28 of the MLIST input control vector. If position 21 of the MLIST is blank this also specifies that the output name is the same as the input name.

Before submitting this run, the list of program member names that will be cataloged in OUTLIB, should be examined to ensure they do not conflict with names already placed there in Run 8d.

MLIST = PGMSET1 This vector should be created from member names selected from the original Copylib vector SYSXCOPY1 created in Run 8a. The members processed here should correspond to the same programs whose Copylib records were used in Run 8d.

WILIST = SYSXWIL Using the member-name field in position 61–70, the data administrator has complete control over the data-names that will be substituted in each program. Those data-names that can be substituted globally will have positions 61–70 set to blanks, while those that are unique to a specific program must have the member name of the program in positions 61–70 of the corresponding line of the WILIST.

9. SUBSTITUTION VALIDATION

If care is exercised in managing the WAS/IS list, with regard to the old name, new name, and the members being modified, a complete system of programs may be retrofitted with complete assurance that the executable code will not have been altered in any way whatsoever.

The accuracy of this procedure can be assured by comparing the complete load module before and after substitution. That is, both before and after substitution is done, each program should be compiled and linked into two different load libraries. Members of these libraries can be easily compared using any compare utility program, such as IEBCOMPR. If differences occur, then the printed address storage map should be examined. In most cases the improper name substitution field can be immediately found and usually obvious corrective action taken. Such reprocessing should be very infrequent, or else a tighter management of the WAS/IS list preparation procedures should be instituted before proceeding with the substitution of other members.

Validation of results, purely on the basis of the load module comparison should be sufficient validation and complete program retesting should not be necessary. As a special note, care must also be taken to assure that both the pre and post compilation runs are done using the exact same version of the Cobol compiler, and the same compiler options.

10. SPECIAL PROBLEMS

The previous discussion described the standard data-name rationalization procedure without any difficult or unusual cases. This section, which will probably be continuously expanded in succeeding versions based upon user contributions, describes some of the more frequently occurring problems.

Common Working Storage Data-Names

Consider the following example:
   Program 1:

```
MOVE TR-AMT-PD TO WORK-8N
MOVE WORK-8N   TO MF-AMOUNT-PD
```

   Program 2:

```
MOVE MF-AMOUNT-PD TO GLA-PD-VALUE
MOVE AMOUNT-DUE    TO WORK-8N
```

In this case, since WORK-8N is related to both AMOUNT-PD and AMOUNT-DUE, both fields will be incorrectly grouped into a single alias group prepared by the @PM.DTRAN (Run 5b). If this is a relatively rare occurrence, the problem can be ignored, since when each data-name of each alias group is studied, it will usually be apparent those names are related as true aliases and those that are not. If there are many instances of using such common working storage fields (usually done in older systems to save storage space), the problem should be dealt with.

To absolutely minimize the coupling coefficient of a system, no such common data-name elements should be used. Theoretically, and ideally, each 'module' of a system, where a module may be defined as either a whole program, ENTRY section, or a paragraph within a program, should have its own set of unique data-names. In most structured programming methodologies, common names would only be used when data is required to cross a program boundary, e.g., a record, or record segment, etc.

Thus, even within a single program it is generally regarded as poorer coding technique (with regard to maintenance difficulty) to share common work areas, simply to save space. If it is determined to actually eliminate this problem as part of the data-name rationalization procedure, some code changes will have to be made.

In this example, all code involving any use of WORK-8N throughout the system should be changed. The change can be as slight as suffixing each use with a unique character. If several different unrelated uses of the same field are located within the same program, a corresponding new data element should be entered in the working storage area of the program. Whenever any changes are made, the program should be recompiled and cataloged for use in the substitution validation step 9 described earlier.

Upon completion of this phase of analysis, Runs 2a and 3a should be redone using the revised set of data transfer groupings. The new alias group report prepared by Run 5b will be a more accurate alias report. This accuracy will have additional payoff in the later manual steps using the Data Transfer Report, and the Worksheets, in making the final determination of alias elements.

Copylib Creation

This is the ideal time to establish better Copylib usage policies. The following are several policies that are commonly used. Naturally, practical variations of these policies should be developed as the programming standards for each organization.

1. Any 01 level record that contains any data element(s) used in more than one compilable load module should be placed in a Copylib.
2. Any 01 level record that contains any data element(s) transferred to or from a system input or output source (or sink), e.g., SYSIN, SYSPRINT, SCREEN, etc., should be placed in a Copylib. These are usually the 'external' data elements that are 'viewed' by the end user, and hence the data that is most subject to maintenance activity.
3. As a more extreme policy that extends the rule stated in 1 above is: Any subordinate level record segment (a non-01 level) that contains any data element(s) used by more than one PERFORMed subroutine within a program, should be rearranged into a separate Copylib record. Thus, paragraph structures, that ideally should also be single function processes, should have separate 01 level records containing only their required data structures. This rule will significantly reduce the coupling coefficient of a program, and in the long run will lead to a much higher ratio of reusable code, which of course, is highly desirable.

11. ENTERING THE DATA ELEMENTS INTO THE DICTIONARY

PM/SS does not write directly into each of the different data dictionary processors. Rather, it provides a general purpose method of creating the actual input file that virtually any data dictionary scheme might require. There are several custom options (in the

PMRUNSTD custom record) that accommodate the slight differences in various dictionary processors e.g., DICTIONARY, DCTYPE.

In PM/SS, the dictionary input file is called a Data Command List (DCLIST). It is created simply by bringing together in one SYNTH run; (1) a set of model instructions of the Data Commands required by the specific data dictionary product; and (2) the data to be entered (ATLIST). There are a number of complete run examples at the end of this application report that show the use of this technique.

Naturally, before the run that will actually create the DCLIST is performed, a new Attribute List, using the fully-substituted records has been created. The final attribute list is produced by performing the same 2 runs as was done in Runs 2a, 2b.

Run 11a: @PM INPUT:

```
---> @PM.ATTRIBUTE   MLIST = SYSXC
---> @PM              SOURCE = COPYLIB
---> @PM              CATAL = SYSXATLC
```

Run 11b: @PM INPUT:

```
---> @PM.ATTRIBUTE   MLIST = SYSXP, COPY = NO
---> @PM              CATAL = SYSXATLP
```

The actual Data Command List being processed depends upon the particular dictionary being used. The following is an example of the @PM control statements required for creating a complete relational input file for the DATAMANAGER dictionary in the INSERT format.

Run 11c: @PM INPUT:

```
---> @PM.DATA   ATLIST = SYSXATL, DCMODEL = SYSXDCM
---> @PM        DICTIONARY = DMAN, DCTYPE = INSERT
---> @PM        CATAL = SYSDCL
```

Simply by changing the DICTIONARY = option, the data in the same ATLIST may be prepared for input to any one of the following dictionaries.

```
DICT-DB/DC    IBM, DB/DC
DICT-DDICT    ADR, DATA DICTIONARY
DICT-DMAN     MSP, DATAMANAGER
DICT-IDD      CULLINET, IDD
```

If the PMRUNSTD record in the PMLIB has been customized to the proper dictionary usage standards, and a standard ATLIST model is used, then only the ATLIST and CATAL options are required. The other options will be automatically invoked based upon the PMRUNSTD option values.

Run 11d: @PM INPUT:

```
---> @PM.DATA    ATLIST = SYSXATL
---> @PM         CATAL = SYSXDCL
```

Note also that the PREFIX-NO or PREFIX-IGNORE (or SUFFIX) option may also be used to control the inclusion or exclusion of a prefix or suffix in the DCLIST. PREFIX-NO is the assumed default.

All that remains now is to actually perform the input run(s) required by each data dictionary product using the Data Command List SYSXDCL. This step is not described here, since it is too specific to each installation's standard operating system procedures. There are a number of complete examples at the end of this Application that show the Data Command Lists that can be created using the same ATLIST.

12. ENTERING OTHER DATA INTO THE DICTIONARY

A Word of Caution

It must be pointed out that because of the ease by which PM/SS can allow users to extract and enter information into data dictionaries, this horsepower should not be abused. *That is, not everything that can be entered into the dictionary should be entered.* For example, since PM/SS can so easily prepare a list of 'where used' COPY member names, it is questionable as to whether this information should be entered in the dictionary, that will also require continuing maintenance. Thus, each user should adopt policies that compromise these and other related questions before building a data dictionary that may eventually become an obsolete dinosaur, rather than the workhorse that it was originally envisioned to be.

The following are a set of runs that can be made to catalog various types of source code information and, thereby, may also be entered into a dictionary.

Function	Description
@PM.ATTRIB	Data element attributes
@PM.DNAMES	Data names
@PM.CALL	Call statements
@PM.COPY	Copy statements
@PM.ROUTINES	Paragraph names
@PM.IONAMES	I/O record names
@PM.DSNAMES	Data set names,
@PM.LIST	Correlated I/O and DSN
@PM.NARRATIVES	REMARKS (or other comments)
@PM.PROC	PROC data
@PM.JOB	Job data

Refer to the following example section of this Application Report for a variety of complete examples of batch lists that may be created by PM/SS, and their corresponding dictionary input files.

Transforming Procedure Division Literals to Data-Name Elements

In almost all Cobol code developed prior to the use of data dictionaries, important keywords were entered as literals in the Procedure Division of the programs. By today's standards, many of these should be defined as data elements in the Data Division, with a corresponding value phrase. PM/SS has the ability to extract literals from the Procedure Division and to catalog them in the PMLIB. Since their member names and line numbers are also retained, they can be readily examined and reformatted in preparation for their entry into the data dictionary.

Run 12a: @PM INPUT:

```
---> @PM.LITERALS   MLIST=SYSXP
---> @PM            CATAL=SYSXLIT


MEMBER      PROGRAM      DATA
NAME        IDENT        NAME
11------    21-------    31---------------------------
PC31        PC31         'DEFINED    '
PC31        PC31         'DELETE     '
PC31        PC31         'DELETED    '
PC31        PC31         'EMP-NO ='
PC31        PC31         'EOB WHEN READY'
PC31        PC31         'FILE CONTROL TOTALS'
PC31        PC31         'HOURS SCHEDULED/NOT WORKED'
PC31        PC31         'INCOMING PROJECTS    '
PC31        PC31         0000
PC31        PC31         100.00
PC31        PC31         850101
PC31        PC31         999999
```

To create the initial version of the WAS/IS list the following run may be made using the output of Run 13a.

Run 12b: @PM.INPUT

```
---> @PM.LIST DNLIST=SYSXLIT
---> @PM       CATAL=(SYSXLIT1,STLIST)
```

13. ENTERING PROCESS INFORMATION INTO THE DICTIONARY

Until now we have only described the method of screening and entering information pertaining to data elements into the data dictionary. The steps described above, of preparing a Data Command List, apply equally well to entering virtually any other data that can be extracted from the current source libraries. For example, many users desire to place in their data dictionary, the names of each of the COPY member names that each program uses. In order to create this DCLIST, a list of such COPY names must first be created and cataloged in the PMLIB.

Run 13a: @PM INPUT:

```
---> @PM.COPY   MLIST = SYSXP = CATALSYSXCOPY


COPY


MEMBER          PROGRAM        DATA
NAME            IDENT          NAME
11---------     21---------    31---------------
PC12            PC12           PCLRDWR
PC21            PC21           PCLRDWR
PC12            PC12           PCMSTREC
PC21            PC21           PCMSTREC
PC22            PC22           PCMSTREC
PC62            PC62           PCMSTREC
PC65            PC65           PCPRNTREC
PC69F           PC69F          PCPRNTREC
PCMSDKTP        PCMSDKTP       PCPRNTREC
PCMSDKTP        PCMSDKTP       PCTRREC
PCMSLD          PCMSTLD        PCTRREC
PC61            PC61           PCTRRECA
PC63            PC63           PCTRRECB
PC69F           PC69F          PCTR14
PC12            PC12           PCTR14
```

It should be obvious, even without an example of the actual DCMODEL (specific to each data dictionary) that performing the SYNTH function similar to Run 14 above will produce an appropriate DCLIST for entering the COPY usage information. Refer to the SYNTH section of the PM/SS Reference Manual for a complete description of the general principals of data dictionary input systhesis.

A Data Element Naming Convention

Jim Odell
Database Design, Inc.

A consistent, coherent data element naming convention is one of the most important standards necessary for a sound data administration. This section describes a convention which I have found to be very useful.

The data element name consists of three basic parts, each of which is separated by a period (see the accompanying illustration). Hyphens are used within multi-word Domains, Qualifiers, and Entities. The process of naming data elements starts with the right-most (or most general) portion of the data element name, and then becomes more specific as the name is constructed to the left.

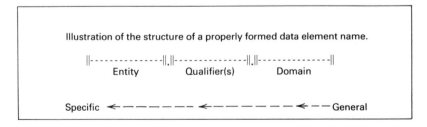

Illustration of the structure of a properly formed data element name.

||----------------||.||----------------||.||--------------||
Entity   Qualifier(s)   Domain

Specific ← — — — — — ← — — — — — ← — —General

Standard Domain and Entity Lists should be maintained for data element definition purposes. Using these, the Analyst constructs the data element name, adding qualifiers as appropriate. The construction of the standard Domain list is viewed as a joint Analyst/ Data Administrator function. The construction of the standard Entity List is the responsibility of the Data Administrator. (The three components comprising the total data element name will be described in greater detail a little later.)

Data element names in abbreviated form are usually limited to 28 characters including periods and hyphens. Use a Standard List of Abbreviations for the Entity and Domain portions of the name; abbreviate Qualifier words only when necessary to reduce the entire data element name to 28 characters or less.

When writing the definition of the data element name, use the following guidelines: Begin with the Domain name (a noun), relate this noun to a verb (such as *represents, indicates, specifies, identifies, provides, quantifies,* etc.), and then use the Qualifiers, in the order that the name was constructed (from right to left). Also refer to the Entity if it increases readability (see Table 1).

Table 1. The Description of the Data Element Name

"EMP.BASE-SALARY.CUR-CD"
could be described as the Currency Code (CUR-CD) that uniquely identifies the currency in which the Base Salary (BASE-SALARY) of the Employee (EMP) is paid.

Pictorially, the definition looks like this:

Domain Name	Verb	Qualifier	Entity
Currency Code	Identifies	Salary (Base)	Employee

If a code uniquely identifies a person, place, or thing, use the word "uniquely" in the item's textual definition as it is an important factor in data analysis. The purpose of this structure for describing data elements is:

- To promote easy identification of incomplete definitions or unnecessary qualifiers
- To establish the exact nature of the relationship between the Domain and the Qualifiers
- To provide clarity by standardizing the format

The three components comprising the total data element are described as follows:

DOMAIN

A named set of data values (such as CURRENCY-CODE). Domains are classified as either "specific" or "generic." A Specific Domain (such as CURRENCY CODE) will have a specified definition, fixed attributes, defined codes and meanings, and specified values and ranges. A Generic Domain (such as AMOUNT) will have a general definition. In this case, attributes, codes, meanings, values, and ranges will be defined at the data element level.

Purpose

The purpose of the Domain portion of the data element name is to identify the sets of possible values over which a data element may range. This will help in controlling data element definitions, analyzing data, referencing existing data elements, and identifying groups of ''code'' elements that will make up tables.

Consideration

Think about the type of values that will be used in the data element, such as employee numbers, currency codes, or dates.

Question to Ask

Into which Domain does the data element to be defined fall? Consult the standard Domain List. If the Domain does not appear on the Domain List, make sure the Domain is properly understood and/or named. When a new Domain must be added to the Domain List, a Domain Definition Form should be completed for the Domain and submitted to the Data Administrator.

Example

One possible Domain is DATE (abbreviated as DT). DATE might be defined as a ''point in time as defined by the Gregorian calendar, consisting of a month, day, and year.''

QUALIFIERS

A further restriction on or qualification of a selected Domain, based on the data element's particular use.

Purpose

The purpose of the Qualifier portion of the data element name is to identify exactly the role of the data element.

Consideration

Be specific. Try to think ahead to all of the potential qualified uses. For example, SALARY AMT (Salary Amount) could have additional qualified uses such as BASE-SALARY.AMT and NET-SALARY.AMT. List the Qualifiers so that the most general

Qualifier is on the right. Additional qualifiers become gradually more specific as each is added to the left.

Question to Ask

What kind of Qualifier is needed? Repeat this question until you feel you have a good Qualifier.

Example

Given the Domain of DATE, you might ask:

- What kind of DT? Answer: EFFECTIVE.
- What kind of EFF.DT? Answer: SALARY.
- What kind of SALARY-EFF.DT? If there are no more Qualifiers that need to be added to insure understanding, stop here.

ENTITY

An organized collection of data elements with a logical and conceptual relationship, i.e., some person, place, or thing (not process) about which we need to keep information.

Purpose

The purpose of the Entity portion of the data element name is to build groups of data that are convenient to manage during data analysis, such as Employee data or Applicant data.

Consideration

Think about who or what the element refers to, or what grouping it should go into; basically, what is the key for this element?

Question to Ask

To whom or to what does the data element refer? Consult the standard Entity List. If an appropriate Entity does not appear on the Entity List, contact the Data Administrator.

Example

Using the element developed in the preceding example for QUALIFIERS, ask: With what person, place, or thing is SALARY-EFF.DT conceptually associated? If this element is associated with an Employee, the data element name would be EMP.SALARY-EFF.DT. If this element is associated with, say, a company standard for salaries, the name would be CO.SALARY-EFF.DT.

DATA DESIGNER User Guide Introduction

Database Design, Inc.

The traditional approach to database design in many corporations has been to understand the user application well enough to translate it into the access method provided by one or more of the company's selected database management systems (DBMS). In this process, the design emphasis was usually placed on the operating efficiency of the resulting programs. Thus, for each application, a separate set of files and access methods were defined that supported this local efficiency.

TRADITIONAL PROBLEMS

As the number of applications proliferated, so did the number and size of files and record types. Consequently, several significant problems arose.

- Additional storage space was required for the duplicated data elements for the various subsystems.
- It was difficult to maintain consistent values of a given data element duplicated in many subsystems.
- It was a complex task to add new applications to existing sets of systems and files.
- It was time consuming to reconfigure the user data requirements as elements changed in importance, use, or were added.

- It was difficult to search for particular data values in response to unanticipated queries.

Traditional Solutions

To solve these problems, it was necessary to identify and eliminate or reduce the amount of duplicate data elements among the information systems of the corporation and to reduce the amount of storage required to maintain this information. Database management systems have been used in the past few years for this purpose.

Unfortunately, many DBMS users continued to employ the same design methodology they used before they "went database", so the problems continued in spite of the DBMS. In addition, even those who use DBMS with new design methods continue to be plagued with problems.

- All of the required access paths to data are not implemented.
- Modifications to both the logical and physical designs are difficult, time consuming, and expensive.
- Every DBMS has its own logical design technique and, therefore, the logical database design is coupled with the physical database design resulting in a substantial loss of logical data independence.
- There is a lack of sufficiently quaified data administrators and database specialists to manage and perform the logical/physical design and implementation functions.

IMPORTANCE OF LOGICAL DATABASE DESIGN

The single factor most critical to the success of a database information system is the overall logical design of the database. Evidence supporting this statement can be found throughout the data processing industry.

In many database installations more than half of the money spent on application development is allocated to so-called maintenance. Here the term maintenance is used to mean the restructuring of data within the database and the consequent rewriting of the programs that use that data. As this situation recurs, the database is unavailable, and both programmers and end-users of the database become increasingly frustrated at the unreliability of the system. Hence, they may develop their own alternatives to circumvent the use of the database, thereby failing to realize the benefits of database technology.

You might ask,

How can a database management system result in this increased cost and user frustration, when one of the strongest arguments favoring the implementation of such systems is that it will greatly reduce such maintenance?

The answer: If the logical design of the database is poorly structured, then physical restructuring to accommodate minor unexpected changes in the future is inevitable.

How to Do It

There are several formal techniques for logically structuring a database in such a way that maintenance costs can be minimized. The most beneficial technique is to organize the data and the relationships among the data into a normalized schema. To do that, all of the data item types must be determined, and relationships among the data, commonly called functional dependencies, specified. Then, all the data and functional dependencies are synthesized into canonical database structures. The result of this process is a logical structure that will usually allow the addition of new types of data items and relationships without the necessity of logical restructuring and, often most importantly, physical restructuring.

A data analyst is responsible for designing the logical structure of the data. In performing the logical database design, the data analyst must work with systems analysts and end users to determine what data items are needed for their operations. Each data item must be defined and catalogued in a data dictionary. The data structures required by different users are collected and must be synthesized into a logical database structure called a schema.

The schema should be as stable as possible. It should accommodate new kinds of data items without substantially affecting the existing schema. If the logical schema has to undergo alterations in the future, it usually forces the physical DBMS schema to change and, therefore, application programs to be rewritten. This can be expensive. It also means that many potential uses of the database will never be implemented.

A database may contain hundreds or even thousands of different types of data items (fields). Each of these data items must have some relationship with the other data items in the database. Corporations often desire a database that contains all of the information for every aspect of that corporation's operation. It is an enormous and difficult task to design such a large corporate database. Is there a methodology available that can assist the database designer with this task? The answer is yes.

DATA DESIGNER

DATA DESIGNER is an automated, easy-to-use tool that assists the database designer in formulating normalized views of the data requirements and synthesizes these views into a canonical normalized form. In addition to developing a logical database design, DATA DESIGNER maintains information needed to physically structure the database for efficient performance. Reports produced by DATA DESIGNER are easily understood by both database designers and end users.

The canonical logical design can subsequently be translated into a schema compatible with any of the database management software systems that are presently available including TOTAL, IMS, SYSTEM 2000, IDMS, DMS 1100, ADABAS, DPL, NOMAD, and many others. Such a logical design can also be translated into efficient file structures for access via COBOL or other non-DBMS tools.

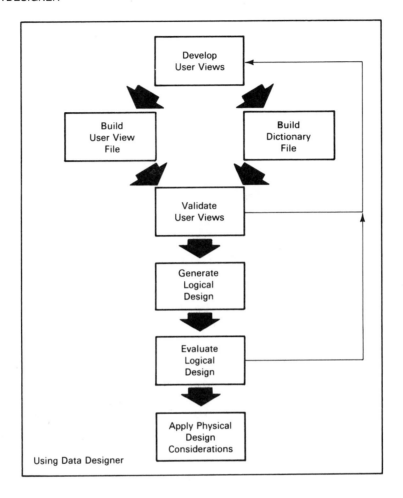

Using Data Designer

A Database Design and Evaluation Workbench: Preliminary Report[1]

David Reiner, Michael Brodie, Gretchen Brown, Mark Chilenskas,
Mark Friedell,[2] David Kramlich, John Lehman, Arnon Rosenthal
Computer Corporation of America

The Database Design and Evaluation Workbench (DDEW), being implemented at CCA, is a graphics workstation for database designers. DDEW provides an interactive support environment for specifying and experimenting with database structures and designs, while automatically maintaining a complete history of the design alternatives investigated. It allows easy and uniform access to an integrated and extensible suite of evaluation, analysis, and design transformation tools that range over the entire database design life-cycle. The system is object oriented, supports multiple screen windows, and has powerful diagram representation and editing capabilities.

On the workstation screen, the designer can build, display, and manipulate objects of two fundamental types, *lists* and *diagrams*. Restricting the number of fundamental object types to two makes designer-system interactions quite uniform. Free-form and formatted textual data (such as requirements, attribute definitions, constraints, and design annotations) are represented primarily as list items, which may be added, deleted, and modified with DDEW's list editor. Database schemas and the design history are represented as diagrams, which may be edited with DDEW's diagram editor. Contrasting colors and graphic icons help clarify design structures. To view related lists and diagrams, the designer can create multiple windows on the screen. Scrolling mechanisms and miniaturized versions of diagrams will help the designer to browse through and keep from getting lost in diagrams and lists that are too large to fit in a window.

[1]This project is supported by the Rome Air Development Center (of the United States Air Force) under contract number F30602-83-C-0073.

[2]Center for Research in Computing Technology, Harvard University.

As the designer moves through the database design life cycle, DDEW keeps a graphic record of the alternatives that are investigated and their interrelationships in the form of a "design tree". This ensures that no design work will be lost, and allows the designer to view the history and track the progress of designs.

One of the main strengths of DDEW is the high degree of integration of its evaluation, analysis, and design transformation tools. The interface to all the tools is uniform, and the designer will not have to memorize invocation conventions, write format translation programs between tools, learn a file system, cope with version control, or know UNIX. The system automatically retrieves and stages tool input data, and the designer need only examine and evaluate the results.

To guide the designer through the complex design process, a context-sensitive help facility is planned. It will be minimal in the first version of DDEW, but later versions will provide information on command formats, data models, tool use, and alternative next steps in the design methodology.

THE DATABASE DESIGN PROCESS

DDEW supports a stepwise methodology for database design that is based on earlier work by Teorey and Fry [TEOR82b]. Starting with the most abstract level of requirements specification, the designer proceeds through increasingly concrete phases of conceptual design (done in terms of a semantic data model), logical design (done in terms of one of the three classical models), distributed design, physical design, and prototyping. The methodology is iterative; earlier decisions always can be reconsidered, and alternatives to them can be explored in parallel. We first discuss the data models that underlie the design process and then describe the methodology.

Data Models

A modified and extended version of the Entity-Relationship model [CHEN77] (referred to as ER +) underlies all phases of DDEW, from conceptual design through physical design. The principal components (or data objects) of the ER + model are entities, binary relationships between entities, and attributes (of both entities and relationships). In ER +, attribute names, qualified by the name of the entity or relationship to which they belong, must be unique within a single schema (diagram). Synonyms for a single data object are not allowed. Multivalued attributes (repeating groups) are represented as (weak) entities. DDEW recognizes and exploits ER + functional dependencies (including keys), inclusion dependencies (referential integrity), and constraints on cardinalities of relationships and on data types of attributes. Transaction specifications take the form of a sequence of operations (query, update, insert, delete) on data objects and on intermediate, set-valued results of other operations.

From the designer's viewpoint, conceptual design is done in the ER + model, and logical design is done in (generic) relational, network, or hierarchical models. The ER + model is semantically rich enough for the system to represent all DDEW designs internally as ER+ schemas, with additional information and restrictions for the logical (and subsequent) levels of design. Examples of data model restrictions on ER+ are: for the relational model, each entity must have a declared key, and no relationships are allowed; and for the network model, no m:n or cyclic relationships are permitted. The (generic) hierarchical model is a subset of the network model where there is at most one incoming relationship for entities, and no cycles. The generic data models in DDEW are intended to capture the essential features of commercial implementations of these models.

Future extensions to the ER+ model may include: aggregation, generalization, and association (set) hierarchies, multivalued dependencies, "null not allowed" declarations for attribute values, derived fields (a feature often implemented in commercial systems), and an ER query language at the level of CQLF [MANO82] or GEM [ZANI83].

Design Methodology

DDEW's integrated and detailed methodology for database design serves as a framework for the efficient use of the system by all designers, as well as an educational aid for novice designers. New and improved tools can be incorporated as they become available. In particular, we envision the later addition of several tools at the physical design level. Contributing to this ease of modification are the use of a common storage system for design data, a relatively general system-tool interface, and a clean division of the methodology into levels of abstraction.

Because the design process is experimental and iterative, and because different efforts are involved in new design versus redesign, there are many pathways through the steps of the methodology. Below, we describe these steps, and the tools that DDEW will provide for them (see Figure 1) (see [DDEW84a] for more details). Preliminary versions of some of these tools were developed at the University of Michigan [TEOR82a] however, improved versions are being built specifically for the DDEW project.

1. Requirements analysis and specification
    1.1. Prepare a global problem statement, in English. Obtain information from interviews with management and from documents describing the organization.
    1.2. Collect local views (detailed information on requirements, processing, and constraints) from end user groups, in text form.
    1.3. For each local view, enter a requirements description list (RDL) into DDEW, using the list editor. An RDL describes processing and constraints (in English), functional dependencies (FDs) among attributes, and a transaction-attribute (T-A) matrix.
    1.4. Review the requirements specification with groups of end users to detect and correct errors.
2. Conceptual design
    2.1. Transform each local view (represented by an RDL) into an ER+ local schema and transactions against it. This may be done manually by the designer or with the help of the usage dependency model (UDM) tool, which constructs

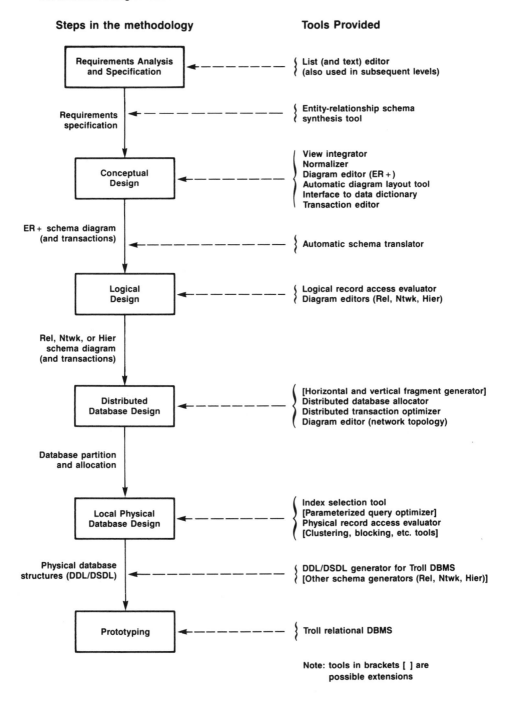

Figure 1: DDEW Methodology and Tools

a first-cut ER + schema from FDs and the T-A matrix. The list editor allows further specification of attributes, constraints, and transactions. The diagram editor and automatic layout tool guide incremental development of the on-screen diagram through cut-and-paste operations. The system prevents the designer from creating illegal structures with the diagram and list editors.

2.2. Integrate the ER + local schemas and transactions against them into an ER + global schema. A facility for synonym and homonym detection is provided, plus graphics support for the view integration process, which may take place over multiple windows. A normalization tool also is available.

2.3. With each end user group, review the appropriate portion of the global conceptual schema and transactions against it.

3. Logical design

3.1. Translate the ER + conceptual schema (and the transactions against it) into a target generic data model (relational, network, or hierarchical). The DDEW translation tools may ask the designer to correct constraint violations, and to choose among feasible alternative translations, perhaps based on semantic knowledge. Structural (schema) translation is supported to a greater extent than behavioral (transaction) translation.

3.2. Refine and augment the logical schema using the diagram and list editors. Also available is a tool, LRA, to display logical record accesses made by transactions.

4. Distributed database design

4.1. Specify the network topology, including bandwidths and costs of communications links, and storage capacities and costs at various sites.

4.2. Allocate files to distributed sites. Given a partitioning of the database into files, data file size in bytes and number of records, network topology, transaction frequency by location, and communication and storage costs, an automated tool proposes a file allocation to distributed sites which minimizes storage and communications costs. (The algorithm for this tool has not yet been chosen.)

4.3. Optimize distributed transactions. Given a network topology, data allocation to distributed sites, transaction frequencies, relation (or record) sizes and cardinalities, and transaction selectivity of domains, an automated tool will produce optimized schedules for individual transactions to minimize either response time or total time for processing across all distributed sites. (The algorithm for this tool has not yet been chosen.) Its results may necessitate changes to design decisions that were made in the previous step.

5. Local physical database design

5.1. Select indexes (or other direct access structures). DDEW's index selection tool relies on its Physical Record Access (PRA) tool, which calculates numbers of physical record and page accesses, given a possible indexing scheme and a transaction mix.

5.2. Use other physical design tools, appropriate to specific data model implementations, which may be added as extensions. Examples for the network model are record clustering, set implementation, and choice of location mode.

5.3. Translate the design (as represented by a schema diagram and associated lists) into the DDL/DSDL of the target DBMS. This translation will be done automatically. For our environment, the relational schemas that are produced initially will be in the form required by the Troll relational DBMS, which will be supported on the DDEW workstation.

6. Prototyping (relational designs only, in our first implementation)

6.1. Compile the DDL/DSDL in the Troll DBMS.

6.2. Load the prototype database with appropriate test data.

6.3. Experiment with the test database. Transactions can be tested using Troll's query language.

In Figure 2, P-C is 1:1, and both PROJ and CONTRACT participate totally in P-C. EMP to PROJ is 1:n through MGR; an employee need not manage any projects, but each project must have a manager. EMP to SKILL is m:n; some skills possessed by no employee may be present, but every employee must have at least one skill.

Network schemas are similar, but half-diamonds (which look like arrowheads) are used to represent set types between record types. (The other half-diamond need not be shown since set members always have a single owner.) The network display includes ER + information that cannot be captured in a network schema (e.g., whether or not a set owner instance must have at least one member instance).

For relational schemas, inclusion dependencies (represented by set inclusion symbols) are shown as graphic links between relations, in a similar way as with set types in network schemas. Translation to the relational model always creates one or two inclusion dependencies (which ensure referential integrity) when a relationship is given a value-based representation. Representing dependencies graphically allows the designer to perceive the structure of the database much more easily than when a relational schema is represented as a collection of unrelated boxes.

Diagram editing commands allow the designer to manipulate single nodes and arcs in a diagram. Basic editing functions for nodes include: create a new instance, delete, move, and rename. Arcs can be moved and reconnected. The designer also can specify collections of nodes, called *affinity groups,* as named subsets of the entire diagram, and move them as a block.

DDEW provides layout assistance ranging from incremental placement and connection of nodes and affinity groups to full automatic layout of design diagrams, drawing partly on placement techniques developed for VLSI design. Fast layout heuristics (e.g., placement of nodes only at grid positions) are used to improve response time and diagram uniformity. The goal is to quickly produce a first-cut layout that the designer can modify if desired.

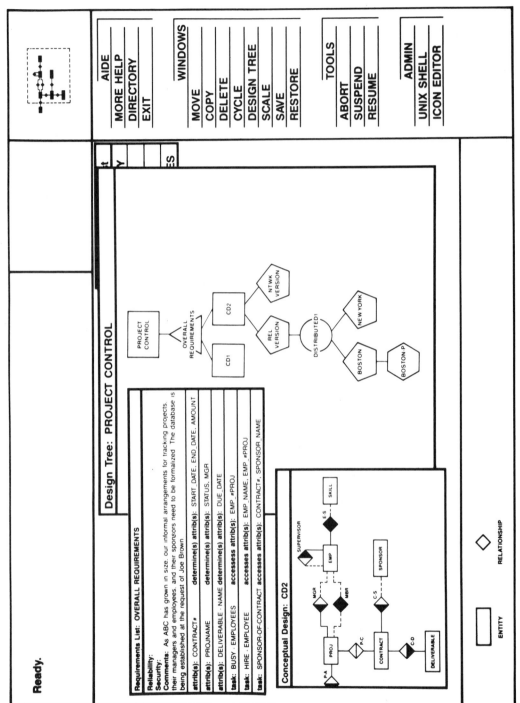

Figure 2: Conceptual Design (workstation screen mockup)

References

[CHEN77]   Chen, P., *The Entity-Relationship Approach to Logical Data Base Design,* QED Monograph Series, Wellesley, Mass., 1977.

[DDEW84a]   Lehman, J., et al., "Overall Design Methodology," DDEW Working Paper 607, Computer Corporation of America, February 1984.

[MANO82]   F. Manola, and Pirotte, A., "CQLF," ACM SIGMOD Conference, Orlando, Fla., June 1982.

[TEOR82a]   Teorey, T. J., and Cobb, R., "Functional Specifications for a Database Design and Evaluation Workbench," Working Paper 82 DE 1.15, Information Systems Research Group, Graduate School of Business Administration, University of Michigan.

[TEOR82b]   Teorey, T. J., and Fry, J. P., *Design of Database Structures,* Prentice-Hall, Englewood Cliffs, N. J., 1982.

[ZANI83]   Zaniolo, C., "The Database Language GEM," ACM SIGMOD Conference, San Jose, Calif., May 1983.

Appendix C

Vendor List

ADPAC Computing Language Corp.
340 Brannan, Suite 501
San Francisco, CA 94107

Advanced Systems Technology Corp.
9111 Edmonston Road
Greenbelt, MD 20770

Applied Data Research (ADR)
Rt. 206 and Orchard Road
Princeton, NJ 08540

Bachman Information Systems
11 Percy Road
Lexington, MA 02173

Composer Technology Corporation
3062 Miller Street
Santa Clara, CA 95051

Computer Corporation of America (CCA)
Four Cambridge Center
Cambridge, MA 02142

Data Design Incorporated (DDI)
2020 Hogback Road
Ann Arbor, MI 48104

Database Research Group, Inc.
23 Sewall Street
Marblehead, MA 01945

Group Operation, Inc.
1110 Vermont Avenue, N.W.
Washington, DC 20005

GUIDE International
111 East Wacker Drive
Chicago, IL 60601

Holland Systems Corporation
3131 South State Street
Ann Arbor, MI 48104

Michael Jackson Systems Limited
22 Little Portland Street
London, England W1N 5AF

Learmonth & Burchett Management Systems
(U.S. Office)
601 Jefferson Avenue, Dresser Tower
Houston, TX 77002

McDonnell Douglas Automation Company
Box 516
St. Louis, MO 63166

MSP, Inc.
21 Worthen Road
Lexington, MA 02173

Ken Orr & Associates, Inc.
1725 Gage Boulevard
Topeka, KS 66604

TSI, International
50 Washington Street
Norwalk, CT 06854

Yourdon, Inc.
1133 Avenue of the Americas
New York, NY 10036

3D Systems
27 Shenley Hill
Radlett, Herts., England WD7 7AU

Glossary

Much of the confusion in the database area is the *multiplicity* of terms used to describe the *same* concepts *or* the use of the *same* term to describe *different* concepts. This glossary integrates the glossaries from ten different sources in reference to data.

1. This book.
2. Travis, *Application 4: Data Name Rationalization and Building the Data Diction- ary,* ADPAC Computing Language Corp., San Francisco, 1984.
3. C. Gane and T. Sarson, *Structured Systems Analysis: Tools and Techniques,* Prentice-Hall, Inc., Englewood Cliffs, N.J., 1979.
4. GUIDE, GPP-41, *DB/DC Data Dictionary Usage Manual,* GUIDE Publications, Chicago, 1980.
5. R. Holland and Cole, *Database: A Builder's Guide,* Holland Systems, Ann Arbor, Mich., 1984.
6. J. King, *Evaluation of Database Management Systems,* Van Nostrand Reinhold Company, New York, 1981.
7. J. Martin, *Computer Data-Base Organization,* 2nd ed., Prentice-Hall, Inc., Englewood Cliffs, N.J., 1977.
8. J. Martin, *Strategic Data-Planning Methodologies,* Prentice-Hall, Inc., Englewood Cliffs, N.J., 1982.
9. T. Teorey and J. Fry, *Design of Database Structures,* Prentice-Hall, Inc., Englewood Cliffs, N.J., 1982.

10. E. Yourdon, C. Gane, T. Sarson, and T. Lister, *Learning to Program in Structured Cobol,* Prentice-Hall, Inc., Englewood Cliffs, N.J. 1979.

I have chosen the most understandable definitions where the definitions are essentially identical. A multiplicity of definitions indicates confusion! The reader is cautioned to examine the sentence context to determine the meaning of a "dubious" term. The number following the definition refers to the reference number above.

ACB. Application Control Block. An IMS control block for on-line programs. It is created by linking information from the Data Base Description (DBD) and the Program Specification Block (PSB) so that these do not have to be resolved at execution time. (4)

Access. The operation of seeking, reading, or writing data on a storage unit. (8)

Accession list. A physical sequential list of pointers to records containing identical values for a particular key item. (9)

Access mechanism. A mechanism for moving one or more reading and writing heads to the position at which certain data are to be read or written. Alternatively, the data medium may be moved to the read/write station. (8)

Access method. A technique for moving data between a computer and its peripheral devices: for example, serial access, random access, virtual sequential access method (VSAM), hierarchical indexed sequential access method (HISAM), access via secondary indices, and relational accesses such as joins, projects, or other relational algebra operations. (8)

Access method routines. A set of software routines that move data between main storage and input/output devices. (6)

Access path length. The number of entity occurrences or logical records accessed to execute a given database application. (9)

Access time. The elapsed time between invoking a command to access some data and the actual availability of the data for processing. (9)

Accuracy. A quality of being free of error. (6)

Action. Something accomplished by a single program access command when using the data base. A *simple action* is a command which creates, reads, updates, or deletes an instance of a single record. A *compound action* is a command which requires multiple instances or records because it performs a sort, search, join, projection, or other relational operation. (8)

Action diagram. A diagrammatic technique of how programs use the data base, specify actions, and control structures which relate to them. In good structured design the action diagram is linked to a data model in which all records are normalized. (8)

Activity. The lowest-level function on a function chart. The activity is a logical description of a function that an enterprise performs. A procedure (computerized or not) is designed for accomplishing that activity. (8)

Activity ratio. The fraction of records in a file or data set which have activity (are updated or inspected) in a given period or during a given run. (8)

Address. An identification (number, name, label) for a location in which data are stored. (8)

Addressing. The means of assigning data to storage locations, and subsequently retrieving them, on the basis of the key of the data. (8)

Adjacency. In data storage, a condition where parts of data are stored consecutively. (6)

Administrative data processing. Automatic data processing used in accounting or in management. (6)

Ad hoc query. A query whose exact specifications (format, key values, and target record volume) are not known in advance. (9)

Aggregation. An abstraction in which a relationship between objects is regarded as a higher-level object. (9)

Algorithm. A set of well-defined rules for the solution of a problem in a finite number of steps. (6)

Alias. Multiple data element names for a single data element. (1) A single data element that has two or more data names pertaining to the same physical element. Each data element will have the same logical length, regardless of the differences in their pictures. (2) A name or symbol which stands for something, and is not its proper name. (3) An alternate "subject name." (4) Different names with the same meaning. One name *is* preferred. (5)

Allocate. To assign a resource for use in performing a specified ask. (6)

Analysis and/or design tool (ADT). Manual or automatic database design tool. (9)

Anomalies (add, delete, update). Three kinds of irregularities due to a relation not being in normal form. It could involve loss of information about a relationship between data items if the last occurrence of that relationship is deleted. (9)

ANSI/SPARC model. Architecture for a database system represented by three levels of schemas (external, conceptual, internal), based on the ANSI/X3/SPARC study group on DBMSs 1975 report, attempting to define standards for database systems. The external schema is based on the application programmer's view, the conceptual schema is a higher-level of all records in the database, and the internal schema is the stored data view [Date. 1975]. (9)

Anticipatory staging. Blocks of data are moved from one storage device to another device with a shorter access time, in anticipation of their being needed by the computer programs. This is to be contrasted with demand staging, in which the blocks of data are moved when programs require them, not before. (8)

Application boundary. The user functions that are to be automated. (1)

Application environment. The application or group of applications for which DBMS implementation is under consideration. (6)

Application independence. Changes to the physical database does not affect any application program that does not use the changed data. (1)

Application program. A program written for or by a user that applies to a particular application. (6)

Area (CODASYL). A named subdivision of the addressable storage space in the data base which may contain occurrences of records and sets or parts of sets of various types. Areas may be opened by a run unit with *usage modes* that permit, or do not permit, concurrent run units to open the same area. An area may be declared in the schema to be a *temporary area*. The effect of this is to provide a different occurrence of the temporary area to each run-unit opening it and at the termination of the run unit, the storage space involved becomes available for reuse. (8)

Argument. A value which is used as the input to some process, often passed through a module-module interface. (3)

Association. A relationship between two entities that is represented in a data model. It is drawn as a line between the entity boxes on the data model. This line is called a *link*. Entity A can be associated with entity B in two ways: one-to-one (drawn A→B). one-to-many (drawn A→→B). The reverse association from entity B to entity A can also be of these two types. If it is possible that there may be no values of entity B associated with entity A, a zero may be drawn on the link by the arrowhead (thus A⊸B). We refer to associations between entities, data items, normalized records, and sometimes unnormalized records. "Association" is a shorthand word meaning either "association type" or "association instance." An association type may be given a name indicating the nature of the association it defines. Usually this is not done because most associations do not change their value. (8)

Association relation or association record. A relation or record containing information about the association. The association name is sometimes stored. In more advanced forms of data model (e.g., intelligent data model), information is stored about the meaning of the association or rules which are applied when using the association. (8)

Associative storage (memory). Storage that is addressed by content rather than by location, thus providing a fast way to search for data having certain contents. (Conventional storage had addresses related to the physical location of the data.) (8)

Asymmetrical distribution. A file whose volatility affects only a small portion of the file. (1)

Atomic condition. The basic qualification condition in a query. It has the form name$\{< = >\}$ value, where name is an item type and value is an item value. (9)

Attribute. A data item containing a single piece of information about an entity. Records are composed of attributes relating to a given entity. An attribute is usually atomic, i.e., it cannot be broken into parts that have meaning of their own. The term *attribute* is a shorthand word meaning either *attribute type* or *attribute value*. All attributes of a given type have the same format, interpretation, and range of acceptable values. An instance of a record has its own (not necessarily unique) value of this attribute. (8) Descriptive information about an entity that might serve as an identifier for an entity. In a stored record an attribute is an item type, which can be used as a primary key, secondary key, or a nonkey. (9)

Attribute relationship. An unqualified ownership between attributes that belong to the same entity or entity relationship. (9)

Attribute value. The number, character string, or other element of information assigned to a given attribute of a given record instance at a given time. The name, format, interpretation, and range of acceptable values of an attribute are determined by its attribute type. Within these constraints, attribute values are free to vary from time to time and from one record instance to another. The shorter term "attribute" may be used to mean attribute value, but only when the context suffices to distinguish it from attribute type. Attributes can have nulls instead of values. These are of two types: (a) value not yet known (but there can potentially be a value), and (b) value not applicable. (An entity type will *never* have a value for a given attribute.) (8) Data representing a specified entity for that property falling into a specified category. (6)

Audit trail. A log in some journal of all changes made to the database. (9)

Automatic navigation. The ability to use high-level relational algebra commands which are automatically executed in the use of a database, rather than accessing records one at a time. (8)

Bachman diagram. *See* DBTG diagram. (1)

Backup copy. A copy of a file or data set that is kept for reference in case the original file or data set is destroyed. (9)

Batch message processing. A method of running IMS batch programs that allows them to process concurrently with IMS on-line programs. (4)

Binding. The firm association of a description of data with the application program. (6) A synonym for *cohesion*. (10)

Black box. A common description of a system whose inputs, outputs, and function are known, but whose inner workings are unknown and irrelevant. (10)

Block index. An ordered index of primary key values, where each value represents the highest key value of all records in a given block. Associated with each key value in the index is a pointer to that block. This forms the basis for the indexed sequential access method. (9)

Blocking. The process of combining several *logical records* into one *physical record*. (9,10) The combining of two or more physical records so that they are jointly read or written by one machine instruction. (8)

Blocking factor. An integer which describes the number of logical records that have been placed in one *physical record*. (10)

Boolean operation. Any operation in which each of the operands and the result take one of two values. An operation that follows the rules of boolean algebra. (6)

Bubble chart. A synonym for *program graph*. (10)

Bubble model. A graphic model that portrays a logical database using ellipses to represent attributes, a single arrowhead ($\rightarrow$) to represent 1:1, and a double arrowhead ($\rightarrow\!\!\!\rightarrow$) to represent 1:M. (1)

Bucket. An area of storage that may contain more than one record and which is referred to as a whole by some addressing technique. The basic unit of storage addressing used by hashing (random or calc) functions. (9)

Buffer. An area of memory into which the operating system reads records from an input/ output device, or from which the operating system writes records onto an input/ output device. (10) These process are not dependent on organizational boundaries remaining constant. (4)

Business systems planning. A methodology to provide an effective plan for integrating data and implementing systems to meet a business's short-term and long-term needs. In a business systems planning study, the major processes or activities of a business are defined in such a way that a systems plan can be developed to support those activities, regardless of changes in the company's organizational structure. (4)

Business user name. The name that a user in the general areas of the business might use to address a data dictionary "subject" (e.g., the business user name for a report could differ from the "subject name" used to record the report definition in the dictionary). (4)

Calc chain (CODASYL). A linked list of logical records that hash (calc) to the same physical block. This allows for keeping track of overflow records. (9)

Calculable data element. An attribute whose value can be arithmetically computed from other attributes. Eliminated in 3NF. (1)

Candidate key. A key that uniquely identifies normalized record instances of a given type. A candidate key must have two properties: (a) Each instance of the record must have a different value on the key, so that given a key value one can locate a single instance, and (b) No attribute in the key can be discarded without destroying the first property. In a bubble chart, a candidate key is a bubble with one or more single-headed arrows leaving it. (8)

Canonical model. A model of data which represents the inherent structure of that data and hence is independent of individual applications of the data and also of the software or hardware mechanisms which are employed in representing and using the data. It is the minimal nonredundant model of a given collection of data items. Neither redundant data items nor redundant associations exist in the canonical model. The canonical model should correctly represent all functional dependencies among the data items in the model. When this is done the model contains third-normal-form groupings of data items. (8)

Canonical synthesis. A formal process for combining separate logical data structures into a canonical model. A recommended technique for designing logical data bases, which can be automated. (8)

Cartesian product. A relational algebra operand that combines two or more tables that have a common column (attribute). (1)

Cellular inverted. An inverted organization in which accession list entries point to physical blocks that contain at least one record that meets the key value criterion. (9)

Cellular multilist. A multilist organization in which the pointers do not go from record to record, but only between physical blocks that contain at least one record that meets the key value criterion. (9)

Central transforms. Those *bubbles* in a *program graph* that are involved in computing, or transforming the inputs to the program into the outputs of the program. (10)

Certification (validation). Error checking of database creation data, before and after database creation. Tests for proper format, value range, uniqueness of key field, and number of occurrences are included. (9)

Chain. A linked list in which the last node has a null link field, or pointer; it may be singly or doubly linked. (9)

Chain file linked. A physical storage method that uses a link or pointer file to implement the association between entity types. (1)

Chain list. A list in which the items may be physically dispersed but each item contains an identifier for locating the next item in logical sequence. (6)

Chaining. A system of storing records in which each record belongs to a list or group of records and has a linking field for tracing the chain. (6)

Circular file. An organization for a file of high volatility, in which new records being added replace the oldest records. (8)

Classification code. A one character designator used to classify data elements (fields) by type (e.g., name, code, amount, date). It is often used in the Cobol or PL/1 name of a data element. (4)

Cluster. Assigning attributes to entity types. (1)

Clustering. The placement of data near related data to improve efficiency of access. Logical clustering places certain items together in records; physical clustering places the same or different record types together in blocks, areas, or storage devices. (9)

Coalesced chaining. A method of chaining for hashing that maintains a global free space list for all the addressable buckets. Each bucket has its own chain, but the next chain entry may reside in any available bucket designated by the free space list head pointer. (9)

CODASYL. COnference on DAta System Languages. The organization that specified the programming language COBOL. It now has specified a set of manufacturer-independent, application-independent languages designed to form the basis of database management. (8)

CODASYL DBTG. Data Base Task Group, a special committee of CODASYL formed in the late 1960s to propose a standard for modern database management systems.(9)

Collision. The transformation of a key value to a physical address that is already occupied. (9)

Combined index. An index in which each entry consists of a concatenation of key item values of different item types. A fully combined index contains positions (and values) for all item types in the records, and a partially combined index only contains positions for a subset of the item types in the records. (9)

Compound indexing. Multiple fully combined indexes, each based on a different order of item types so that each possible order is represented. (9)

Compound key. A primary key composed of two or more data elements of which at least one data element is an odometer (counter) and is meaningless by itself. (1)

Concatenate. To link together. A *concatenated* data set is a collection of logically connected data sets. A *concatenated key* is composed of more than one data item. (8)

Concatenated key. A primary key composed of two or more data elements. (1)

Conceptual design. Analysis of formally specified processing-independent information requirements and the formulation of a DBMS-independent information structure, or conceptual schema, that accurately models the real-world organization and its important data elements and relationships. (9)

Conceptual schema. A term used to mean the same as conceptual model. The word schema often refers to the logical representation of data which is used by a particular class of database management systems (e.g., CODASYL). It is recommended that the word model be used for software independent data structures, and schema be used for those linked to a specific class of software. (8)

Concurrent reorganization. A reorganization strategy in which users have access to the reorganized portion of the database while one or more reorganization processes are modifying it. (9)

Conjunct. A record condition, a conjunction (AND function) of item conditions in a query. A conjunctive query is any query of Boolean form of conjunctions and disjunctions of data elements. (9)

Consistency. A property of databases, particularly those with duplicate data and multiple users, such that at any instant in time the database will respond with the same result to a query for all users. To maintain consistency when updating occurs, read operations are restricted from the changing data until all copies are updated properly. (9)

Containment. The placement of repeating groups within logical records, the only recourse available with flat file organizations. (9)

Continuous data element. One which can take so many values within its range that it is not practical to enumerate them (e.g., a sum of money). (3)

Copylib. A COBOL facility that allows standard data definitions and common instructions to be copied into COBOL programs. (9)

Currency. The knowledge that an application programmer requires of the physical structure of the database in order to navigate it successfully. (1) Method of saving the addresses of the most recently accessed record occurrences of each type or set occurrences (in CODASYL) of each type (i.e., owner record, etc.) so that they can be quickly retrieved if database navigation is to be continued from one or more of those points at a later time. (9)

Data. Something that is either known from being experientially encountered or from being admitted or assumed for specific purposes; a fact or principle granted; something upon which an inference or an argument is based or from which an intellectual system of any sort is constructed. (9)

Data administration (DA). A function responsible for developing and administering the policies, procedures, practices, and plans for the definition, organization, protection, and efficient utilization of data within a corporate enterprise. This function is chartered to manage data as a valuable corporate resource. (4)

Data administrator. The person(s) responsible for the data administration funtion. (4)

Data aggregate (CODASYL definition). A named collection of data items within a record. There are two types: vectors and repeating groups. A vector is a one-dimensional, ordered collection of data items, all of which have identical charateristics. A repeating group is a collection of data that occurs an arbitrary number of times within a record occurrence. The collection may consist of data items, vectors, and repeating groups. (8) A named collection of data items (data elements) within a record. (3) *See also* Group.

Data bank. A collection of data relating to a given set of subjects. (7)

Database. A computerized collection of stored operational data that serves the needs of multiple users within an organization or some defined subset of the organization. (9)

Database administrator (DBA). An individual, possibly aided by a staff, who manages the organization's database resource over the life cycle of database applications. (9)

Database design. The process of developing an implementable database structure from user requirements. (9)

Database design methodology. A collection of tools and techniques employed within an organizational framework that can be consistently applied to successive database structure development projects. (9)

Database key. A unique identifier which is associated with every record occurrence in the database. (9)

Database management system (DBMS). A generalized tool for manipulating large databases; it is made available through special software for the interrogation, maintenance, and analysis of data. Its interfaces generally provide a broad range of language to aid all users—from clerk to data administrator. (9)

Database system. The combination of DBMS software, applications software, database, and operating system-hardware environment brought together to provide information services for users. (9)

Database system life cycle. The major steps in the process of designing, implementing, and reorganizing a database and its application software. (9)

Data clustering. *See* Clustering.

Data collection. Assembling the data for a user requirement. (1)

Data compression. A technique that saves storage space by eliminating gaps, empty fields, redundancies, or unnecessary data to shorten the length of records or blocks. (6)

Data correctness. A correct or acceptable answer for each and every transaction. (1)

Data decomposition. An analysis technique that decomposes data into its atomic components. (1)

Data definition. Generally consists of a statement of the names of elements, their properties (such as character or numerical type), and their relationship to other elements (including complex grouping) that make up the database. (9)

Data definition language (DDL). A language for defining a data model together with (part of) its mapping to storage; a subschema DDL is a language for defining a data submodel. (9)

Data dictionary. A catalogue of all data types, giving their names and structures, and information about data usage. Advanced data dictionaries have a directory function which enables them to represent and report on the cross-references between components of data and business models. (8)

Data dictionary types

Active: Uses the host DBMS to maintain its metadata but also controls the data operations of its host DBMS. (1)

Automated: A software package that automates the functions of a data dictionary. (1)

Integrated: Uses the host DBMS to maintain its metadata. (1)

Manual: Metadata is maintained on 8 x 5 cards. (1)

Passive: Uses the host DBMS to maintain its metadata but does not control the host DBMS. (1)

Stand-alone: Uses its own access method to maintain its meta-data. (1)

Subsumed: Host DBMS creates data dictionary; can be active or passive. (1)

Data directory. A data store, usually machine-readable, that tells *where* each piece of data is stored in a system. (3)

Data division (COBOL). That division of a COBOL program which consists of entries used to define the nature and characteristics of the data to be processed by the object program. (7)

Data element (data item, field). The smallest unit of data that is meaningful for the purpose at hand. (3) A primitive data object in the real world; an entity. (9) An attribute of an entity type. (1)

Data file. A collection of related data records organized in a specific manner. (6)

Dataflow diagram (DFD). A picture of the flows of data through a system of any kind, showing the external entities which are sources or destinations of data, the processes which transform data, and the places where the data is stored. (3)

Data group. A single packet of related data elements. (1)

Data hierarchy. A data structure consisting of sets and subsets such that every subset of a set is of lower rank than the data of the set. (6)

Data immediate-access diagram (DIAD). A picture of the immediate access paths into a data store, showing what the users require to retrieve from the data store without searching or sorting it. (3)

Data independence. The ability to modify the database structure without having to revise application programs that access that database. Logical data independence inplies the ability to change the logical database structure (implementation schema) without affecting application programs, and physical data independence implies the ability to change physical structure without affecting application programs. (9) The concept of separating the definitions of logical and physical data such that application programs need not be dependent on where or how physical units of data are stored. (6)

Data integrity. The concept that all units of data must be protected against accidental or deliberate invalidation. (6)

Data item. The smallest unit of data that has meaning in describing information; the smallest unit of named data. Synonymous with data element or field. (8) The smallest amount of data available to a program. (6) The smallest unit of data that has meaning in describing information; the smallest unit of named data. (9) *See* Data element. (3)

Data management. A general term that collectively describes those functions of the system that provide creation of and access to stored data, enforce data storage conventions, and regulate the use of input/output devices. (7)

Data manipulation language. The language which the programmer uses to cause data to be transferred between his program and the data base. The data manipulation language is not a complete language by itself. It relies on a host programming language to provide a framework for it and to provide the procedural capabilities required to manipulate data. (7)

Data model. A representation of data and its interrelationships which describes ideas about the real world. A data model may present either a conceptual view or an implementation view of data. (9)

Data name. A character or group of characters used to identify an item of data. (6)

Data processing. The execution of a systematic sequence of operations performed upon data. (6)

Data purification. The process of eliminating homonyms, aliases, and synonyms from a data set. (1)

Data record. A collection of data items. (6)

Data security. That property pertaining to the protection of data from accidental or intentional, but unauthorized modification, destruction, or disclosure. (6)

Data set. A named collection of logically related data items, arranged in a prescribed manner, and described by control information to which the programming system has access. (7)

Data store. Any place in a system where data is stored between transactions or between executions of the system (includes files—manual and machine readable, databases, and tables). (3)

Data structure. One or more data elements in a particular relationship, usually used to describe some entity. (3)

Data translation. The modification of the physical (and sometimes logical) representation of data used in one hardware/software environment so that it is compatible with a different hardware/software environment. (9)

Data value. Actual data contained in data element. (1)

Data verification. The process of ascertaining that all data in a data set is entered, maintained, and used. (1)

Data volume. The number of occurrences of each record type currently stored in the database. (9)

DBD. Database description. An IMS control block containing descriptive information about logical relationships and physical storage of a database. (4)

DBprototype. An IMS productivity aid which can be used to determine what the performance of a database design will be. (4)

DBTG diagram. A graphic representation of either logical or physical databases recommended by the CODASYL DBTG committee. (1)

Degree (of normalized relation). The number of domains making up the relation. (If there are 7 domains, the relation is 7-ary or of degree 7.) (3)

Demand staging. Blocks of data are moved from one storage device to another device with a shorter access time (possibly including main memory), when programs request them and they are not already in the faster-access storage. *Contrast with* Anticipatory staging. (8)

Derivable data element. An attribute whose value can be ascertained from another attribute. Eliminated in 3NF. (1)

Descriptive name. The English language descriptive title of a dictionary subject, usually limited to 40 or 80 characters and often stored in the first description segment. (4)

Design. The (iterative) process of taking a logical model of a system, together with a strongly stated set of objectives for that system, and producing the specification of a physical system that will meet those objectives. (3)

Designer. A software package that produces either a feasible database structure (logical or physical), given some requirements, or produces a database structure that optimizes on some clearly defined measure or measures. (9)

Design review. A walkthrough of the current design specifications for a database structure. It is often conducted in conjunction with a review of the applications software for a database system. (9)

Design tool. Any analytical, heuristic, or procedural technique relevant to database design that is implementable in software. (9)

Device/media control language. A language for specifying the physical layout and organization of data. (8)

DFD. *See* Dataflow diagram. (3)

DIAD. *See* Data immediate access diagram. (3)

Dialogue. A generic word for a preplanned human-machine interaction; it encompasses formal programming languages, languages for interrogating data bases, and innumerable nonformal conversational interchanges, many of which are designed for one specific application. (8)

DIAM model. The data-independent accessing model is a formal conception of data in a DBMS based on a four-level architecture from a logical (entity) model to a physical device model. (8)

Direct access. Retrieval or storage of data by a reference to its location on a volume, rather than relative to the previously retrieved or stored data. The access mechanism goes directly to the data in question, as is normally required with on-line use of data. (8)

Direct access method. A method for mapping every possible value of a primary key identifier to a unique position in storage. Tends to be high on storage overhead, but quite useful for entry-point access when there are very few primary key values. (9)

Direct-access storage device (DASD). A data storage unit on which data can be accessed directly at random without having to progress through a serial file such as tape. A disc unit is a direct-access storage device. (8)

Directory. A table giving the relationships between items of data. Sometimes a table (index) giving the addresses of data. (8)

Discrete data element. One which takes up only a limited number of values, each of which usually has a meaning. *See also* Continuous data element. (3)

Distributed database. A single database partitioned into disjoint (or redundant and overlapping) subunits at separate locations. (9)

Distributed free space. Space left empty at intervals in a data layout to permit the possible insertion of new data. (8)

DL/1. IBM's Data Language/1, for describing logical and physical data structures. (8)

Domain. The collection of data items (fields) of the same type, in a relation (flat file). (8)

Doubly chained tree. An inverted file organization in which the index hierarchy consists of one level for each key item type, the index entries consist of key item values, and the data records do not contain the key item values used to index them. (9)

Embedded pointers. Pointers in the data records rather than in a directory. (8)

End user. The ultimate source or destination of information flowing through a system. An end user may be an application program, an operation, or a data medium. (6)

Enterprise. An endeavor, activity, or process (e.g., a task force, government, computer room, school, or business). (6)

Entity. A person, place, thing, or event of interest to the enterprise. An element of an enterprise is anything that can be perceived. (6) A person, place, thing, or concept that has characteristics of interest to the enterprise. An entity is something about which we store data. Examples of entities are: CUSTOMER, PART, EMPLOYEE, INVOICE, MACHINE TOOL, SALESPERSON, BRANCH OFFICE, SALES TV AREA, WAREHOUSE, WAREHOUSE BIN, SHOP ORDER, SHIFT REPORT, PRODUCT, PRODUCT SPECIFICATION, LEDGER ACCOUNT, PAYMENT, DEBTOR, and DEBTOR ANALYSIS RECORD. An entity has various attributes which should be recorded, such as COLOR, SIZE, MONETARY VALUE, PERCENTAGE UTILIZATION, or NAME. For each entity type there is at least one record type. Sometimes more than one record type is used to store the data about one entity type (because of normalization). An entity type has one data item type or a group of data item types which uniquely identifies it. *Entity* is a shorthand word meaning either *entity type* or *entity instance*. (8) External entity: a source or destination of data on a dataflow diagram; something about which information is stored in a data store (e.g., customer, employees). (3) A single occurrence of an entity type. (1) A primitive data object that represents elements of the real world (persons, places, things). (9)

Entity-attribute relationship. A functional dependency between an entity and one of its attributes. (9)

Entity chart. A diagram showing entities or entity records, and associations among them. (9)

Entity class. A class (set) of entity types. (1)

Entity identifier. A key that uniquely identifies an entity. (8)

Entity record. A record containing the attributes pertaining to a given entity. (8)

Entity relationship. The property of qualified or unqualified ownership between entities of different type. (9)

Entity set. A set of entities. (6)

Entity type. A particular kind of entity. (6) A class of objects that an enterprise desires to maintain independent data elements about. (1)

Entity type analysis. The process of identifying entity types. (1)

Error. A discrepancy between a computed, observed, or measured value or condition and the true, specified, or theoretically correct value or condition. (6)

Evaluator. A software package that evaluates a given database structure (logical or physical) in terms of one or more clearly defined performance measures. (9)

Exclusive control. A facility to prevent multiple concurrent interaction with a specific unit of data in the database such that the integrity of the data is preserved. (6)

Extent. A contiguous area of data storage. (8)

External coupling. A severe form of intermodule coupling in which one module refers to elements inside another module, and such elements have been declared to be accessible to other modules. (3)

External entity. A source or destination of data on a dataflow diagram. (3)

External schema (ANSI-SPARC). The application programmer view of data, usually represented in an implementation schema, a logical database structure. (9)

Factored. A function or logical module is factored when it is decomposed into subfunctions or submodules. (3)

False drop. A record that appears to satisfy a query, based on index pointers to a block, but is not a target record of that query. (9)

Field. *See* Data item. (8) An item type (IMS). (9)

File. A set of similarly constructed records. (8)

Filial set. The set of all existing child nodes for a parent node. (9)

File organization. A representation of data records that make up a file that shows the interrecord relationships and accounts for physical parameters such as pointers and indices. (9)

Final normal form (FNF). The ''last'' level of normalization. (1)

First normal form (1NF). A relation without repeating groups (a normalized relation), but not meeting the stiffer tests for second or third normal form. (3)

Flat file. A two-dimensional array of data items. (8) A physical sequential structure, a file. (9)

Foreign key. An attribute that provides a logical pathway to another entity set. (1)

Format. The arrangement or layout of data on a data medium. (6)

Fourth-generation language (4GL). A nonprocedural query language that is user friendly or user lazy. (1)

Fourth normal form (4NF). A 3NF relation without key data element anomolies. (1)

Full functional dependence. Attribute Y is fully functionally dependent on attribute X if it is functionally dependent on X and not functionally dependent on any subset of X (X must be composite). (9)

Full index. A file organization in which an index entry is necessary for each individual record occurrence in the file. An index entry consists of a primary key value and a pointer to the record containing that value. Normally, this method is too high on storage overhead to be practical, except for small files. It is also known as the indexed random organization. (9)

Fully concatenated key (IMS). The concatenation of the sequence field values of all segments in the hierarchical path from the root down to the retrieved segment. (9)

Function. A mathematical entity whose value depends in a specific manner on the values of one or more independent variables, not more than one value of the dependent variable corresponding to each permissible combination of values from the respective ranges of the independent variables. (6)

Functional decomposition. Breaking the operations of an enterprise into a hierarchy of functions which are represented on a funtion chart. (8) An analysis technique that decomposes a function into its atomic component. (1)

Function chart. A chart showing the *logical* operations carried out in an enterprise. A hierarchical breakdown of these operations is usually drawn. The lowest-level function in the hierarchy is called an activity and is the basis for the design of *physical* procedures. (8)

Functional dependence. Attribute B of a relation R is functionally dependent on attribute A of R if, at every instant in time, each value of A has no more than one value of B associated with it in relation R. (Equivalent to saying that A identifies B.) An attribute or collection of attributes, B, or a relation, R, is said to be *fully functionally dependent* on another collection of attributes, A, of R, if B is functionally dependent on the whole of A but not on any subset of A. (8) A data element A is functionally dependent on another data element B, if given the value of B, the corresponding value of A is determined. (3)

Generalization. The process of determining if all root tables represent entity types or entities. (1) An abstraction in which a set of similar objects is regarded as a generic object. (4)

Global information structure. An efficient consolidation of two or more local information structures that minimizes redundancy and record access path length. (4)

Global name. Data name created by using the OF language naming standards. Basic syntax is classword/connector/prime word/ . . . (1)

Granularity of lockout. The option of locking a field, record, or entire file. (6)

Graphic model. A pictorial model of a database (logical or physical). (1)

Group (item). A data structure composed of a small number of data elements, with a name, referred to as a whole. *See also* Data aggregate. (3)

Hash-code search. A searching algorithm in which the desired table entry is used to compute a probable index in the table. The algorithm used to compute the probable address is used both to store entries in the table and to retrieve entries from the table. (10)

Hashing. An access method that directly addresses data by transforming, through a randomization function, a key value into a relative or absolute physical address. (9)

Hash total. A total of the values of a certain field in a file, maintained for control purposes to ensure that no items are lost or changed invalidly, and having no meaning of its own. (8)

Header record or header table. A record containing common, constant, or identifying information for a group of records that follows. (8)

Hidden key. A data element required for correct normalization that is ''lost'' in the table name or undiscovered because a data ''element'' has not been broken into its atomic components. (1)

Hierarchical blocking. A physical storage technique that places data elements in continuous physical locations according to their hierarchical relationship. (1)

Hierarchical file. A file in which some records are subordinate to others in a tree structure. Storage units linked together to form a storage subsystem, in which some are fast but small and others are large but slow. Blocks of data are moved from the large slow levels to the small fast levels when required. (8)

Hierarchical order (or sequence). For an IMS database, it is the sequence of segment occurrences defined by ascending values of the hierarchical sequence key, which consists of the sequence field value for that segment, prefixed with the type code for that segment, prefixed with hierarchical sequence key value of its parent, if any. (9)

Hierarchy. A set of directed relationships between two or more units of data such that some units are considered owners while others are members. This is distinguished from a network because in a hierarchy, each member can have one and only one owner; a set of relationships among entities of a set defining a tree structure for the set. (6)

HIPO (hierarchical input process output). A graphical technique similar to the structure chart showing a logical model of a modular hierarchy. A HIPO overview diagram shows the hierarchy of modules: details of each module's input processing and output are shown on a separate detail diagram, one per module. (3)

Hit rate. A measure of the number of records in a file which are expected to be accessed in a given run. Usually expressed as a percentage:

$$\frac{number\ of\ input\ transactions\ \times\ 100\%}{number\ of\ records\ in\ the\ file} \qquad (8)$$

Hit ratio. The ratio of the number of records in the file or database that satisfy a query to the total number of records in the file or database. (9)

Home address.

    a. The address of a physical storage location (e.g., a home bucket) into which a data record is logically assigned; as opposed to overflow address. (8)

    b. A field that contains the physical address of a track, recorded at the beginning of a track. (8)

Homonym. Two or more different data elements that have the same data element name. (1) Two data elements with identical data names but with different logical lengths. (2) Different meaning with same name. Must uniquely identify. (5)

Huffman code. A code for data compaction in which frequently used characters are encoded with a smaller number of bits than infrequently used characters. (8)

Identifier. A character or group of characters used to identify or name an item of data and possibly to indicate certain properties of that data. (6) An attribute that uniquely defines each occurrence of some real-world entity; an item type that uniquely identifies occurrences of a particular record type (i.e., a primary key). (9)

Immediate access. Retrieval of a piece of data from a data store faster than it is possible to read through the whole data store searching for the piece of data, or to sort the data store. (3)

Implementation design. The phase of database design that transforms and refines a conceptual schema into a DBMS-processable schema. (9)

Index. A table which maps each data item of a specific column into the remaining data of the same row. A table which maps an identifier of an entity into one or more attribute values of that entity. (6) A table containing information on records or data items and their location. (9) A data store that, as part of a retrieval process, takes information about the value(s) of some attribute(s) and returns with information that enables the record(s) with those attributes to be retrieved quickly. (3)

Index chains. Chains within an index. (8)

Indexed random. Full index. (9)

Indexed sequential access method. An access method associated with an ordered sequential file that uses a hierarchy of block indexes, each ordered by primary key values (same way the data are ordered), to reduce the access time for randomly requested records while maintaining efficiency for sequential processing. When overflow occurs due to database additions, the efficiency goes down quickly. (9)

Indexed-sequential storage. A file structure in which records are stored in ascending sequence by key. Indices showing the highest key on a cylinder/track/bucket, etc., are used for the selected retrieval of records. (7)

Indicative data. Data that identifies or describes; e.g., in a stock file, the product number, description, pack size. Normally, indicative data does not change on a regular, frequent basis during processing (as in, for example, an account balance). (7)

Indirect addressing. Any method of specifying or locating a storage location whereby the key (of itself or through calculation) does not represent an address. For example, locating an address through indices. (7)

Information. The meaning implied by data that is assigned by means of known conventions used in representations. (6)

Information processing system. A computer system and its collection of user programs and data. (9)

Information requirements. Process-independent information requirements are requirements that certain types of data be represented in the database to represent the organization accurately, not necessarily to satisfy the current applications, integrity, and security constraints. Process-dependent requirements include the efficient and correct execution of application programs using the final database structure. (9)

Information structure. Diagram of primitive data objects or entities and their relationships that is totally independent of DBMS characteristics. Entities are normally represented by boxes and relationships by arcs or arrows. (9)

Information structure perspective (ISP). Information describing the natural and conceptual relationships of all data in the database and not bound to any applications; process-independent information. (9)

Information system. Contrasted with production system, to mean a system in which the data stored will be used in spontaneous ways which are not fully predictable in advance for obtaining information. (8)

Input data. Data being received or to be received into a device or into a computer program. (6)

Inquiry. A request for information from storage. (6)

Integrated database. A database which has been consolidated from diverse overlapping data sets. (6)

Integrity. A database is defined to have the integrity property when it satisfies data value (range) constraints and preserves this property under all modifications of the database. (9)

Intelligent database. A database which contains shared logic as well as shared data, and automatically invokes that logic when the data are accessed. Logic, constraints, and controls relating to the usage of the data are represented in an intelligent data model. (8)

Intelligent data model. A conventional (unintelligent) data model contains descriptions of normalized records and associations. However these data have properties inherent to them which relate to the logic, controls, and constraints which we code into programs which use the conventional (unintelligent) database. An intelligent data model represents the logic, controls, and constraints which should be applied whenever the data are accessed, independently of the specific application. The logic, controls, and constraints may be associated with the records themselves, or with the associations among records. (8)

Intermediate file. A file produced as output by one program, and used as input in another program, but which is not saved for any other purpose after the programs have finished executing. (10)

Internal schema (ANSI-SPARC). The physical structure of data; the system view of data as they actually appear in the storage media, usually represented in a storage structure. (9)

Interrecord gap. An area between two *physical records* on an input-output device (typically, magnetic tape or disk). Used by the computer hardware to detect the end of one record and the beginning of another record. (10)

Intersection data. Data that is associated with the conjunction of two or more entities or record types but which have no meaning if associated with only one of them. (8)

Intersection of entities. Some characteristics which are represented in attributes belong not to individual entity instances, but to specific combinations of two or more entity instances. Such cases require a separate data grouping called *intersection data*. The intersection is represented in a logical data model by a normalized record type whose primary key is the concatenation of the keys that identify the entities involved, and whose other attributes represent characteristics belonging to the interaction. Usually an intersection relates to entities of different types (e.g., SUPPLIER and PART). Less commonly it relates to entities of the same type (e.g., SUBASSEMBLY and SUBASSEMBLY, when a product or subassembly contains multiple other subassemblies). (8)

Inversion. The process of converting a data element to an index. (1)

Inverted file. A file organization that permits fast searching for general queries based on secondary key item values. It consists of a multiple-level index structure plus a collection of accession lists pointing to data that meet specific key item value criteria. A partially inverted file is inverted on (has index entries for) some item types, and a fully inverted file is inverted on all item types. (9) A file in which the entity identifiers are assigned to the possible attribute values of the file. A file whose sequence has been reversed. (6) One in which multiple indexes to the data are provided; the data may itself be contained within the indexes. (3)

Inverted list. A list organized by a secondary key, not a primary key. (8)

I/O time. The access time to retrieve data from secondary storage to main storage; includes the data transfer time. (9)

Item type. A data item type or field. The basic unit of data that describes an entity; the basic component of a record. (9)

Item value. A value of an item in a record occurrence. (9)

Join. A relational algebra operand that combines two or more tables sharing a common column(s). (1)

Journal. A record of all environmental conditions and changes relative to the data base. It may include time and date stamps, user identification, attempted security breaches, changes to a database, etc. (9)

Journalling. Recording transactions against a database so that it can be reconstructed by applying the transactions in the journal against a previous version. (9)

Key. A data element (or group of data elements) used to find or identify a record (tuple). (3)

Key compression. A technique for reducing the number of bits in keys; used in making indices occupy less space. (8)

Key data element. A data element that forms part of or the entire primary key. (1)

Key, primary. A key that is used to uniquely identify a record instance (or other data grouping). (8)

Key, secondary. A key that does not uniquely identify a record instance; that is, more than one record instance can have the same key value. A key that contains the value of an attribute (data item) other than the unique identifier. Secondary keys are used to search a file or extract subsets of it, e.g., "all the engineers" or "all employees living in Boston." (8)

Keyword. One of the predefined words of an artificial language. (6)

Keyword in context. An analysis made of textual material listing everywhere specific words or phrases are used. The words and phrases may represent a predefined list of keywords or all words in the textual material may be listed, except those specifically excluded. (4)

Label. A set of symbols used to identify or describe an item, record, message, or file. Occasionally, it may be the same as the address in storage. (8)

Language. A set of characters, conventions, and rules that is used to convey information. The three aspects of language are pragmatics, semantics, and syntax. (6)

LFU. Least frequently used. A replacement algorithm in which when new data have to replace existing data in an area of storage, the least frequently used items are replaced. (*Contrast with* LRU.) (8)

Link. An association or relationship between entities or records. (*See also* Association.) A link is drawn as a line connecting entities or records on an entity chart or data model. The word *link* is more visual than *association* or *relationship* and so is sometimes preferred when referring to such lines drawn on charts. The word *link* sometimes refers to link relation or link record. A distinction should be made between link types and link instances. This is important when the attribute instances associated with a link can change as they might in an intelligent database. (8) The attachment, joining of two nodes of a structure. (6)

Linkage. A mechanism for connecting one unit of data to another. (6)

Link relation or link record. A relation or record containing information about the link. *See also* Association relation. (8)

List. A string, all nodes of which are data conforming to a single format; a string of data with the same format. (6) An ordered set of data items, a chain. (8)

Local information structure. An information structure that satisfies the basic processing requirement for individual application. (9)

Lockout. A programming technique used in multiprocessing to prevent access to critical data by two (or more) processing units at the same time. (6)

Logical. An adjective describing the form of data organization, hardware, or system that is perceived by an application program, programmer, or user; it may be different from the real (physical) form. (8)

Logical data. That data which the application program presents to, or receives from the database management system. Program data in the context of processing rather than storing. (9)

Logical database. A database as perceived by its users; it may be structured differently from the physical database structure. In IBM's Data Language/I, a logcial database is a tree-structured collection of segments derived from one or more physical databases by means of pointer linkages. (8)

Logical database description. A schema. A description of the overall database structure as perceived for the users, which is employed by the database management software. (8)

Logical database structure. A DBMS-processible schema or data definition which results from implementation design. (9)

Logical file. A file as perceived by an application program; it may be in a completely different form from that in which it is stored on the storage units. (8)

Logical length. The length of the item that would result if all edit characters were removed from its PICTURE clause, except for the codes X, A, B, or 9. Thus an item's logical length is not affected by the picture codes V or P used to specify an implied decimal point, or any of the special edit characters, such as: $, . * CR DB, etc. Note also that an item's logical length is also not affected by its COMP, SYNCH, OCCURS, or VALUE clauses. (2)

Logical record. A view of the physical database that is independent of the physical structure. (1) A data record as seen by the computer programmer, and as defined in the COBOL program. Usually contrasted with *physical record*. (10) A collection of one or more related data values (6).

Logical record facility (LRF). A DBMS option that implements logical records. (1)

Logical relationship. The relationship that exists between two units of logical data. (6)

LRU. Least recently used. A replacement algorithm in which when new data has to replace existing data in an area of storage, the least recently used items are replaced. (*Contrast with* LFU.) (8)

L view. A user's view of data. Synonymous with subschema. (8)

Maintenance of a file. Periodic reorganization of a file to accommodate more easily items that have been added or deleted. (8)

Map. To associate, assign, or match one element to another of the same or a different set. To resolve the physical storage of data to the symbolic request for the data. (8)

Mapping. A definition of the way records are associated with one another. (8)

Message. In information theory, an ordered series of characters intended to convey information. (6)

Metadata. Data about data, i.e., the information about data which is stored in data dictionaries, data models, schemas, and their computerized representation. (8)

Migration. Frequently used items of data are moved to areas of storage where they are more rapidly accessible; infrequently used items are moved to areas that are less rapidly accessible and possibly less expensive. (8)

Minimal cover. The smallest quantity of data elements required to satisfy a user requirement. (1)

M:N relationship. Two entities A and B are M:N related if elements of A are associated with several elements of B and also elements of B are associated with several elements of A. (9)

Multi-list. A data structure that passes multiple lists through data records using the chained list technique. (6)

Multilist file. A collection of linked sequential structures (linked lists), each consisting of stored records containing the same value for a particular item type. Typically, the lists are indexed to permit rapid access to records related by secondary key values. (9)

Multilist organization. A chained file organization in which the chains are divided into fragments in each fragment indexed, to permit faster searching. (8)

Multiple-key retrieval. Retrieval that requires searches of data based on the values of several key fields (some or all of which are secondary keys). (8)

Network. In data structures, a set of directed relationships between two or more units of data such that some units of data are considered owners while others are members. Unlike a hierarchy, each member may have more than one owner. (6) *See also* Plex structure. (1,8)

Node. An element of a set in the context of a data structure. (6)

Nonprime attribute. An attribute that is not part of the primary key of a normalized record. Attributes that are part of the primary key are called prime attributes. (8)

Normalization. The decomposition of complex data structures into a set of one or more flat files (relations); analysis of functional dependencies is necessary to formulate the different levels of normalization (i.e., normal forms). (9)

Normalized (relation). A relation (file), without repeating groups, such that the values of the data elements (domains) could be represented as a two-dimensional table. (3)

Normalized record. A named set of attributes representing some or all of the characteristics of some entity or intersection of entities. One entity is represented by one or more records in third normal form, and an intersection of two or more entities (if that intersection has nonprime attributes) is represented by one normalized record. Every normalized record has a primary key. ''Record'' may be used as a shorthand for ''normalized record'' in contexts where there is no possible confusion with other uses of ''record'' that are prevalent in the field (e.g., IMS logical records or physical records). Moreover, the term ''normalized record'' is a shorthand term meaning either *normalized record type* or *normalized record instance*. (8)

Occurrence. A specific representation of the value of a unit of data that is usually associated with a value called its identifier. (6) An individual instance of an entity, record, item, CODASYL set, and so on, containing a set of values for its constituent parts. (9)

Odometer. A data element that is a sequential counter that has no meaning unless attached to a defining data element. Part of a compound key. (1)

Of language. *See* Global name. (1)

Optimization. The process of combining tables with identical primary keys. (1)

Organization. A logical grouping of people and information required to accomplish the mission of an enterprise. (6)

Output data. Data being delivered, or to be delivered from a device or from a computer program. (6)

Overflow. The condition when a record (or segment) cannot be stored in its home address, that is, the storage location logically assigned to it on loading. It may be stored in a special overflow location, or in the home address of other records. (8)

Packed decimal. A form of data representation that permits two decimal digits to be stored in one byte of computer memory. (10)

Page blocking. A physical storage method that permits a database designer to assign specific owner-member sets to a specified block of storage media. (1)

Path. A route between any two nodes in a data network. (6)

Percent fill. A parameter (0 to 100%) that specifies how much each physical block is to be allocated for data at the initial load of the file or database. It allows for subsequent database growth such that new records that are to be inserted in a particular order or clustered near each other reside in their proper block without having to resort to overflow. (9)

Personnel subsystem. The data flows and processes, within a total information system, that are carried out by people: the documentation and training needed to establish such a subsystem. (3)

Physical. An adjective, contrasted with logical, which refers to the form in which data or systems exist in reality. Data are often converted by software from the form in which they are *physically* stored to a form in which a user or programmer perceives them. (8) To do with the particular way data or logic is represented or implemented at a particular time. A physical statement cannot be assigned more than one real-world implementation. (3)

Physical block accesses (PBAs). The total number of physical blocks accessed to execute a database application. Sequential block accesses (sba) on disk incur a rotational delay plus transfer time (I/O time); random or pointer block accesses (rba) incur an additional average seek delay. (9)

Physical database. A database in the form in which it is stored on the storage media, including pointers or other means of interconnecting it. Multiple logical databases may be derived from one or more physical databases. (8)

Physical database structure. Stored record format, logical and physical ordering of stored records, access paths, and device allocation for a multiple-record-type database. (9)

Physical record. A collection of bits that are physically recorded on the storage medium and which are read or written by one machine input/output instruction. (8) A record of data, as stored on an input-output device. A physical record contains one or more *logical records*. (10)

Physical sequential organization. A file or physical database organization in which records are stored in contiguous locations so that logical and physical ordering coincide. (9)

Plex structure. A relationship between records (or other groupings) in which a child record can have more than one parent record. Also called network structure. (8)

Pointer. The address of a record (or other data groupings) contained in another record so that a program may access the former record when it has retrieved the latter record. The address can be absolute, relative, or symbolic, and hence the pointer is referred to as absolute, relative, or symbolic. (8) An address indicating the next node of a structure. An address representing a link. (6)

Pointer array. A list of pointers to records meeting a specific criterion; an accession list. (9)

Pointer types.

Backward:	Parent (owner) to "last" child (member) to last-1 child to. . . . (1)
Embedded:	Pointer is inserted by DBMS into the data records. (1)
External:	Pointer is stored in pointer array by DBMS that is separate from the data records. (1)
Forward:	Parent (owner) to "first" child (member) to second child to. . . . (1)
Parent (owner):	Any child (member) to its parent (owner). (1)
Twin (IMS):	Forward or backward to specified segment occurrence of a specified segment type of a specified parent. (1)

Populating. Initial loading of data into the database. (9) Loading of metadata from existing application programs into a data dictionary. (1)

Portable. The ability to generate multiple physical databases from a single logical database. (1)

Primary key. A key which uniquely identifies a record (tuple). (3) The dictionary subject may be accessed by using other names and because of the relationships established between names, will actually pick up the data stored. (4)

Prime attribute. An attribute that forms all or part of the primary key of a record. Other attributes are called nonprime attributes. (8)

Processing frequency. The frequency at which an individual query or update transaction (database application) is estimated to be executed. (9)

Processing volume. The combination of processing frequency and data volume. (9)

Program graph. A diagram that shows the flow of data elements through a program, and the transformations of data from one form to another form. (10)

Programmer navigation. The knowledge that an application programmer requires of the *physical* structure of the database to program their user system. (1)

Program translation. Modification of source program code written originally to manipulate data in one hardware/software environment, so that it can do the equivalent functions on the translated data when running in a new hardware/software environment. (9)

Progressive overflow. A method of handling overflow in a randomly stored file which does not require the use of pointers. An overflow record is stored in the first available space and is retrieved by a forward serial search from the home address. (8)

Project. A relational algebra operand that extracts specific columns from a specific *single* table. (1)

Purge date. The date on or after which a storage area is available to be overwritten. Used in conjunction with a file label, it is a means of protecting file data until an agreed release date is reached. (8)

Qualifier. Criteria used to select a logical record. (6)

Query. A retrieval request for specific data from a database, often generalized in terms of Boolean functions consisting of logical conjunctions (AND) and disjunctions (OR). (9)

Query language. A high-level data manipulation language for interacting with the file or database. (9)

Random access. To obtain data directly from any storage location regardless of its position with respect to the previously referenced information. Also called direct access. (8)

Random access method. Access method utilizing a hashing function to derive record addresses from key item values. (9)

Random access storage. A storage technique in which the time required to obtain information is independent of the location of the information most recently obtained. This strict definition must be qualified by the observation that we usually mean relatively random. Thus magnetic drums are relatively nonrandom access when compared to magnetic cores for main memory, but relatively random access when compared to magnetic tapes for file storage. (8)

Randomizing. An old word for hashing. (8)

Random processing. The combination of database organization and target record selection by user applications that result in a random target record physical location with respect to the previous record accessed. (9)

Record.
  a. A group of related data items treated as a unit by an application program. (8)

    b. CODASYL definition: A named collection of zero, one, or more data items or data aggregates. There may be an arbitrary number of occurrences in the database of each record type specified in the schema for that database. For example, there would be one occurrence of the record type PAYROLL-RECORD for each employee. This distinction between the actual occurrences of a record and the type of the record is an important one. (8)

    c. IBM's DL/1 terminology: A logical database record consists of a named hierarchy (tree) of related segments. There may be one or more segment types, each of which may have a different length and format. (8)

Record clustering. The clustering of stored records in a collection of contiguous extents. (9)

Recording density. A measure of the amount of data that can be stored on one unit (e.g., a block or a track) of a physical input/output device. (10)

Record segmentation. Record partitioning; the allocation of individual data items in a stored record to separate physical extents, possibly on different physical devices. (9)

Recovery. The designed capability of a DBMS to restore the integrity (correct state) of a database following any type of system failure. (9)

Recursive foreign key. An attribute that provides an alternate logical pathway to the table that contains it. (1)

Redundancy. A situation where there are multiple occurrences of a particular unit of data in a database. (6)

Reformatting. Physical reorganization of data (e.g., changing character representation, word length, or purging overflow records back into the primary data area). (9)

Relation. A flat file or table; a file whose records (called tuples) cannot have repeating groups. (9)

Relational algebra. A collection of data manipulation operations that operate on one or more relations as its operands and produces a relation as its result. (9)

Relational calculus. A language in which the user states the results he requires from manipulating a relational database. (8)

Relational database. A database made up of relations (as defined above) which use a database management system has the capability to recombine the data items to form different relations thus giving great flexibility in the usage of data. If the database management system does not provide the functions of or equivalent to a relational algebra the term *relational data base* should not be used. (8)

Relationship. A property shared by two or more entities; the condition of two or more entities being members of the same set. (6) An association between occurrences of primitive or aggregated data objects (entities or records)(e.g., 1:1, 1:*m*, *m*:*n*). (9)

Reorganization. The process of changing the conceptual, implementation (logical), or physical structure of a database. The change of a logical structure is called restructuring, and the change of a physical structure is called reformatting. (9)

Repeating group. A named collection of data items that has a variable number of occurrences. (9) A data group that can have zero to many sets of data value per data store. (1)

Response. An answer to an inquiry. (6)

Response time. The elapsed time between the end of an inquiry or demand on a data processing system and the beginning of the response, e.g., the length of time between an indication of the end of an inquiry and the display of the first character of the response at a user terminal. (6)

Restart. The resumption of the execution of a computer program using the data recorded at a checkpoint. (6)

Restructuring. Logical reorganization of data (e.g., schema redesign). A restructurer is a software package that reorganizes record occurrences to be compatible with a modified schema. (9)

Ring structure. Data organized with chains such that the end of the chain points to its beginning, thus forming a ring. (8)

Role. A defined function that a specific attribute has within a table. For instance, an instructor can have roles of teacher, student advisor, alumnus, etc. (1)

Root. The base node of a tree structure. Data in the tree may be accessed starting at its root. (8)

Root table. A table that contains 1:1 attributes defining a specific *single* entity type. (1)

Scatter table. A pointer array associated with a hashing function that allows one level of indirection to data to be randomly accessed, and thus facilitates flexibility in the physical ordering of the data areas. (9)

Schema.

    a. A map of the overall logical structure of a database. (Contrast with data model.) (8)

    b. CODASYL definition: A *schema* consists of DDL (Data Description Language) entries and is a complete description of all the area, set occurrences, record occurrences, and associated data items and data aggregates as they exist in the database. (8)

Schema language. Logical database description language. (8)

Search. To examine a series of items for any that have a desired property or properties. (8)

Search argument. The attribute value(s) which are used to retrieve some data from a data store, whether through an index, or by a search. *See also* Argument. (3)

Search key. The key or identifier used in a query upon which data are searched. A complete description of all record types, set types, data item types as they exist in the database. Many DBMS implementations include physical structure in their schemas; however, we refer to (logical or implementation) schema as separate from the physical schema in the analysis. (9)

Search mechanism. An algorithm that defines a specific access path to be taken in a database structure and traverses that access path for transactions that invoke it. (9)

Secondary access method. A collection of techniques designed to access efficiently all the target records associated with a set of stated secondary key values in a query. (9)

Secondary data set group (IMS). A physical clustering of segments that does not contain the root segment (IMS). (9)

Secondary index. An index composed of secondary keys rather than primary keys. (8) An index of a file based on an attribute other than the identity attribute. (6)

Secondary key. An attribute or item type that is used to index records but does not necessarily uniquely identify those records (i.e., the same key value can appear in more than one record occurrence). (9)

Second normal form (2NF). A normalized table in which all of the nonkey attributes are fully functionally dependent on the primary key. (1)

Security. The protection of data against intentional or unintentional disclosure, modification, or loss. (9)

Segment. A named fixed-format quantum of data containing one or more data items. A segment is the basic quantum of data that is passed to and from the application programs when IBM Data Language/1 is used. (IBM definition.) (8)

Select. A relational algebra operand that allows qualification of an inquiry. (1)

Sensitivity. A programmer may view only certain of the data in a logical database. His program is said to be sensitized to those data. (8)

Sequence set index. The lowest level in a tree-structured index. The entries in this level are in sequence. Searches and other operations may be carried out in the sequence set index; those are called sequence set operations. (8)

Sequential access. A method of accessing records from a file in which the Nth record may be obtained only by first reading the first N-1 records of the file. Usually contrasted with *direct access*. (10)

Sequential access method. The sequential processing of a sequential file. (9)

Sequential file. A file stored in contiguous physical addresses. (9)

Sequential processing. Accessing records in ascending sequence by key; the next record accessed will have the next higher key, irrespective of its physical position in the file. (8)

Serial-access storage. Storage in which records must be read serially one after the other (e.g., tape). (8)

Serial processing. Accessing records in their physical sequence. The next record accessed will be the record in the next physical position/location in the field. (8)

Set (CODASYL definition). A Set is a named collection of record types. As such, it establishes the characteristics of an arbitrary number of occurrences of the named set. Each set type specified in the schema must have one record type declared as its OWNER and one or more record types declared as its MEMBER records. Each occurrence of a set must contain one occurrence of its owner record and may contain an arbitrary number of occurrences of each of its member record types. (7)

Set, singular. A CODASYL set without owner records; the owner is declared to be "SYSTEM." A singular set is used to provide simple nonhierarchical files such as a file of customer records. (7)

Skew. The processing of modifying the physical database to fulfill user requirements. (1)

Skip-searched chain. A chain having pointers which permit it to be searched by skipping, not examining every link in the chain. (7)

Sort. Arrange a file in sequence by a specified key. (7)

Sorting. The process of rearranging the records of a file so that they appear in sequential order. (10)

Stable. The nonvolatile quality of a logical database. (1)

Staging. Blocks of data are moved from one storage device to another with a shorter access time, either before or at the time they are needed. (8)

Storage hierarchy. Storage units linked together to form a storage subsystem, in which some are fast but small and others are large but slow. Blocks of data are moved (staged) from the large slow levels to the small fast levels as required. (8)

Storage structure. Describes the way data is physically stored in the system: pointers, character representations, floating point, blocking, access method, and so on. (9)

Stored record. A collection of related data items that correspond to one or more logical records and includes all necessary pointers, record length and other overhead data, and coding schemes for character representation. (9)

Structure. A generic term which refers to the aggregation of units of data, their formats, and their relationships; a pattern or arrangement among the elements of a set such that some elements are joined (explicitly or implicitly) to others. (6)

Structure chart. A logical model of a modular hierarchy, showing invocation, intermodular communication (data and control), and the location of major loops and decisions. (3)

Submodel. A user's or programmer's view of the data. (8)

Subschema. A map of a programmer's view of the data he uses. It is derived from the global logical view of the data—the schema, and external schema. Also called LView. (8)

Subset. A defined entity occurrence of a generalized entity type. For instance, student is a subset of the generalized entity type of student: instructor: alumni. (1)

Supertype. A generalized entity type. (1)

Synonym. Two data elements with identical data names and the *same logical lengths,* but with different picture clauses. (2) Different names with same meaning. No name preferred over others. (5) Multiple physical representations for a single data element. (1)

Table. An array of data each item of which may be unambiguously identified by means of one or more arguments. (6) A normalized data group. (1) A collection of data suitable for quick reference, each item being uniquely identified either by a label or by its relative position. (8)

Target record. A record that satisfies the qualification conditions of a query. (9)

Terabit storage. Storage that can hold 10^{12} bits of data. (8)

Third normal form (3NF). A normalized table in which all of the nonkey attributes are fully functionally dependent on the primary key and all of the nonkey attributes are mutually independent. (1)

Transaction. An input record applied to an established file. The input record describes some "event" that will either cause a new file record to be generated, an existing record to be changed, or an existing record to be deleted. (8)

Transfer rate. A measure of the speed with which data are moved between a direct-access device and the central processor. (Usually expressed as thousands of characters per second or thousands of bytes per second.) (8)

Transparent data. Complexities in the data structure are hidden from the programmers or users (made transparent to them) by the software. (8)

Transport volume. The total number of bytes transferred to satisfy (execute) a database application. (9)

Tree. A set, each of whose nodes is connected to only one predecessor and at least one of whose nodes is connected to more than one successor. (6)

Tree index. An index in the form of a tree structure. (8)

Tree structure. A hierarchy of groups of data such that (a) the highest level in the hierarchy has only one group, called a *root*; (b) all groups except the root are related to one and only one group on a higher level than themselves. A simple master/detail file is a two-level tree. Also called a hierarchical structure. (8)

Trie structure. A random access method based on individual character values in the primary key; it utilizes a multiway tree structure at each level, corresponding to the many possible values of character $i + 1$, given a particular value of character i. (9)

Tuple. A group of related fields. N related fields are called an N-tuple. (8) A specific set of values for the domains making up a relation. The "relational" term for a record. (3)

Union. See Cartesian Product. (1)

Unjoin. A relational algebra operand that combines two or more tables that do *not* have matching values in a common column. (1)

Unnormalized relation. A relation that is not in first normal form. (9)

Update. Any modification of a database, whether via additions, deletions, or changes to data. (9)

Usage perspective (UP). Information describing the processing requirements; process-dependent information. (9)

User. Anyone who requires the services of a computing system. (6)

User extensibility. A feature supplied with the dictionary product beginning with Release 3 that allows an installation to define its own unique subjects, attributes for those subjects, and relationships among subjects. (4)

User view. The logical data required to satisfy a user requirement. (1)

Value. The specific property of a data item at a specified time in the context of the occupant of some unit of data space. (6)

View integration. Consolidation of individual users' requirements and representation of those requirements in a common form. It may or may not be done separately for process-independent and process-dependent requirements. (9)

Virtual. Conceptual or appearing to be, rather than actually being. An adjective which implies that data, structures, or hardware appear to the application programmer or user to be different from what they are in reality, the conversion being performed by software. (8)

Virtual data. A logical unit of data that is materialized and does not exist as a physical unit of data. (9)

Virtual field (or record). A field or record that appears to be but is not physically stored; rather, it is formulated physically when its value is requested by an application program. It is constructed or derived from existing physical data. (9)

Virtual memory. Memory that can appear to the programs to be larger than it really is because blocks of data or program are rapidly moved to or from secondary storage when needed. (8)

Volatile file. A file with a high rate of additions and deletions. (8)

Volatile storage. Storage that loses its contents when the power supply is cut off. Solid-state (LSI) storage is volatile; magnetic storage is not. (8)

Volatility. A measure of the rate at which a file's contents change, especially in terms of addition of new records and deletion of old. (3)

Volume. Demountable tapes, discs, and cartridges are referred to as *volumes*. The word also refers to a nondemountable disc or other storage medium. It has been defined as "that portion of a single unit of storage medium which is accessible to a single read/write mechanism"; however, some devices exist in which a volume is accessible with two or more read/write mechanisms. (8)

Volume table of contents (VTOC). A table associated with a volume that describes each file or data set on the volume. (8)

Z. The end. (1)

Bibliography

TOOLS

DeMarco, T. *Structured Analysis and System Specification,* Yourdon Press, Inc., New York, 1979.

Finkelstein, C., Information Engineering, *Computerworld,* 1981.

Gane, C., and T. Sarson, *Structured Systems Analysis,* Prentice-Hall, Inc., Englewood Cliffs, N.J., 1979.

Hansen, K., *Data Structured Program Design,* Ken Orr & Associates, Inc., Topeka, Kans., 1983.

Jackson, M. A., *Principles of Program Design,* Academic Press, Inc., New York, 1975.

Jackson, M. A., *System Development,* Prentice-Hall, Inc., Englewood Cliffs, N.J., 1983.

Martin, J., *An Information Systems Manifesto,* Prentice-Hall, Inc., Englewood Cliffs, N.J., 1984.

Myers, G. J., Composite Structured Design, Van Nostrand Reinhold Company, Inc., New York, 1978.

Orr, K., *Structured Requirements Definition,* Ken Orr & Associates, Inc., Topeka, Kans., 1981.

Orr, K., *Structured Systems Development,* Yourdon Press, Inc., New York, 1977.

Warnier, J. D., *Logical Construction of Systems,* Van Nostrand Reinhold Company, Inc., New York, 1980.

Warnier, J. D., *Program Modification,* Leiden, The Netherlands, 1975.

Yourdon, E., *Techniques of Program Structure and Design,* Prentice-Hall, Inc., Englewood Cliffs, N.J., 1976.

Yourdon, E., and L. L. Constantine, *Structured Design,* Yourdon Press, Inc., New York, 1975.

DATA DICTIONARIES

GPP-41, *DB/DC Data Dictionary Usage Manual,* GUIDE Publications, Chicago, 1980.

Lelkovits, Sibley, Lelkovits, *Information Resource/Data Dictionary Systems,* QED Information Sciences.

Ross, *Data Dictionaries* and *Data Administration,* Database Research Group, Inc.

Travis, A., *Application 4: Data Name Rationalization and Building the Data Dictionary,* ADPAC Computing Language Corp., San Francisco, 1985.

DATABASES

Curtice, R. M., and P. E. Jones, *Logical Data Base Design,* Van Nostrand Reinhold Company, Inc., New York, 1982.

Date, C. J., *An Introduction to Database Systems,* 3rd ed., Addison-Wesley Publishing Co., Inc., Reading, Mass., 1981.

GJP-1, *Material on Data Base Management,* GUIDE Publications, Chicago, 1971.

GJP-3, *ANSI/X3/SPARC/DBSD Interim Report on DBMS,* GUIDE Publications, Chicago, 1975.

GJP-4, *ANSI/X3/SPARC/DBMS Framework,* GUIDE Publications, Chicago, 1977.

GPP-5, *Data Base Design Guide,* GUIDE Publications, Chicago, 1973.

GPP-12, *Conceptual Model of an Information Processsing System,* GUIDE Publications, Chicago, 1975.

GPP-68, *Data Base Sharing and Distribution (from an IMS View),* GUIDE Publications, Chicago, 1981.

GPP-105, *Designing IMS Data Bases Using Data Models,* GUIDE Publications, Chicago, 1983.

Hubbard, G., *Computer-Assisted Data Base Design,* Van Nostrand Reinhold Company, Inc., New York, 1981.

King, J., *Evaluation of Database Management Systems,* Van Nostrand Reinhold Company, Inc., New York, 1981.

Martin, J., *An End-User's Guide to Data Base,* Prentice-Hall, Inc., Englewood Cliffs, N.J., 1981.

Martin, J., *Computer Data-Base Organization,* 2nd ed., Prentice-Hall, Englewood Cliffs, N.J., 1977.

Martin, J., *Principles of Data-Base Management,* Prentice-Hall, Inc., Englewood Cliffs, N.J., 1976.

Teorey, T., and J. Fry, *Design of Database Structures,* Prentice-Hall, Inc., Englewood Cliffs, N.J., 1982.

Ullman, *Principles of Database Systems,* Computer Science Press, Inc., Rockville, Md., 1982.

Unger, E. A., J. Slonim, and P. S. Fisher, *Advances in Data Base Management,* John Wiley & Sons, Inc., New York, 1983.

OTHER

Cohen, L., *Creating and Planning the Corporate Data Base System Project,* Prentice-Hall, Inc., Englewood Cliffs, N.J., 1984.

GPP-6, *Guidelines for Planning and Design of Information Systems,* GUIDE Publications, Chicago, 1971.

GPP-30, *Data Administration Methodology,* GUIDE Publications, Chicago, 1982.

GPP-34, *Data Resource Management Planning Methodology,* GUIDE Publications, Chicago, 1982.

GPP-79, *Data Administration in a Distributed Data Environment,* GUIDE Publications, Chicago, 1983.

Hsiao, D., ed., *Advanced Database Machine Architecture,* Prentice-Hall, Inc., Englewood Cliffs, N.J., 1983.

Martin, J., *Application Development without Programmers,* Prentice-Hall, Inc., Englewood Cliffs, N.J., 1982.

Martin, J., *Strategic Data-Planning Methodologies,* Prentice-Hall, Inc., Englewood Cliffs, N.J., 1982.

Ramanamoorthy, C. V., and R. T. Yeh, *Tutorial: Software Methodology,* IEEE Computer Society, Silver Spring, Md., 1978.

Yourdon, E., C. Gane, T. Sarson, and T. Lister, *Learning to Program in Structured Cobol,* Yourdon Press, Inc., New York, 1979.

PERIODICALS

Database Management, Auerbach Publishers, Inc., Pennsauken, N.J.
Database Newsletter, Database Research Group, Inc., Marblehead, Md.

INDEX